THREE PLAYS BY BRIEUX

Brieux.

THREE PLAYS BY BRIEUX
MEMBER OF THE FRENCH ACADEMY · WITH PREFACE BY BERNARD SHAW · ENGLISH VERSIONS BY MRS BERNARD SHAW, ST JOHN HANKIN AND JOHN POLLOCK

BRENTANO'S · NEW YORK
MCMXI

Third Edition

THE UNIVERSITY PRESS, CAMBRIDGE, U. S. A.

CONTENTS

PREFACE

By Bernard Shaw

From Molière to Brieux

AFTER the death of Ibsen, Brieux confronted Europe as the most important dramatist west of Russia. In that kind of comedy which is so true to life that we have to call it tragi-comedy, and which is not only an entertainment but a history and a criticism of contemporary morals, he is incomparably the greatest writer France has produced since Molière. The French critics who take it for granted that no contemporary of theirs could possibly be greater than Beaumarchais are really too modest. They have never read Beaumarchais, and therefore do not know how very little of him there is to read, and how, out of the two variations he wrote on his once famous theme, the second is only a petition in artistic and intellectual bankruptcy. Had the French theatre been capable of offering a field to Balzac, my proposition might have to be modified. But as it was no more able to do that than the English theatre was to enlist the genius of Dickens, I may say confidently that in that great comedy which Balzac called " the comedy of humanity," to be played for the amusement of the gods rather than for that of the French public, there is no summit in the barren plain that stretches from Mount Molière to our own times until we reach Brieux.

How the Nineteenth Century found itself
out

It is reserved for some great critic to give us a study
of the psychology of the nineteenth century. Those of
us who as adults saw it face to face in that last moiety
of its days when one fierce hand after another — Marx's,
Zola's, Ibsen's, Strindberg's, Turgenief's, Tolstoy's —
stripped its masks off and revealed it as, on the whole,
perhaps the most villainous page of recorded human history, can also recall the strange confidence with which it
regarded itself as the very summit of civilization, and
talked of the past as a cruel gloom that had been dis-
pelled for ever by the railway and the electric telegraph.
But centuries, like men, begin to find themselves out in
middle age. The youthful conceit of the nineteenth had
a splendid exponent in Macaulay, and, for a time, a glo-
riously jolly one during the nonage of Dickens. There
was certainly nothing morbid in the air then: Dickens
and Macaulay are as free from morbidity as Dumas
père and Guizot. Even Stendhal and Prosper Merimée,
though by no means burgess optimists, are quite sane.
When you come to Zola and Maupassant, Flaubert and
the Goncourts, to Ibsen and Strindberg, to Aubrey
Beardsley and George Moore, to D'Annunzio and Eche-
garay, you are in a new and morbid atmosphere. French
literature up to the middle of the nineteenth century was
still all of one piece with Rabelais, Montaigne and
Molière. Zola breaks that tradition completely: he is as
different as Karl Marx from Turgot or Darwin from
Cuvier.

In this new phase we see the bourgeoisie, after a century and a half of complacent vaunting of its own prob-
ity and modest happiness (begun by Daniel Defoe in
Robinson Crusoe's praises of "the middle station of

life "), suddenly turning bitterly on itself with accusations of hideous sexual and commercial corruption. Thackeray's campaign against snobbery and Dickens's against hypocrisy were directed against the vices of respectable men; but now even the respectability was passionately denied: the bourgeois was depicted as a thief, a tyrant, a sweater, a selfish voluptuary whose marriages were simple legalizations of unbridled licentiousness. Sexual irregularities began to be attributed to the sympathetic characters in fiction not as the blackest spots in their portraits, but positively as redeeming humanities in them.

Jack the Ripper

I am by no means going here either to revive the old outcry against this school of iconoclasts and disillusioners, or to join the new reaction against it. It told the world many truths: it brought romance back to its senses. Its very repudiation of the graces and enchantments of fine art was necessary; for the artistic morbidezza of Byron and Victor Hugo was too imaginative to allow the Victorian bourgeoisie to accept them as chroniclers of real facts and real people. The justification of Zola's comparative coarseness is that his work could not have been done in any other way. If Zola had had a sense of humor, or a great artist's delight in playing with his ideas, his materials, and his readers, he would have become either as unreadable to the very people he came to wake up as Anatole France is, or as incredible as Victor Hugo was. He would also have incurred the mistrust and hatred of the majority of Frenchmen, who, like the majority of men of all nations, are not merely incapable of fine art, but resent it furiously. A wit is to them a man who is laughing at them: an artist is a man of loose character who lives by telling lying stories and

pandering to the voluptuous passions. What they like to
read is the police intelligence, especially the murder
cases and divorce cases. The invented murders and di-
vorces of the novelists and playwrights do not satisfy
them, because they cannot believe in them; and belief
that the horror or scandal actually occurred, that real
people are shedding real blood and real tears, is indispensable to their enjoyment. To produce this belief by
works of fiction, the writer must disguise and even dis-
card the arts of the man of letters and assume the style
of the descriptive reporter of the criminal courts. As an
example of how to cater for such readers, we may take
Zola's Bête Humaine. It is in all its essentials a simple
and touching story, like Prévost's Manon Lescaut. But
into it Zola has violently thrust the greatest police sensation of the nineteenth century: the episode of Jack the
Ripper. Jack's hideous neurosis is no more a part of
human nature than Cæsar's epilepsy or Gladstone's miss-
ing finger. One is tempted to accuse Zola of having borrowed it from the newspapers to please his customers
just as Shakespear used to borrow stories of murder and
jealousy from the tales and chronicles of his time, and
heap them on the head of convivial humorists like Iago
and Richard III, or gentle poets like Macbeth and Hamlet. Without such allurements, Shakespear could not
have lived by his plays. And if he had been rich enough
to disregard this consideration, he would still have had to
provide sensation enough to induce people to listen to
what he was inspired to say. It is only the man who has
no message who is too fastidious to beat the drum at the
door of his booth.

Rise of the Scientific Spirit

Still, the Shakesperean murders were romantic murders: the Zolaesque ones were police reports. The old mad heroines, the Ophelias and Lucies of Lammermoor, were rhapsodists with flowers in their hands: the new ones were clinical studies of mental disease. The new note was as conspicuous in the sensational chapters as in the dull chapters, of which there were many. This was the punishment of the middle class for hypocrisy. It had carried the conspiracy of silence which we call decorum to such lengths that when young men discovered the suppressed truths, they felt bound to shout them in the streets. I well remember how when I was a youth in my teens I happened to obtain access to the papers of an Irish crown solicitor through a colleague who had some clerical work to do upon them. The county concerned was not one of the crimeless counties: there was a large camp in it; and the soldier of that day was not the respectable, rather pious, and very low-spirited youth who now makes the King's uniform what the curate's black coat was then. There were not only cases which were tried and not reported: there were cases which could not even be tried, the offenders having secured impunity by pushing their follies to lengths too grotesque to be bearable even in a criminal court — also because of the silly ferocity of the law, which punished the negligible indecencies of drunken young soldiers as atrocious crimes. The effect produced by these revelations on my raw youth was a sense of heavy responsibility for conniving at their concealment. I felt that if camp and barrack life involved these things, they ought to be known. I had been caught by the great wave of scientific enthusiasm which was then passing over Europe as a result of the discovery of Natural Selection by Darwin, and of

the blow it dealt to the vulgar Bible worship and re-
demption mongering which had hitherto passed among
us for religion. I wanted to get at the facts. I was prepared for the facts being unflattering: had I not already
faced the fact that instead of being a fallen angel I was
first cousin to a monkey? Long afterwards, when I was
a well-known writer, I said that what we wanted as the
basis of our plays and novels was not romance, but a
really scientific natural history. Scientific natural history is not compatible with taboo; and as everything
connected with sex was tabooed, I felt the need for mentioning the forbidden subjects, not only because of their
own importance, but for the sake of destroying taboo
by giving it the most violent possible shocks. The same
impulse is unmistakably active in Zola and his contemporaries. He also wanted, not works of literary art, but
stories he could believe in as records of things that really
happen. He imposed Jack the Ripper on his idyll of
the railwayman's wife to make it scientific. To all
artists and Platonists he made it thereby very unreal;
for to the Platonist all accidents are unreal and negligible; but to the people he wanted to get at — the anti-
artistic people — he made it readable.

The scientific spirit was unintelligible to the Philis-
tines and repulsive to the dilettanti, who said to Zola:
" If you must tell us stories about agricultural laborers,
why tell us dirty ones? " But Zola did not want, like
the old romancers, to tell a story. He wanted to tell
the world the scientific truth about itself. His view was
that if you were going to legislate for agricultural laborers, or deal with them or their business in any way,
you had better know what they are really like; and in
supplying you with the necessary information he did not
tell you what you already knew, which included pretty
nearly all that could be decorously mentioned, but what
you did not know, which was that part of the truth that

was tabooed. For the same reason, when he found a generation whose literary notions of Parisian cocotterie were founded on Marguerite Gauthier, he felt it to be a duty to show them Nana. And it was a very necessary thing to do. If some Irish writer of the seventies had got himself banished from all decent society, and perhaps convicted of obscene libel, by writing a novel showing the side of camp life that was never mentioned except in the papers of the Crown Solicitor, we should be nearer to a rational military system than we are to-day.

Zolaism as a Superstition

It is, unfortunately, much easier to throw the forces of art into a reaction than to recall them when the reaction has gone far enough. A case which came under my own notice years ago illustrates the difficulty. The wife of an eminent surgeon had some talent for drawing. Her husband wrote a treatise on cancer; and she drew the illustrations. It was the first time she had used her gift for a serious purpose; and she worked hard enough at it to acquire considerable skill in depicting cancerous proliferation. The book being finished and published, she resumed her ordinary practice of sketching for pleasure. But all her work now had an uncanny look. When she drew a landscape, it was like a cancer that accidentally looked like a landscape. She had acquired a cancerous technique; and she could not get rid of it.

This happens as easily in literature as in the other arts. The men who trained themselves as writers by dragging the unmentionable to light, presently found that they could do that so much better than anything else that they gave up dealing with the other subjects. Even their quite mentionable episodes had an unmentionable air. Their imitators assumed that unmentionability was an end in itself — that to be decent was to be out of the movement. Zola and Ibsen could not, of course, be confined to mere reaction against taboo. Ibsen was to the last fascinating and full of a strange moving beauty; and Zola often broke into sentimental romance. But neither Ibsen nor Zola, after they once took in hand the work of unmasking the idols of the bourgeoisie, ever again wrote a happy or pleasant play or novel. Ibsen's suicides and catastrophes at last produced the cry of "People don't do such things," which he ridiculed through Judge Brack in Hedda Gabler. This was easy enough: Brack was so far wrong that people do do such things occasionally. But on the whole Brack was right. The tragedy of Hedda in real life is not that she commits suicide but that she continues to live. If such acts of violent rebellion as those of Hedda and Nora and Rebecca and the rest were the inevitable or even the probable consequences of their unfitness to be wives and mothers, or of their contracting repugnant marriages to avoid being left on the shelf, social reform would be very rapid; and we should hear less nonsense as to women like Nora and Hedda being mere figments of Ibsen's imagination. Our real difficulty is the almost boundless docility and submission to social convention which is characteristic of the human race. What balks the social reformer everywhere is that the victims of social evils do not complain, and even strongly resent being treated as victims. The more a dog suffers from being chained the more dangerous it is to release him: he bites savagely at the hand that dares touch his collar. Our Rougon-Macquart families are usually enormously proud of themselves; and though they have to put up with their share of drunkards and madmen, they do not proliferate into Jack-the-Rippers. Nothing that is admittedly and unmistakably horrible matters very much, because it frightens people into seeking a remedy: the serious horrors are those which seem entirely respectable and normal to respectable and normal men. Now the formula of tragedy had come down to the nineteenth century from days in which this was not recognized, and when life was so thoroughly accepted as a divine institution that in order to make it seem tragic, something dreadful had to happen and somebody had to die. But the tragedy of modern life is that nothing happens, and that the resultant dulness does not kill. Maupassant's Une Vie is infinitely more tragic than the death of Juliet.

In Ibsen's works we find the old traditions and the new conditions struggling in the same play, like a gudgeon half swallowed by a pike. Almost all the sorrow and the weariness which makes his plays so poignant are the sorrow and weariness of the mean dull life in which nothing happens; but none the less he provides a final catastrophe of the approved fifth-act-blank-verse type. Hedwig and Hedda shoot themselves: Rosmer and Rebecca throw themselves into the mill-race: Solness and Rubeck are dashed to pieces: Borkman dies of acute stage tragedy without discoverable lesions. I will not again say, as I have said before, that these catastrophes are forced, because a fortunate performance often makes them seem inevitable; but I do submit that the omission of them would leave the play sadder and more convincing.

The Passing of the Tragic Catastrophe and the Happy Ending

Not only is the tradition of the catastrophe unsuitable to modern studies of life: the tradition of an ending, happy or the reverse, is equally unworkable. The moment the dramatist gives up accidents and catastrophes, and takes " slices of life " as his material, he finds himself committed to plays that have no endings. The curtain no longer comes down on a hero slain or married: it comes down when the audience has seen enough of the

life presented to it to draw the moral, and must either
leave the theatre or miss its last train.

The man who faced France with a drama fulfilling all
these conditions was Brieux. He was as scientific, as
conscientious, as unflinching as Zola without being in the
least morbid. He was no more dependent on horrors
than Molière, and as sane in his temper. He threw over
the traditional forced catastrophe uncompromisingly.
You do not go away from a Brieux play with the feeling
that the affair is finished or the problem solved for you
by the dramatist. Still less do you go away in " that
happy, easy, ironically indulgent frame of mind that is
the true test of comedy," as Mr. Walkley put it in *The
Times* of the 1st October, 1909. You come away with
a very disquieting sense that you are involved in the
affair, and must find the way out of it for yourself and
everybody else if civilization is to be tolerable to your
sense of honor.

The Difference between Brieux and Molière or Shakespear

Brieux's task is thus larger than Molière's. Molière
destroyed the prestige of those conspiracies against
society which we call the professions, and which thrive
by the exploitation of idolatry. He unmasked the doctor, the philosopher, the fencing master, the priest. He
ridiculed their dupes: the hypochondriac, the acade-
mician, the devotee, the gentleman in search of accom-
plishments. He exposed the snob: he showed the gentleman as the butt and creature of his valet, emphasizing
thus the inevitable relation between the man who lives
by unearned money and the man who lives by weight of
service. Beyond bringing this latter point up to a later
date Beaumarchais did nothing. But Molière never indicted society. Burke said that you cannot bring an in-

dictment against a nation; yet within a generation from
that utterance men began to draw indictments against
whole epochs, especially against the capitalistic epoch.
It is true that Molière, like Shakespear, indicted human
nature, which would seem to be a broader attack; but
such attacks only make thoughtful men melancholy and
hopeless, and practical men cynical or murderous. Le
Misanthrope, which seems to me, as a foreigner perhaps,
to be Molière's dullest and worst play, is like Hamlet in
two respects. The first, which is that it would have been
much better if it had been written in prose, is merely
technical and need not detain us. The second is that the
author does not clearly know what he is driving at. Le
Festin de Pierre, Molière's best philosophic play, is as
brilliant and arresting as Le Misanthrope is neither the
one nor the other; but here again there is no positive
side: the statue is a hollow creature with nothing to
say for himself; and Don Juan makes no attempt to
take advantage of his weakness. The reason why
Shakespear and Molière are always well spoken of and
recommended to the young is that their quarrel is really
a quarrel with God for not making men better. If they
had quarrelled with a specified class of persons with incomes of four figures for not doing their work better, or
for doing no work at all, they would be denounced as
seditious, impious, and profligate corruptors of morality.
Brieux wastes neither ink nor indignation on Providence. The idle despair that shakes its fist impotently
at the skies, uttering sublime blasphemies, such as

'As flies to wanton boys are we to the gods:
They kill us for their sport,'

does not amuse Brieux. His fisticuffs are not aimed
heavenward: they fall on human noses for the good of
human souls. When he sees human nature in conflict
with a political abuse he does not blame human nature,

knowing that such blame is the favorite trick of those
who wish to perpetuate the abuse without being able
to defend it. He does not even blame the abuse: he exposes it, and then leaves human nature to tackle it with
its eyes open. And his method of exposure is the dramatic method. He is a born dramatist, differing from
the ordinary dramatists only in that he has a large mind
and a scientific habit of using it. As a dramatist he must
take for his theme a conflict of some sort. As a dramatist of large mind he cannot be satisfied with the trum-
pery conflicts of the Divorce Court and the Criminal
Court: of the husband with the seducer, of the policeman with the murderer. Having the scientific conscience
in a higher degree than Zola (he has a better head), he
cannot be interested in imaginary conflicts which he himself would have to invent like a child at play. The conflict which inspires his dramatic genius must be a big one
and a real one. To ask an audience to spend three hours
hanging on the question of which particular man some
particular woman shall mate with does not strike him as
a reasonable proceeding; and if the audience does not
agree with him, why, it can go to some fashionable
dramatist of the boulevard who does agree with it.

Brieux and the Boulevard

This involves Brieux in furious conflict with the boulevard. Up to quite recent times it was impossible for an
Englishman to mention Brieux to a Parisian as the only
French playwright who really counted in Europe, without being met with astonished assurances that Brieux is
not a playwright at all; that his plays are not plays; that
he is not (in Sarcey's sense of the phrase) " du théâtre ";
that he is a mere pamphleteer without even literary style.
And when you expressed your natural gratification at
learning that the general body of Parisian dramatists

were so highly gifted that Brieux counted for nothing
in Paris — when you respectfully asked for the names of
a few of the most prominent of the geniuses who had
eclipsed him, you were given three or four of which you
had never heard, and one or two known to you as those of
cynically commercial manipulators of the *menage a trois,*
the innocent wife discovered at the villain's rooms at
midnight (to beg him to spare the virtue of a sister, the
character of a son, or the life of a father), the compro-
mising letter, the duel, and all the rest of the claptraps
out of which dramatic playthings can be manufactured
for the amusement of grown-up children. Not until the
Academie Française elected Brieux did it occur to the
boulevardiers that the enormous difference between him
and their pet authors was a difference in which the supe-
riority lay with Brieux.

The Pedantry of Paris

Indeed it is difficult for the Englishman to understand
how bigotedly the Parisians cling to the claptrap theatre.
The English do not care enough about the theatre to
cling to its traditions or persecute anyone for their sake;
but the French do. Besides, in fine art, France is a
nation of born pedants. The vulgar English painter
paints vulgar pictures, and generally sells them. But the
vulgar French painter paints classical ones, though
whether he sells them or not I do not know: I hope not.
The corresponding infatuation in the theatre is for
dramas in alexandrines; and alexandrines are far worse
than English blank verse, which is saying a good deal.
Racine and Corneille, who established the alexandrine
tradition, deliberately aimed at classicism, taking the
Greek drama as their model. Even a foreigner can hear
the music of their verse. Corneille wrote alexandrines as
Dryden wrote heroic couplets, — in a virile, stately, hand-

some and withal human way; and Racine had tenderness
and beauty as well. This drama of Racine and Corneille,
with the music of Gluck, gave the French in the seventeenth and eighteenth centuries a body of art which was
very beautiful, very refined, very delightful for cultivated people, and very tedious for the ignorant. When,
through the spread of elementary education, the ignorant
invaded the theatre in overwhelming numbers, this exquisite body of art became a dead body, and was practised
by nobody except the amateurs — the people who love
what has been already done in art and loathe the real
life out of which living art must continually grow afresh.
In their hands it passed from being a commercial failure
to being an obsolete nuisance.

Commercially, the classic play was supplanted by a
nuisance which was not a failure: to wit, the " well made
play " of Scribe and his school. The manufacture of
well made plays is not an art: it is an industry. It is
not at all hard for a literary mechanic to acquire it: the
only difficulty is to find a literary mechanic who is not
by nature too much of an artist for the job; for nothing
spoils a well made play more infallibly than the least
alloy of high art or the least qualm of conscience on the
part of the writer. " Art for art's sake " is the formula
of the well made play, meaning in practice " Success for
money's sake." Now great art is never produced for its
own sake. It is too difficult to be worth the effort. All
the great artists enter into a terrible struggle with the
public, often involving bitter poverty and personal humil-
iation, and always involving calumny and persecution,
because they believe they are apostles doing what used
to be called the Will of God, and is now called by many
prosaic names, of which " public work " is the least con-
troversial. And when these artists have travailed and
brought forth, and at last forced the public to associate
keen pleasure and deep interest with their methods and

morals, a crowd of smaller men — art confectioners, we may call them — hasten to make pretty entertainments out of scraps and crumbs from the masterpieces. Offenbach laid hands on Beethoven's Seventh Symphony and produced J'aime les militaires, to the disgust of Schumann, who was nevertheless doing precisely the same thing in a more pretentious way. And these confectioners are by no means mere plagiarists. They bring all sorts of engaging qualities to their work: love of beauty, desire to give pleasure, tenderness, humor, everything except the high republican conscience, the identification of the artist's purpose with the purpose of the universe, which alone makes an artist great.

But the well made play was not confectionery: it had not even the derived virtue of being borrowed from the great playwrights. Its formula grew up in the days when the spread of elementary schooling produced a huge mass of playgoers sufficiently educated to want plays instead of dog-fights, but not educated enough to enjoy or understand the masterpieces of dramatic art. Besides, education or no education, one cannot live on masterpieces alone, not only because there are not enough of them, but because new plays as well as great plays are needed, and there are not enough Molières and Shakespears in the world to keep the demand for novelty satisfied. Hence it has always been necessary to have some formula by which men of mediocre talent and no conscience can turn out plays for the theatrical market. Such men have written melodramas since the theatre existed. It was in the nineteenth century that the demand for manufactured plays was extended to drawing room plays in which the Forest of Bondy and the Auberge des Adrets, the Red Barn and the Cave at Midnight, had to be replaced by Lord Blank's flat in Whitehall Court and the Great Hall, Chevy Chace. Playgoers, being by that time mostly poor playgoers, wanted

to see how the rich live; wanted to see them actually
drinking champagne and wearing real fashionable dresses
and trousers with a neatly ironed crease down the knee.

How to Write a Popular Play

The formula for the well made play is so easy that I
give it for the benefit of any reader who feels tempted to
try his hand at making the fortune that awaits all successful manufacturers in this line. First, you "have an
idea" for a dramatic situation. If it strikes you as a
splendidly original idea, whilst it is in fact as old as the
hills, so much the better. For instance, the situation of
an innocent person convicted by circumstances of a crime
may always be depended on. If the person is a woman,
she must be convicted of adultery. If a young officer, he
must be convicted of selling information to the enemy,
though it is really a fascinating female spy who has en-
snared him and stolen the incriminating document. If
the innocent wife, banished from her home, suffers
agonies through her separation from her children, and,
when one of them is dying (of any disease the dramatist
chooses to inflict), disguises herself as a nurse and at-
tends it through its dying convulsion until the doctor,
who should be a serio-comic character, and if possible a
faithful old admirer of the lady's, simultaneously an-
nounces the recovery of the child and the discovery of
the wife's innocence, the success of the play may be regarded as assured if the writer has any sort of knack for
his work. Comedy is more difficult, because it requires
a sense of humor and a good deal of vivacity; but the
process is essentially the same: it is the manufacture of
a misunderstanding. Having manufactured it, you place
its culmination at the end of the last act but one, which
is the point at which the manufacture of the play begins.
Then you make your first act out of the necessary intro-

duction of the characters to the audience, after elaborate explanations, mostly conducted by servants, solicitors, and other low life personages (the principals must all be dukes and colonels and millionaires), of how the misunderstanding is going to come about. Your last act consists, of course, of clearing up the misunderstanding, and generally getting the audience out of the theatre as best you can.

Now please do not misunderstand me as pretending that this process is so mechanical that it offers no opportunity for the exercise of talent. On the contrary, it is so mechanical that without very conspicuous talent nobody can make much reputation by doing it, though some can and do make a living at it. And this often leads the cultivated classes to suppose that all plays are written by authors of talent. As a matter of fact the majority of those who in France and England make a living by writing plays are unknown and, as to education, all but illiterate. Their names are not worth putting on the playbill, because their audiences neither know nor care who the author is, and often believe that the actors improvise the whole piece, just as they in fact do sometimes improvise the dialogue. To rise out of this obscurity you must be a Scribe or a Sardou, doing essentially the same thing, it is true, but doing it wittily and ingeniously, at moments almost poetically, and giving the persons of the drama some touches of real observed character.

Why the Critics are always Wrong

Now it is these strokes of talent that set the critics wrong. For the talent, being all expended on the formula, at least consecrates the formula in the eyes of the critics. Nay, they become so accustomed to the formula that at last they cannot relish or understand a play that has grown naturally, just as they cannot admire the

Venus of Milo because she has neither a corset nor high
heeled shoes. They are like the peasants who are so accustomed to food reeking with garlic that when food is
served to them without it they declare that it has no taste
and is not food at all.

This is the explanation of the refusal of the critics of
all nations to accept great original dramatists like Ibsen
and Brieux as real dramatists, or their plays as real
plays. No writer of the first order needs the formula
any more than a sound man needs a crutch. In his
simplest mood, when he is only seeking to amuse, he does
not manufacture a plot: he tells a story. He finds no
difficulty in setting people on the stage to talk and act
in an amusing, exciting or touching way. His characters
have adventures and ideas which are interesting in themselves, and need not be fitted into the Chinese puzzle of
a plot.

The Interpreter of Life

But the great dramatist has something better to do
than to amuse either himself or his audience. He has to
interpret life. This sounds a mere pious phrase of literary criticism; but a moment's consideration will discover
its meaning and its exactitude. Life as it appears to us
in our daily experience is an unintelligible chaos of happenings. You pass Othello in the bazaar in Aleppo, Iago
on the jetty in Cyprus, and Desdemona in the nave of
St. Mark's in Venice without the slightest clue to their
relations to one another. The man you see stepping into
a chemist's shop to buy the means of committing murder
or suicide, may, for all you know, want nothing but a
liver pill or a toothbrush. The statesman who has no
other object than to make you vote for his party at the
next election, may be starting you on an incline at the
foot of which lies war, or revolution, or a smallpox epi-

demic, or five years off your lifetime. The horrible murder of a whole family by the father who finishes by killing himself, or the driving of a young girl on to the streets, may be the result of your discharging an employee in a fit of temper a month before. To attempt to understand life from merely looking on at it as it happens in the streets is as hopeless as trying to understand public questions by studying snapshots of public demonstrations. If we possessed a series of cinematographs of all the executions during the Reign of Terror, they might be exhibited a thousand times without enlightening the audiences in the least as to the meaning of the Revolution: Robespierre would perish as " un monsieur " and Marie Antoinette as " une femme." Life as it occurs is senseless: a policeman may watch it and work in it for thirty years in the streets and courts of Paris without learning as much of it or from it as a child or a nun may learn from a single play by Brieux. For it is the business of Brieux to pick out the significant incidents from the chaos of daily happenings, and arrange them so that their relation to one another becomes significant, thus changing us from bewildered spectators of a monstrous confusion to men intelligently conscious of the world and its destinies. This is the highest function that man can perform — the greatest work he can set his hand to; and this is why the great dramatists of the world, from Euripides and Aristophanes to Shakespear and Molière, and from them to Ibsen and Brieux, take that majestic and pontifical rank which seems so strangely above all the reasonable pretensions of mere strolling actors and theatrical authors.

How the Great Dramatists torture the Public

Now if the critics are wrong in supposing that the formula of the well made play is not only an indispensable factor in playwriting, but is actually the essence of the play itself — if their delusion is rebuked and confuted by the practice of every great dramatist, even when he is only amusing himself by story telling, what must happen to their poor formula when it impertinently offers its services to a playwright who has taken on his supreme function as the Interpreter of Life? Not only has he no use for it, but he must attack and destroy it; for one of the very first lessons he has to teach to a play-ridden public is that the romantic conventions on which the formula proceeds are all false, and are doing incalculable harm in these days when everybody reads romances and goes to the theatre. Just as the historian can teach no real history until he has cured his readers of the romantic delusion that the greatness of a queen consists in her being a pretty woman and having her head cut off, so the playwright of the first order can do nothing with his audiences until he has cured them of looking at the stage through the keyhole, and sniffing round the theatre as prurient people sniff round the divorce court. The cure is not a popular one. The public suffers from it exactly as a drunkard or a snuff taker suffers from an attempt to conquer the habit. The critics especially, who are forced by their profession to indulge immoderately in plays adulterated with falsehood and vice, suffer so acutely when deprived of them for a whole evening that they hurl disparagements and even abuse and insult at the merciless dramatist who is torturing them. To a bad play of the kind they are accustomed to they can be cruel through superciliousness, irony, impatience, contempt, or even a Rochefoucauldian pleasure in a friend's misfortune. But the hatred provoked by deliberately inflicted pain, the frantic denials as of a prisoner at the bar accused of a disgraceful crime, the clamor for vengeance thinly disguised as artistic justice, the suspicion that the dramatist is using private information and making a personal attack: all these are to be found only when the playwright is no mere *marchand de plaisir,* but, like Brieux, a ruthless revealer of hidden truth and a mighty destroyer of idols.

Brieux's Conquest of London

So well does Brieux know this that he has written a play, La Foi, showing how truth is terrible to men, and how false religions (theatrical romance, by the way, is the falsest and most fantastically held of all the false religions) are a necessity to them. With this play he achieved, for the first time on record, the feat of winning a success in a fashionable London theatre with a cold-blooded thesis play. Those who witnessed the performance of False Gods at His Majesty's Theatre this year were astonished to see that exceptionally large theatre filled with strangely attentive ordinary playgoers, to whose customary requirements and weaknesses no concession was made for a moment by the playwright. They were getting a lesson and nothing else. The same famous acting, the same sumptuous *mise en scène,* had not always saved other plays from failure. There was no enthusiasm: one might almost say there was no enjoyment. The audience for once had something better to do than to amuse themselves. The old playgoers and the critics, who, on the first night, had politely regretted an inevitable failure after waiting, like the maturer ladies at the sack of Ismail in Byron's poem, for the adultery to begin, asked one another incredulously whether there could really be money in this sort of thing. Such feats had been performed before at coterie theatres where the expenses were low and where the plays were seasoned with a good deal of ordinary amusing comedy; but in this play there was not a jest from beginning to end; and the size of the theatre and the expenses of produc-

tion were on a princely scale. Yet La Foi held its own.
The feat was quite unprecedented; and that it should
have been achieved for the first time by a Frenchman is
about a million times more remarkable than that the first
man to fly across the channel (the two events were almost
simultaneous) should also have been a Frenchman.

Parisian Stupidity

And here I must digress for a moment to remark that
though Paris is easily the most prejudiced, old-fashioned,
obsolete-minded city in the west of Europe, yet when she
produces great men she certainly does not do it by
halves. Unfortunately, there is nothing she hates more
than a Frenchman of genius. When an Englishman says
that you have to go back to Michael Angelo to find a
sculptor who can be mentioned in the same breath as
Rodin without manifest absurdity, the Parisians indignantly exclaim that only an ignorant foreigner could
imagine that a man who was not a pupil at the Beaux
Arts could possibly be a sculptor at all. And I have
already described how they talk about Brieux, the only
French dramatist whose fame crosses frontiers and
channels, and fills the continent. To be quite frank, I
cannot to this day understand why they made him an Aca-
demician instead of starving him to death and then giving him a statue. Can it be that in his early days, before
he could gain his living by the theatre, he wrote a spell-
ing book, or delivered a course of lectures on the use of
pure line in Greek design? To suppose that they did it
because he is a great man is to imply that they know a
great Frenchman when they see him, which is contrary
to all experience. They never know until the English
tell them.

Brieux and the English Theatre

In England our knowledge of Brieux has been delayed by the childishness of our theatre. This childishness is by no means to be deplored: it means that the theatre is occupied with the elementary education of the masses instead of with the higher education of the classes. Those who desire dramatic performances of the higher sort have procured them only by forming clubs, hiring theatres, engaging performers, and selecting plays for themselves. After 1889, when Ibsen first became known in London through A Doll's House, a succession of these clubs kept what may be called the serious adult drama fitfully alive until 1904, when Messrs. Vedrenne and Barker took the field with a regular theatrical enterprise devoted to this class of work, and maintained it until the National Theatre project was set on foot, and provisional repertory schemes were announced by established commercial managements. It was through one of these clubs, the Stage Society, that Brieux reached the English stage with his Bienfaiteurs. Then the first two plays in this volume were performed, and, later on, Les Hannetons. These performances settled for English connoisseurs the question of Brieux's rank among modern playwrights. Later on his Robe Rouge introduced the ordinary playgoers to him; and he is now no longer one of the curiosities of the coterie theatre, as even Ibsen to some extent still is, but one of the conquerors of the general British public.

The Censorship in France and England

Unfortunately, he has not yet been able to conquer our detestable, discredited, but still all-powerful censorship. In France he was attacked by the censorship just as in England; but in France the censorship broke itself against him and perished. The same thing would probably have occurred here but for the fact that our Censor, by a grotesque accident of history — to be precise, because Henry VIII began the censorship of the theatre by appointing an officer of his own household to do the work — remains part of the King's retinue; and his abolition involves the curtailment of that retinue and therefore the reduction of the King's State, always a very difficult and delicate matter in a monarchical country. In France the censorship was exercised by the Minister of Fine Arts (a portfolio that does not exist in our Cabinet), and was in the hands of two or three examiners of plays, who necessarily behaved exactly like our Mr. Redford; for, as I have so often pointed out, the evils of censorship are made compulsory by the nature of the office, and are not really the fault of the individual censor. These gentlemen, then, prohibited the performance of Brieux's best and most useful plays, just as Mr. Redford did here. But as the French Parliament, having nobody to consider but themselves and the interests of the nation, presently refused to vote the salaries of the Censors, the institution died a natural death. We have no such summary remedy here. Our Censor's salary is part of the King's civil list, and is therefore sacred. Years ago, our Playgoers' Club asked me how the censorship could be abolished. I replied, to the great scandal of that loyal body, — You must begin by abolishing the monarchy.

Brieux and the English Censorship

Nevertheless, Brieux has left his mark even on the English censorship. This year (1909) the prohibition of his plays was one of the strongest items in the long list of grievances by which the English playwrights compelled the Government to appoint a Select Committee of

both houses of Parliament to enquire into the working
of the censorship. The report of that Committee admits
the charge brought against the Censor of systematically
suppressing plays dealing seriously with social problems
whilst allowing frivolous and even pornographic plays to
pass unchallenged. It advises that the submission of
plays to the Censor shall in future be optional, though it
does not dare to omit the customary sycophantic recommendation that the Lord Chamberlain shall still retain
his privilege of licensing plays; and it proposes that the
authors and managers of plays so licensed, though not
exempt from prosecution, shall enjoy certain immunities
denied in the case of unlicensed plays. There are many
other conditions which need not be gone into here; but
to a Frenchman the main fact that stands out is that the
accident which has made the Censor an officer of the
King's Household has prevented a parliamentary committee from recommending the abolition of his control
over the theatre in a report which not only has not a
word to say in his defence, but expressly declares that his
license affords the public no guarantee that the plays he
approves are decent, and that authors of serious plays
need protection against his unenlightened despotism.

Taboo

We may therefore take it on the authority of the
Select Committee that the prohibition by the English
censorship of the public performances of the three plays
in this book does not afford the smallest reasonable
ground for condemning them as improper — rather the
contrary. As a matter of fact, most men, if asked to
guess the passages to which the Censor took exception,
would guess wrongly. Certainly a Frenchman would.
The reason is that though in England as in France what
is called decency is not a reasoned discrimination between

what needs to be said and what ought not to be said, but simply the observance of a set of taboos, these taboos are not the same in England as in France. A Frenchman of scrupulously correct behavior will sometimes quite innocently make an English lady blush by mentioning something that is unmentionable in polite society in England though quite mentionable in France. To take a simple illustration, — an Englishman, when he first visits France, is always embarrassed, and sometimes shocked, on finding that the person in charge of a public lavatory for men is a woman. I cannot give reciprocal instances of the ways in which Englishmen shock the French nation, because I am happily unconscious of all the *cochonneries* of which I am no doubt guilty when I am in France. But that I do occasionally shock the brave French bourgeois to the very marrow of his bones by my indelicacy, I have not the smallest doubt. There is only one epithet in universal use for foreigners. That epithet is " dirty."

The Attitude of the People to the Literary Arts

These differences between nation and nation also exist between class and class and between town and country. I will not here go into the vexed question of whether the peasant's way of blowing his nose or the squire's is the more cleanly and hygienic, though my experience as a municipal councillor of the way in which epidemics are spread by laundries makes me incline to the side of the peasant. What is beyond all question is that each seems disgusting to the other. And when we come from physical facts to moral views and ethical opinions we find the same antagonisms. To a great section — perhaps the largest section — of the people of England and France, all novels, plays, and songs are licentious; and the habit of enjoying them is a mark of a worthless character. To these people the distinctions made by the literary classes between books fit for young girls to read and improper books — between Paul and Virginia and Mademoiselle de Maupin or Une Vie, between Mrs. Humphry Ward and Ouida — have no meaning: all writers of love stories and all readers of them are alike shameless. Cultivated Paris, cultivated London, are apt to overlook people who, as they seldom read and never write, have no means of making themselves heard. But such simple people heavily outnumber the cultivated; and if they could also outwit them, literature would perish. Yet their intolerance of fiction is as nothing to their intolerance of fact. I lately heard an English gentleman state a very simple fact in these terms: "I never could get on with my mother: she did not like me, and I did not like her: my brother was her pet." To an immense number of living English and French people this speech would suggest that its utterer ought to be burned alive, though the substitution of stepmother for mother and of half-brother for brother would suffice to make it seem quite probable and natural. And this, observe, not in the least because all these horrified people adore and are adored by their mothers, but simply because they have a fixed convention that the proper name of the relation between mother and son is love. However bitter and hostile it may in fact be in some cases, to call it by any other name is a breach of convention; and by the instinctive logic of timidity they infer that a man to whom convention is not sacred is a dangerous man. To them the ten commandments are nothing but arbitrary conventions; and the man who says to-day that he does not love his mother, may, they conclude, to-morrow steal, rob, murder, commit adultery, and bear false witness against his neighbor.

The Dread of the Original Thinker

This is the real secret of the terror inspired by an original thinker. In repudiating convention he is repudiating that on which his neighbors are relying for their sense of security. But he is usually also doing something even more unpopular. He is proposing new obligations to add to the already heavy burden of duty. When the boy Shelley elaborately and solemnly cursed his father for the entertainment of his friends, he only shocked us. But when the man Shelley told us that we should feed, clothe and educate all the children in the country as carefully as if they were our immediate own, we lost our tempers with him and deprived him of the custody of his own children.

It is useless to complain that the conventional masses are unintelligent. To begin with, they are not unintelligent except in the sense in which all men are unintelligent in matters in which they are not experts. I object to be called unintelligent merely because I do not know enough about mechanical construction to be able to judge whether a motor car of new design is an improvement or not, and therefore prefer to buy one of the old type to which I am accustomed. The brave bourgeois whom Brieux scandalizes must not be dismissed with ridicule by the man of letters because, not being an expert in morals, he prefers the old ways and mistrusts the new. His position is a very reasonable one. He says, in effect, " If I am to enjoy any sense of security, I must be able to reckon on other people behaving in a certain ascertained way. Never mind whether it is the ideally right way or the ideally wrong way: it will suit me well enough if only it is convenient and, above all, unmistakable. Lay it down if you like that people are not to pay debts and are to murder one another whenever they .

get a chance. In that case I can refuse to give credit, and can carry weapons and learn to use them to defend myself. On the other hand, if you settle that debts are to be enforced and the peace kept by the police, I will give credit and renounce the practice of arms. But the one thing that I cannot stand is not knowing what the social contract is."

The Justification of Conventionality

It is a cherished tradition in English politics that at a meeting of Lord Melbourne's Cabinet in the early days of Queen Victoria, the Prime Minister, when the meeting threatened to break up in confusion, put his back to the door and said, in the cynically profane manner then fashionable: " Gentlemen: we can tell the House the truth or we can tell it a lie: I do not care a damn which. All I insist on is that we shall all tell the same lie; and you shall not leave the room until you have settled what it is to be." Just so does the bourgeois perceive that the essential thing is not whether a convention is right or wrong, but that everybody shall know what it is and observe it. His cry is always: " I want to know where I stand." Tell him what he may do and what he may not do; and make him feel that he may depend on other people doing or not doing the same; and he feels secure, knowing where he stands and where other people stand. His dread and hatred of revolutions and heresies and men with original ideas is his dread of disorientation and insecurity. Those who have felt earthquakes assure us that there is no terror like the terror of the earth swaying under the feet that have always depended on it as the one immovable thing in the world. That is just how the ordinary respectable man feels when some man of genius rocks the moral ground beneath him by denying the validity of a convention. The popular phrases by which such innovators are described are always of the same kind. The early Christians were called men who wished to turn the world upside down. The modern critics of morals are reproached for " standing on their heads." There is no pretence of argument, or of any understanding of the proposals of the reformers: there is simply panic and a demand for suppression at all costs. The reformer is not forbidden to advance this or that definite opinion, because his assailants are too frightened to know or care what his opinions are: he is forbidden simply to speak in an unusual way about morals and religion, or to mention any subject that is not usually mentioned in public.

This is the terror which the English censorship, like all other censorships, gives effect to. It explains what puzzles most observers of the censorship so much: namely, its scandalous laxity towards and positive encouragement of the familiar and customary pornographic side of theatrical art simultaneously with its intolerance of the higher drama, which is always unconventional and super-bourgeois in its ethics. To illustrate, let me cite the point on which the English censorship came into conflict with Brieux, when Les Hannetons was first performed by the Stage Society.

Why Les Hannetons was Censored

Les Hannetons is a very powerful and convincing demonstration of the delusiveness of that sort of freedom which men try to secure by refusing to marry, and living with a mistress instead. The play is a comedy: the audience laughs throughout; but the most dissolute man present leaves the theatre convinced that the unfortunate hero had better have been married ten times over than fallen into such bondage as his liaison has landed him in. To witness a performance might very wisely be made part of the curriculum of every university college and polytechnic in the country.

Now those who do not know the ways of the censorship may jump to the conclusion that the objection of the Censor was to the exhibition on the stage of two persons living together in immoral relations. They would be greatly mistaken. The Censor made no difficulty whatever about that. Even the funny but ruthless scene where the woman cajoles the man by kissing him on a certain susceptible spot on his neck — a scene from which our shamed conscience shrinks as from a branding iron — was licensed without a word of remonstrance. But there is a searching passage in the play where the woman confesses to a girl friend that one of the lies by which she induced the man to enter into relations with her was that he was not her first lover. The friend is simple enough to express surprise, thinking that this, far from being an inducement, would have roused jealousy and disgust. The woman replies that, on the contrary, no man likes to face the responsibility of tempting a girl to her first step from the beaten path, and that girls take care accordingly not to let them know it.

This is one of those terrible stripping strokes by which a master of realism suddenly exposes a social sore which has been plastered over with sentimental nonsense about erring Magdalens, vicious nonsense about gaiety, or simply prudish silence. No young man or young woman hearing it, however anarchical their opinions may be as to sexual conduct, can possibly imagine afterwards that the relation between " les hannetons " is honest, charming, sentimentally interesting, or pardonable by the self-respect of either. It is felt instinctively to have something fundamentally dishonorable in it, in spite of the innocence of the natural affection of the pair for one another. Yet this is precisely the passage that the Censor refused to pass. All the rest was duly licensed. The

exhibition of the pretty, scheming, lying, sensual girl
fixing herself with triumphant success on the meanly
prudent sensual man, and having what many women
would consider rather a good time of it, was allowed and
encouraged by the court certificate of propriety. But
the deadly touch that made it impossible for even the
most thoughtless pair in the audience to go and do like-
wise without loathing themselves, was forbidden.

Misadventure of a Frenchman in Westminster Abbey

In short, the censorship did what it always does: it left
the poison on the table and carefully locked up the anti-
dote. And it did this, not from a fiendish design to
destroy the souls of the people, but solely because the
passage involved a reference by a girl to her virginity,
which is unusual and therefore tabooed. The Censor
never troubled himself as to the meaning or effect of the
passage. It represented the woman as doing an unusual
thing: therefore a dangerous, possibly subversive thing.
In England, when we are scandalized and can give no
direct reason why, we exclaim " What next? " That is
the continual cry of the Censor's soul. If a girl may
refer to her virginity on the stage, what may she not
refer to? This instinctive regard to consequences was
once impressed painfully on a pious Frenchman who, in
Westminster Abbey, knelt down to pray. The verger,
who had never seen such a thing happen before, promptly
handed him over to the police and charged him with
" brawling." Fortunately, the magistrate had compassion on the foreigner's ignorance; and even went the
length of asking why he should not be allowed to pray
in church. The reply of the verger was simple and
obvious. " If we allowed that," he said, " we should
have people praying all over the place." And to this

day the rule in Westminster Abbey is that you may stroll about and look at the monuments, but you must not on any account pray. Similarly, on the stage you may represent murder, gluttony, sexual vice, and all the crimes in the calendar and out of it, but you must not say anything unusual about them.

Marriage and Malthus

If Brieux found himself blocked by the censorship when he was exposing the vice of illicit unions, it will surprise no one to learn that his far more urgently needed exposures of the intemperance and corruption of marriage itself was fiercely banned. The vulgar, and consequently the official, view of marriage is that it hallows all the sexual relations of the parties to it. That it may mask all the vices of the coarsest libertinage with added elements of slavery and cruelty has always been true to some extent; but during the last forty years it has become so serious a matter that conscientious dramatists have to vivisect legal unions as ruthlessly as illegal ones. For it happens that just about forty years ago the propaganda of Neo-Malthusianism changed the bearing of children from an involuntary condition of marriage to a voluntary one. From the moment this momentous discovery was made, childless marriage became available to male voluptuaries as the cheapest way of keeping a mistress, and to female ones as the most convenient and respectable way of being kept in idle luxury by a man. The effects of this have already been startling, and will yet be revolutionary as far as marriage is concerned, both in law and custom. The work of keeping the populations of Europe replenished received a sudden check, amounting in France and England to a threat of actual retrogression. The appointment of a Royal Commission to enquire into the decline of the birthrate in the very sections of the population which most need to be maintained, is probably not very far off: the more far-seeing of those who know the facts have prophesied such a step for a long time past. The expectation of the Neo-Malthusians that the regulation of births in our families would give the fewer children born a better chance of survival in greater numbers and in fuller health and efficiency than the children of the old unrestricted families, and of the mother exhausted by excessive childbearing, has no doubt been fulfilled in some cases; but, on the whole, artificial sterility seems to be beating natural fertility; for as far as can be judged by certain sectional but typical private censuses, the average number of children produced is being dragged down to one and a half per family by the large proportion of intentionally childless marriages, and the heavy pressure of the cost of private childbearing on the scanty incomes of the masses.

That this will force us to a liberal State endowment of parentage, direct or indirect, is not now doubted by people who understand the problem: in fact, as I write, the first open step has already been taken by the Government's proposal to exempt parents from the full burden of taxation borne by the childless. There has also begun a change in public opinion as to the open abuse of marriage as a mere means by which any pair can procure a certificate of respectability by paying for it, which may quite possibly end in the disuse of the ceremony for all except fertile unions. From the point of view of the Church, it is a manifest profanation that couples whose only aim is a comfortable domesticity should obtain for it the sacrament of religious marriage on pretence of unselfish and publicly important purposes which they have not the smallest intention of carrying out. From the secular point of view, there is no reason why couples who do not intend to have children should be allowed to enslave one another by all the complicated legal restrictions of their liberty and property which are attached to marriage solely to secure the responsibility of parents to the State for their children.

Brieux and the Respectable Married Man

All these by no means remote prospects, familiar though they are to the statesman and sociologist, are amazing to the bourgeois even when he is personally implicated in the change of practice that is creating the necessity for a change in law and in opinion. He has changed his practice privately, without talking about it except in secret, or in passages of unprintable Rabelaisian jocosity with his friends; and he is not only unable to see why anyone else should talk publicly about the change, but terrified lest what he is doing furtively and hypocritically should be suddenly dragged into the light, and his own case recorded, perhaps, in public statistics in support of innovations which vaguely suggest to him the destruction of morals and the break-up of the family. But both his pruderies and his terrors must give way before the absolute necessity for re-examining the foundations of our social structure after the shock they have received from the discovery of artificial sterilization, and their readjustment to the new strains they have to bear as a consequence of that discovery.

Tolstoy, with his Kreutzer Sonata, was the first to carry the war into the enemy's country by showing that marriage intensified instead of eliminating every element of evil in sexual relations; but Brieux was the first dramatist to see not only the hard facts of the situation, but its political importance. He has seen in particular that a new issue has arisen in that eternal conflict of the sexes which is created by the huge difference between the transient pleasure of the man and the prolonged suffering of the woman in maintaining the population.

Malthusianism, when it passed from being the specula-
tion of an economist to being the ardent faith of a devoted band of propagandists, touched our feelings mainly
as a protest against the burden of excessive childbearing
imposed on married women. It was not then foreseen
that the triumph of the propaganda might impose a still
worse burden on them, — the burden of enforced sterility.
Before Malthus was born, cases were familiar enough in
which wives who had borne two or three children as an
inevitable consequence of their conjugal relations had
thereupon rebelled against further travail, and discon-
tinued the relations by such a resolute assertion of selfishness as is not easy to an amiable woman and practically
not possible to a loving or a jealous wife. But the case
of a man refusing to fulfil his parental function and
thereby denying the right of his wife to motherhood was
unknown. Yet it immediately and inevitably arose the
moment men became possessed of the means of doing this
without self-denial. A wife could thus be put in a position intolerable to a woman of honor as distinguished
from a frank voluptuary. She could be condemned to
barren bodily slavery without remedy. To keep silence
about so monstrous a wrong as this merely because the
subject is a tabooed one was not possible to Brieux.
Censorship or no censorship, it had to be said, and indeed shouted from the housetops, if nothing else would
make people attend, that this infamy existed and must be
remedied. And Brieux touched the evil at its worst spot,
— in that section of the middle class in which the need
for pecuniary prudence has almost swallowed up every
more human feeling. In this most wretched of all classes
there is no employment for women except the employment of wife and mother, and no provision for women
without employment. The fathers are too poor to provide. The daughter must marry whom she can get: if
the first chance, which she dares not refuse, is not that

of a man whom she positively dislikes, she may consider herself fortunate. Her real hope of affection and self-respect lies in her children. And yet she above all women is subject to the danger that the dread of poverty, which is the ruling factor in her husband's world, may induce him to deny her right and frustrate her function of motherhood, using her simply as a housekeeper and a mistress without paying her the market price of such luxuries or forfeiting his respectability. To make us understand what this horror means, Brieux wrote Les Trois Filles de Monsieur Dupont, or, in equivalent English, The Three Daughters of Mr. Smith. Mr. Smith, in the person of the Censor, immediately shrieked "You must not mention such things." Mr. Smith was wrong: they are just the things that must be mentioned, and mentioned again and yet again, until they are set right. Surely, of all the anomalies of our marriage law, there is none more mischievously absurd than that a woman can have her marriage annulled for her husband's involuntary, but not for his voluntary sterility. And the man is in the same predicament, though his wife now has the same power as he of frustrating the public purpose of all marriages.

Brieux shows the Other Side

But Brieux is not, as the ordinary man mostly is, a mere reactionist against the latest oversights and mistakes, becoming an atheist at every flaw discovered in popular theology, and recoiling into the grossest superstition when some Jesuit who happens by exception to be a clever and subtle man (about the last thing, by the way, that a real live Jesuit ever is) shows him that popular atheism is only theology without mind or purpose. The ordinary man, when Brieux makes him aware of the fact that Malthusianism has produced an unexpected and revolting situation, instantly conceives a violent prejudice against it, pointing to the declining population as evidence that it is bringing ruin on the human race, and clamoring for the return of the conjugal morality of his grandmother, as Theodore Roosevelt did when he was President of the United States of America. It therefore became necessary for Brieux to head him off in his frantic flight by writing another play, Maternity, to remind him of the case for Malthusianism, and to warn him — if he is capable of the warning — that progress is not achieved by panic-stricken rushes back and forward between one folly and another, but by sifting all movements and adding what survives the sifting to the fabric of our morality. For the fact that Malthusianism has made new crimes possible should not discredit it, and cannot stop it, because every step gained by man in his continuous effort to control Nature necessarily does the same. Flying, for instance, which has become practical as a general human art for the first time this year, is capable of such alarming abuse that we are on the eve of a clamor for its restriction, and even for its prohibition, that will speedily make the present clamor against motor cars as completely forgotten as the clamor against bicycles was when motor cars appeared. But the motor car cannot be suppressed: it is improving our roads, improving the manners and screwing up the capacity and conduct of all who use them, improving our regulation of traffic, improving both locomotion and character as every victory over Nature finally improves the world and the race. Malthusianism is no exception to the rule: its obvious abuses, and the new need for protecting marriage from being made a mere charter of libertinage and slavery by its means, must be dealt with by improvements in conduct and law, and not by a hopeless attempt to drive us all back to the time of Mrs. Gamp. The tyranny which denies to the wife the right to become a mother has become possible through the discovery of the

means of escape from the no less unbearable tyranny
which compelled her to set another child at the table
round which those she had already borne were starving
because there was not enough food for them. When the
French Government, like Colonel Roosevelt, could think
of no better cure for the new tyranny than a revival of
the old, Brieux added a play on the old tyranny to his
play on the new tyranny.

This is the explanation of what stupid people call the
inconsistencies of those modern dramatists who, like
Ibsen and Brieux, are prophets as well as playwrights.
Ibsen did not write The Wild Duck to ridicule the
lesson he had already taught in Pillars of Society and
An Enemy of the People: he did it to head off his
disciples when, in their stampede from idealism, they
forgot the need of ideals and illusions to men not strong
enough to bear the truth. Brieux's La Foi has virtually the same theme. It is not an ultramontane tract to
defend the Church against the sceptic. It is a solemn
warning that you have not, as so many modern sceptics
assume, disposed of the doctrine when you have proved
that it is false. The miracle of St. Januarius is worked,
not by men who believe in it, but by men who know it to
be a trick, but know also that men cannot be governed by
the truth unless they are capable of the truth, and yet
must be governed somehow, truth or no truth. Maternity and The Three Daughters of Mr. Smith are
not contradictory: they are complementary, like An
Enemy of the People and The Wild Duck. I myself
have had to introduce into one of my plays a scene in
which a young man defends his vices on the ground that
he is one of my disciples. I did so because the incident
had actually occurred in a criminal court, where a young
prisoner gave the same reason and was sentenced to six
months' imprisonment, less, I fear, for the offence than
for the attempt to justify it.

The Most Unmentionable of All Subjects

Finally, Brieux attacked the most unmentionable subject of all, — the subject of the diseases that are supposed to be the punishment of profligate men and worthless women. Here the taboo acquires double force. Not only must not the improper thing be mentioned, but the evil must not be remedied, because it is a just retribution and a wholesome deterrent. The last point may be dismissed by simply inquiring how a disease can possibly act as a deterrent when people are kept in ignorance of its existence. But the punishment theory is a hideous mistake. It might as well be contended that fires should not be put out because they are the just punishment of the incendiary. Most of the victims of these diseases are entirely innocent persons: children who do not know what vice means, and women to whom it is impossible to explain what is the matter with them. Nor are their fathers and husbands necessarily to blame. Even if they were, it would be wicked to leave them unwarned when the consequences can spread so widely beyond themselves; for there are dozens of indirect ways in which this contagion can take place exactly as any other contagion can. The presence of one infected person in a house may lead to the infection of everybody else in it, even if they have never seen one another. In fact it is impossible to prove in any given case that the sufferer is in any way culpable: every profligate excuses himself or herself to the doctor on this ground; and though the excuse may not be believed, its truth is generally possible. Add to the chances of contagion the hereditary transmission of the disease, and the fact that an innocent person receiving it from a guilty partner without other grounds for divorce has no legal redress; and it becomes at once apparent that every guilty case may produce several innocent ones. Under such circumstances, even if it were possible in a civilized community to leave misconduct to be checked by its natural or accidental consequences, or by private vengeance instead of by carefully considered legal measures, such an anarchical solution must be ruled out in the present case, as the disease strikes blindly at everyone whom it reaches, and there are as many innocent paths for its venom as guilty ones. The taboo actually discriminates heavily against the innocent, because, as taboos are not respected in profligate society, systematic profligates learn the danger in their loose conversations, and take precautions, whereas the innocent expose themselves recklessly in complete ignorance, handling possibly contaminated articles and entering possibly infected places without the least suspicion that any such danger exists. In Brieux's play the husband alone is culpable; but his misconduct presently involves his wife, his child, and his child's nurse. It requires very little imagination to see that this by no means exhausts the possibilities. The nurse, wholly guiltless of the original sin, is likely to spread its consequences far more widely than the original sinner. A grotesque result of this is that there is always a demand, especially in France, for infected nurses, because the doctor, when he knows the child to be infected, feels that he is committing a crime in not warning the nurse; and the only way out of the difficulty is to find a nurse who is already infected and has nothing more to fear. How little the conscience of the family is to be depended on when the interests of a beloved child are in the scale against a mere cold duty to a domestic servant, has been well shown by Brieux in the second act of his play. But indeed anyone who will take the trouble to read the treatise of Fournier, or the lectures of Duclaux, or, in English, the chapters in which Havelock Ellis has dealt with this subject, will need no further instruction to convince

him that no play ever written was more needed than
Les Avariés.

It must be added that a startling change in the ur-
gency of the question has been produced by recent advances in pathology. Briefly stated, the facts of the
change are as follows. In the boyhood of those of us
who are now of middle age, the diseases in question were
known as mainly of two kinds. One, admittedly very
common, was considered transient, easily curable, harm-
less to future generations, and, to everyone but the
sufferer, dismissible as a ludicrous incident. The other
was known to be one of the most formidable scourges of
mankind, capable at its worst of hideous disfigurement
and ruinous hereditary transmission, but not at all so
common as the more trifling ailment, and alleged by some
authorities to be dying out like typhus or plague. That is
the belief still entertained by the elderly section of the
medical profession and those whom it has instructed.

This easy-going estimate of the situation was alarm-
ingly upset in 1879 by Neisser's investigation of the sup-
posedly trivial disease, which he associated with a ma-
lignant micro-organism called the gonococcus. The
physicians who still ridicule its gravity are now confronted by an agitation led by medical women and professional nurses, who cite a formidable array of authorities for their statements that it is the commonest cause
of blindness, and that it is transmitted from father to
mother, from mother to child, from child to nurse, pro-
ducing evils from which the individual attacked never
gets securely free. If half the scientific evidence be
true, a marriage contracted by a person actively affected
in either way is perhaps the worst crime that can be
committed with legal impunity in a civilized community.
The danger of becoming the victim of such a crime is
the worst danger that lurks in marriage for men and
women, and in domestic service for nurses.

Stupid people who are forced by these facts to admit that the simple taboo which forbids the subject to be mentioned at all is ruinous, still fall back on the plea that though the public ought to be warned, the theatre is not the proper place for the warning. When asked "What, then *is* the proper place?" they plead that the proper place is out of hearing of the general public: that is, not in a school, not in a church, not in a newspaper, not in a public meeting, but in medical text-books which are read only by medical students. This, of course, is the taboo over again, only sufficiently ashamed of itself to resort to subterfuge. The commonsense of the matter is that a public danger needs a public warning, and the more public the place the more effective the warning.

Why the Unmentionable must be Mentioned on the Stage

But beyond this general consideration there is a special need for the warning in the theatre. The best friends of the theatre cannot deny, and need not seek to deny, that a considerable proportion of our theatrical entertainments stimulate the sexual instincts of the spectators. Indeed this is so commonly the case that a play which contains no sexual appeal is quite openly and commonly written of, even by professional critics of high standing, as being "undramatic," or "not a play at all." This is the basis of the prejudice against the theatre shown by that section of English society in which sex is regarded as original sin, and the theatre, consequently, as the gate of hell. The prejudice is thoughtless: sex is a necessary and healthy instinct; and its nurture and education is one of the most important uses of all art; and, for the present at all events, the chief use of the theatre.

Now it may be an open question whether the theatre

has proved itself worthy of being entrusted with so serious a function. I can conceive a community passing a law forbidding dramatic authors to deal with sex as a motive at all. Although such a law would consign the great bulk of existing dramatic literature to the waste-paper basket, it would neither destroy it wholly nor paralyze all future playwrights. The bowdlerization of Molière and Shakespear on the basis of such a law would leave a surprising quantity of their work intact. The novels of Dickens and his contemporaries are before us to prove how independent the imaginative writer is of the theme so often assumed to be indispensable in fiction. The works in which it is dragged in by the ears on this false assumption are far more numerous than the tales and plays — Manon Lescaut is an example — of which it forms the entire substance. Just as the Euro-pean dramatist is able to write plays without introducing an accouchement, which is regarded as indispensable in all sympathetic Chinese plays, he can, if he is put to it, dispense with any theme that law or custom could conceivably forbid, and still find himself rich in dra-matic material. Let us grant therefore that love might be ruled out by a written law as effectually as cholera is ruled out by an unwritten one without utterly ruining the theatre.

Still, it is none the less beyond all question by any reasonable and thoughtful person that if we tolerate any subject on the stage we must not tolerate it by halves. It may be questioned whether we should allow war on the stage; but it cannot sanely be questioned that, if we do, we must allow its horrors to be represented as well as its glories. Destruction and murder, pestilence and famine, demoralization and cruelty, robbery and job-bery, must be allowed to contend with patriotism and military heroism on the boards as they do in actual war: otherwise the stage might inflame national hatreds and lead to their gratification with a recklessness that would make a cockpit of Europe. Again, if unscrupulous authors are to be allowed to make the stage a parade of champagne bottles, syphons, and tantaluses, scrupulous ones must be allowed to write such plays as L'Assommoir, which has, as a matter of simple fact, effectively deterred many young men from drunkenness. Nobody disputes the reasonableness of this freedom to present both sides. But when we come to sex, the taboo steps in, with the result that all the allurements of sex may be exhibited on the stage heightened by every artifice that the imagination of the voluptuary can devise, but not one of its dangers and penalties. You may exhibit seduction on the stage, but you must not even mention illegitimate conception and criminal abortion. We may, and do, parade prostitution to the point of intoxicating every young person in the theatre; yet no young person may hear a word as to the diseases that follow prostitution and avenge the prostitute to the third and fourth generation of them that buy her. Our shops and business offices are full of young men living in lonely lodgings, whose only artistic recreation is the theatre. In the theatre we practise upon them every art that can make their loneliness intolerable and heighten the charm of the bait in the snares of the street as they go home. But when a dramatist is enlightened enough to understand the danger, and sympathetic enough to come to the rescue with a play to expose the snare and warn the victim, we forbid the manager to perform it on pain of ruin, and denounce the author as a corrupter of morals. One hardly knows whether to laugh or cry at such perverse stupidity.

Brieux and Voltaire

It is a noteworthy fact that when Brieux wrote Les Avariés (Damaged Goods) his experience with it recalled in one particular that of Voltaire.

It will be remembered that Voltaire, whose religious opinions were almost exactly those of most English Nonconformists to-day, took refuge from the Established Church of France near Geneva, the city of Calvin, where he established himself as the first and the greatest of modern Nonconformist philanthropists. The Genevese ministers found his theology so much to their taste that they were prevented from becoming open Voltaireans only by the scandal he gave by his ridicule of the current Genevese idolatry of the Bible, from which he was as free as any of our prominent Baptists and Congregationalists. In the same way, when Brieux, having had his Les Avariés condemned by the now extinct French censorship, paid a visit to Switzerland, he was invited by a Swiss minister to read the play from the pulpit; and though the reading actually took place in a secular building, it was at the invitation and under the auspices of the minister. The minister knew what the Censor did not know: that what Brieux says in Les Avariés needs saying. The minister believed that when a thing needs saying, a man is in due course inspired to say it, and that such inspiration gives him a divine right to be heard. And this appears to be the simple truth of the matter in terms of the minister's divinity. For most certainly Brieux had every worldly inducement to refrain from writing this play, and no motive for disregarding these inducements except the motive that made Luther tear up the Pope's Bull, and Mahomet tell the idolatrous Arabs of Mecca that they were worshipping stones.

The reader will now understand why these three great plays have forced themselves upon us in England as they

forced themselves upon Brieux's own countrymen. Just
as Brieux had to write them, cost what it might, so we
have had to translate them and perform them and finally
publish them for those to read who are out of reach of
the theatre. The evils they deal with are as rampant in
England and America as they are in France. The gonococcus is not an exclusively French microbe: the possibility of sterilizing marriage is not bounded by the
Channel, the Rhine, or the Alps. The furious revolt of
poor women against bringing into the world more mouths
to eat the bread that is already insufficient for their first
born, rages with us exactly as it does in the final scene
of Maternity. Therefore these three plays are given
to the English speaking peoples first. There are others
to follow of like importance to us. And there are some,
like La Française, which we may read more lightheart-
edly when we have learnt the lesson of the rest. In La
Française an American (who might just as well be an
Englishman) has acquired his ideas of France and
French life, not from the plays of Brieux, but from the
conventional plays and romances which have only one
theme, — adultery. Visiting France, he is received as a
friend in an ordinary respectable French household,
where he conceives himself obliged, as a gallant man of
the world, to invite his hostess to commit with him the
adultery which he imagines to be a matter of course in
every French *ménage*. The ignominious failure of his
enterprise makes it much better comedy than his success
would have made it in an ordinary fashionable play.

As Good Fish in the Sea

The total number of plays produced by Brieux up to
the date on which I write these lines is fifteen. The
earliest dates as far back as 1890. It is therefore high
time for us to begin to read him, as we have already

begun to act him. The most pitiful sort of ignorance is
ignorance of the few great men who are men of our own
time.   Most of us die without having heard of those
contemporaries of ours, for our opportunities of seeing
and applauding whom posterity will envy us.   Imagine
meeting the ghost of an Elizabethan cockney in heaven,
and, on asking him eagerly what Shakespear was like,
being told either that the cockney had never heard of
Shakespear, or knew of him vaguely as an objectionable
writer of plays full of regrettable errors of taste.   To
save our own ghosts from disgracing themselves in this
manner when they are asked about Brieux, is one of the
secondary uses of this first instalment of his works in
English.   G. B. S.

PARKNASILLA AND AYOT ST. LAWRENCE.
1909.

MATERNITY

A PLAY IN THREE ACTS

BY BRIEUX

Translated from the French

BY MRS. BERNARD SHAW

Cast of the original production before the Stage Society at the King's Hall, London, on April 8, 9 and 10, 1906.

LUCIE BRIGNAC	Suzanne Sheldon
JULIEN BRIGNAC	Dennis Eadie
LIORET	Robert Grey
ANNETTE	Muriel Ashwynne
CATHERINE	Betty Castle
MME. BERNIN	Lilian M. Revell
PIERRE POIRET	Fred Grove
LAURENT	Charles Dodsworth
LE SOUS-INTENDANT	Michael Sherbrooke
LE COLONEL	Frank H. Denton
M. CHEVILLOT	Vincent Sternroyd
JACQUES POIRET	Trevor Lowe
MME. CHEVILLOT	Charles Maltby
LE PRÉSIDENT	Kenyon Musgrave
L'AVOCAT	C. Herbert Hewetson
MME. THOMAS	Claire Greet
MARIE GAUBERT	Italia Conti
TUPIN	Blake Adams
MME. TUPIN	Eily Malyon
LE PROCUREUR	Charles A. Dovan

ACT I

Brignac's drawing-room. Doors right, left, and at the back. Furniture of a government official. When the curtain rises Lucie, a woman of about thirty, is alone. Brignac, a man of thirty-eight, opens a door outside and calls gaily from the anteroom.

BRIGNAC. Here I am. [*He takes off his cloak, gives it to a maid-servant, and enters*].

LUCIE [*gaily*] Good-morning, sous-préfet.

BRIGNAC [*He is in the uniform of a sous-préfet. A tunic or dolman, with simple embroidery and two rows of buttons; a cap with an embroidered band, a sword with a mother-o'-pearl handle and a silver-plated sheath. His belt is of silk; his trousers blue with a silver stripe; and he wears a black cravat. He comes forward, taking off his sword and belt during the following conversation. He is finishing a large cigar*] Have you been bored all alone?

LUCIE. With three children one has n't time to be bored.

BRIGNAC [*taking his sword into the anteroom*] By Jove, no!

LUCIE. Well, how did the luncheon go off?

BRIGNAC [*throwing away his cigar-end*] Very well. I 'll tell you all about it in a minute. [*Going to the door to the right and calling through*] Has M. Mouton come?

A VOICE [*from outside*] Yes, monsieur le sous-préfet. Shall I tell him he 's wanted?

3

BRIGNAC. No. Bring me my letters. [*He closes the door and comes back*] Shall I never catch that fellow out?

LUCIE. Why do you want to?

BRIGNAC. I want to get rid of him, of course, and get a young chap. An unmarried man would n't ask half the salary I give this one.

A clerk enters bringing letters.

CLERK. The letters, monsieur le sous-préfet.

BRIGNAC. All right.

The clerk goes out. Brignac glances at the addresses and sorts the letters into several piles without opening the envelopes.

LUCIE. That little ceremony always amuses me.

BRIGNAC. What ceremony? Sorting my letters?

LUCIE. Without opening them.

BRIGNAC. I know what 's inside by looking at them.

LUCIE. Nonsense!

BRIGNAC. Don't you believe it? Well, look. Here 's one from the mayor of St. Sauveur. Something he asks me to forward to the préfet. [*He opens it and hands the letter to his wife, who does not take it*] There!

LUCIE. Why does n't he send it direct to the préfet?

BRIGNAC. What would be the use of *us* then?

LUCIE [*laughing*] That 's true.

BRIGNAC. Now I suppose you 'll make some more jokes about sous-préfets and their work. It 's easy, and not particularly clever. Perhaps some of us don't take our jobs very seriously, but I 'm not like that. If we *are* useless, our business is to make ourselves indispensable. Just take to-day for example and see if I 'm not busy enough. This morning I signed thirty documents; afterwards I went to the meeting of the Council of Revision.[1] Then came this luncheon of the mayor's to all these gentlemen. Now I shall have an hour of office-

[1] The Board appointed to inspect conscripts, and see if they are fit for military service.— *Note by the Translator.*

work, and then I shall have to go and meet our guests and bring them here, to our own dinner. [*Pause*] Oh! and I forgot — after dinner there will be that reception at the Club that they put off to suit me. That's a fairly full official day, is n't it?

LUCIE. Yes.

BRIGNAC. We shall only have part of the Committee at dinner. Some of the members have refused. [*With interest*] Hullo! I did n't see this. A letter from the Minister of the Interior.

LUCIE. Perhaps it's your promotion.

BRIGNAC [*opening the letter*] One never knows — No, it's a circular [*pause*] upon the decline of the population. [*He runs his eye through the paper*] *Most* important. [*He goes to the door on the right*] M. Lioret! *A clerk comes in.*

CLERK. Yes, monsieur le sous-préfet?

BRIGNAC [*giving him papers*] Give that to M. Mouton. It must be done by five o'clock, and *well* done. This for M. Lamblin — M. Rouge — And put this upon my desk. I will see to it myself and give it the attention it requires.

The clerk goes out.

LUCIE. Perhaps it's not worth attention.

BRIGNAC. It needs an acknowledgment, anyway; and the terms used in the original must be most carefully reproduced in the acknowledgment.

LUCIE. Now tell me how the luncheon went off.

BRIGNAC. I *have* told you. It went off very well. Too well. The mayor wanted to be even with us. All the same, our dinner to-night will be better. [*He takes a cigar out of his pocket*] I brought away a cigar to show it to you. Are ours as big?

LUCIE. Pretty much the same.

BRIGNAC. He does n't give you cigars like that at his big receptions. There's the menu.

Lucie [*glancing at it*] Oh! I say!

Brignac. The champagne was decanted!

Lucie. Well, we 'll have ours decanted. [*Brightly*] Only, you know, it 'll cost money. We should n't have much left if we had to give many dinners to Councils of Revision.

Brignac. Don't worry about that. You know very well that when Balureau gets back into power he 'll have us out of this dead-alive Châteauneuf, and give us a step up.

Lucie. Yes; but *will* he get back into power?

Brignac. Why should n't he?

Lucie. He was in such a short time.

Brignac. Precisely. They had n't time to find him out.

Lucie [*laughing*] If he heard you!

Brignac. You misunderstand me. I have the greatest respect for —

Lucie [*interrupting*] I know, I know. I was only joking.

Brignac. You 're always worrying about the future; now what makes me the man I am is my persistent confidence in the future. If Balureau does n't get into office again we 'll stay quietly at Châteauneuf, that 's all. *You* can't complain, as you were born here.

Lucie. But it 's *you* who complain.

Brignac. I complain of the want of spirit in the people. I complain that I cannot get them to love and respect our political institutions. I complain above all of the society of Châteauneuf: a set of officials entertaining one another.

Lucie. Society in Châteauneuf does n't open its arms to us, certainly.

Brignac. It does n't think us important enough.

Lucie. To have a larger acquaintance we ought to entertain the commercial people. You won't do that.

BRIGNAC.   I have to consider the dignity of my position.

LUCIE.   As you often say, we are in the enemy's camp.

BRIGNAC.   That's true.   But the fact that people hate me shows that I am a person of some importance.   We must look out for the unexpected.   How do you know some great opportunity won't come in my way to-morrow, or next month, or in six months?   An opportunity to distinguish myself and force the people in Paris to pay attention to me.

LUCIE.   Yes; you've been waiting for that opportunity for eleven years.

BRIGNAC.   Obviously then it is so much the nearer.

LUCIE.   And what will it be?

BRIGNAC.   Some conflict, some incident — trouble.

LUCIE.   Trouble at Châteauneuf?

BRIGNAC.   I'm quite aware that Châteauneuf is most confoundedly peaceable.   One gets no chance.   I count more upon Balureau than on anything else.   [*Pause*]   Is Annette with her friend Gabrielle?

LUCIE.   No.

BRIGNAC.   But this is Tuesday.

LUCIE.   It's not time for her to go yet.

BRIGNAC.   Yes, but if she puts it off till too late.

LUCIE.   I've wanted for some time to speak to you about Annette.   Don't you think she goes to the Bernins a little too often?

BRIGNAC.   Not at all.   They're very influential people and may be useful to me.   Call her.   [*He goes to the door to the left and calls himself*]   Annette!   [*Coming back*]   Annette goes three times a week to practise with Mademoiselle Bernin, who goes everywhere.   That's an excellent thing for us, and may be of consequence.   [*Annette comes in*]   Annette, don't forget how late it is. It's time you were with your friend.

ANNETTE [*going out*] Yes, yes. I 'll go and put on my hat.

LUCIE [*to Brignac*] They want Annette to spend a few days with them in the country. Ought we to let her?

BRIGNAC. Why not? She wants to go. You know how fond she is of Gabrielle.

LUCIE. Yes; but Gabrielle has a brother.

BRIGNAC. Young Jacques. But he 's going to be married, my dear.

LUCIE. Is he?

BRIGNAC. Yes, yes, of course. [*Annette comes in from the left*] Make haste, Annette.

LUCIE. What does it matter if she 's five minutes late?

ANNETTE. No — no — Where *is* my music?

LUCIE. You look quite upset. Would you rather not go?

ANNETTE. Yes, yes, I 'll go — Good-bye. [*She hurries off, forgetting her music*].

LUCIE [*calling*] Your music! [*She holds out the music-case*].

ANNETTE. Oh, thank you. Good-bye. [*She goes out*].

LUCIE. Don't you think Annette has been a little depressed lately?

BRIGNAC. Eh? Yes — no — has she? Have you found a new parlor-maid?

LUCIE. Yes.

BRIGNAC. There, you see! You were worrying about that.

LUCIE. I had good reason to worry. I 've been without a parlor-maid for a week. I liked a girl who came yesterday very much; but she would n't take the place.

BRIGNAC. Why not?

LUCIE. She said there were too many children here.

BRIGNAC. Too many children! Three!

LUCIE. Yes: but the eldest is three years old and the youngest two months.

BRIGNAC. There's a nurse.

LUCIE. I told her that, of course.

BRIGNAC. Well, I declare! And when you consider that it meant coming to the sous-préfet!

LUCIE. I suppose she's not impressed by titles.

BRIGNAC. And what about the one you have engaged?

LUCIE. She's elderly. Perhaps she'll be steady.

BRIGNAC. Yes, and have other vices. Still —

LUCIE. The unhappy woman has two children out at nurse, and two older ones at Bordeaux. Her husband deserted her.

BRIGNAC. Too bad of Céline to force us to turn her out of doors.

LUCIE. Her conduct was bad, certainly. All the same —

BRIGNAC. Oh, it was not her *conduct!* She might have conducted herself ten times worse if only she had had the sense to keep up appearances. Outside her duty to me her life was her own. But we have to draw the line at a confinement in the house. You admit that, don't you? [*A pause. Lucie does not answer*] It was getting quite unmistakable — you know it was. Those wretched grocer's boys are a perfect scourge to decent houses. [*He takes up a paper*] This circular is admirable.

LUCIE. Is it?

BRIGNAC. And of the greatest importance. Such style, too. Listen. [*He reads*] "Our race is diminishing! Such a state of affairs demands the instant attention of the authorities. The Legislature must strenuously endeavor to devise remedial measures against the disastrous phenomenon now making itself manifest in our midst." The Minister of the Interior has done this very well. The end is really fine — quite touching. Listen. "Truth will triumph: reason will prevail: the noble sentiment of nationality and the divine spirit of self-sacrifice will

bear us on to victory. We who know the splendid re-
cuperative power of our valiant French race look forward
with confidence and security to the magnificent moral
regeneration of this great and ancient people." [*He
looks at his wife*].

LUCIE. It's well written, certainly.

BRIGNAC [*continuing to read*] "Let each one, in his
own sphere of action and influence, work with word and
pen to point out the peril and urge the immediate necessity of a remedy. Committees must be formed all over
France to evolve schemes and promote measures by which
the birth-rate may be raised."

LUCIE. Does it suggest any scheme?

BRIGNAC. Yes. The rest of the circular is full of the
ways and means. I shall read it aloud this evening.

LUCIE. This evening!

BRIGNAC. Yes. [*He goes to the right-hand door and
calls*] Monsieur Lioret!

CLERK [*coming in*] Monsieur le sous-préfet.

BRIGNAC. Make me two copies of this circular *yourself;* you will understand its great importance. And
bring the original back *yourself* and place it upon this
table.

CLERK. Yes, monsieur le sous-préfet. [*He goes out*].

BRIGNAC [*returning to Lucie*] The covering letter
from my official superior ends with these words: "Have
the goodness, M. le sous-préfet, to send me at once a sta-
tistical schedule of all committees or associations of this
nature at present existing in your district, and let me
know what measures you think of taking in response to
the desiderata of the Government." Well, I shall take
advantage of the dinner we give to-night to the members
of the Council of Revision to set on foot some associations of the sort, and then I can write up to the authorities, "There were no associations: *I* created them!"

LUCIE. But is the dinner a suitable —

BRIGNAC. Listen to me. This morning there was a Council of Revision at Châteauneuf.

LUCIE. Yes.

BRIGNAC. The mayor invited the members to luncheon and we have invited them to dinner.

LUCIE. Well?

BRIGNAC. The Council of Revision is composed of a Councillor to the Préfecture, a general Councillor, a district Councillor — I leave out the doctor — and the mayors of the communes concerned — *the mayors of the communes concerned.* I shall profit by the chance of having them all together after dinner to-night — after a dinner where the champagne will be decanted, mind you — to impress them with my own enthusiasm and conviction. *They* shall create local committees, and *I* shall presently announce the formation of those committees to the authorities. So even if Balureau does n't get into power, I shall sooner or later force the Minister to say, " But why don't we give a man like Brignac a really active post?" This is a first-rate opening for us: I saw it at a glance. After dinner I shall show them my diagram. You must make my office into a cloak-room, and —

LUCIE [*interrupting*] Why? There's room in the hall.

BRIGNAC. I can't put the diagram in the hall, and I want an excuse for bringing them all through the office. Some day the Colonel may meet the Minister of the Interior and say to him: " I saw in the sous-préfecture at Châteauneuf " —

LUCIE [*interrupting again*] All right. As you like.

BRIGNAC. You trust to me. You don't understand anything about it. You did n't even know how a Council of Revision was made up, — you, the wife of a sous-préfet. And yet every year we give them a dinner. And we 've been married four years.

LUCIE [*gently and pleasantly*] Now think for a minute. We 've been married four years, that 's true. But this time three years was just after Edmée was born: two years ago I was expecting little Louise; and last year after weaning her I was ill. Remember too that if I had nursed the last one myself I could not be at dinner to-night, as she is only two months old.

BRIGNAC. You complain of that?

LUCIE [*laughing*] No: but I am glad to be having a holiday.

BRIGNAC [*gaily*] You know what I said: as long as we have n't a boy —

LUCIE [*brightly*] We ought to have a trip to Switzerland first.

BRIGNAC. No, no, no. We have only girls: I want a boy.

LUCIE [*laughing*] Is it the Minister's circular that —

BRIGNAC. No, it is *not* the Minister's circular.

LUCIE. Then let me have time to breathe.

BRIGNAC. You can breathe afterwards.

LUCIE. Before.

BRIGNAC. After.

LUCIE. Would n't you rather have a holiday?

BRIGNAC. No.

LUCIE [*gently*] Listen, Julien, since we 're talking about this. I wanted to tell you — I have n't had much leisure since our marriage. We 've not been able to take advantage of a single one of your holidays. And if you don't agree to let — [*tenderly*] Maurice — wait another year it will be the same thing this time. [*Smiling*] I really have a right to a little rest. Consider. We 've not had any time to know one another, or to love one another. Besides, remember that we already have to find dowries for three girls.

BRIGNAC. I tell you this is going to be a boy.

LUCIE. A boy is expensive.

BRIGNAC. We are going to be rich.

LUCIE. How?

BRIGNAC. Luck may come in several ways. I may stay in the Civil Service and get promoted quickly. I may go back to the Bar: I was a fairly successful barrister once. I may have some unexpected stroke of luck. Anyway, I 'm certain we shall be rich. [*Smiling*] After all, it 's not much good you 're saying no, if I say yes.

LUCIE [*hurt*] Evidently. My consent was asked for before I was given a husband, but my consent is not asked for before I am given a child.

BRIGNAC. Are you going to make a scene?

LUCIE. No. But all the same — this slavery —

BRIGNAC. What?

LUCIE. Yes, *slavery*. After all you are disposing of my health, my sufferings, my life — of a year of my existence, calmly, without consulting me.

BRIGNAC. Do I do it out of selfishness? Do you suppose I am not a most unhappy husband all the time I have a future mother at my side instead of a loving wife? " A father is a man all the same."

LUCIE [*ironically*] Oh, you are *most* unhappy, are n't you?

BRIGNAC. Yes.

LUCIE. Rubbish!

BRIGNAC. Rubbish?

LUCIE. You evidently take me for a fool.

BRIGNAC. I don't understand.

LUCIE. I know what you do at those times. *Now* do you understand?

BRIGNAC. No.

LUCIE [*irritated*] Don't deny it. You must see that I know all about it. The best thing you can do is to be silent, as I have pretended so far to know nothing.

BRIGNAC [*coming off his high-horse*] I assure you —

LUCIE. Do you want me to tell you the name of the

person you go to see over at Villeneuve, while I am
nursing, or a " future mother " as you call it?

BRIGNAC. If you 're going to believe all the gossip
you hear —

LUCIE. We had better say no more about it.

BRIGNAC. I beg to observe that it was not I who
started the subject. There, there — you 're in a bad
temper. I shall go and do some work, and then I must
join those gentlemen. Only, you know, you 're mistaken.

LUCIE. Oh, yes, of course.

*He goes out to the right, shrugging his shoulders.
Lucie rings. Catherine comes in.*

LUCIE. Are Nurse and Joséphine out with the
children?

CATHERINE. Yes, madame.

LUCIE [*beaming*] Were my little ones well and happy?

CATHERINE. Oh, yes, madame.

LUCIE [*sincerely*] Are n't my little girls pretty?

CATHERINE. Yes: pretty and clever.

LUCIE. The other day Edmée was talking about playing horses, and Louise said " 'orses " quite distinctly.
It 's wonderful at her age.

CATHERINE. I 've seen lots of children, but I never
saw such nice ones before.

LUCIE. I 'm so glad. You 're a good creature,
Catherine.

Annette comes in. She pulls off her hat, wild with joy.

ANNETTE. Lucie! Sister! News! Great news!
Good news!

LUCIE. What is it?

ANNETTE [*giving her hat to Catherine*] Take this,
Catherine, and go. [*She pushes her out gently*].

LUCIE [*laughing*] Well!

ANNETTE. I must kiss you, *kiss* you! I wanted to
kiss the people in the street. [*She bursts into a laugh
which ends in a sob*].

LUCIE. Little sister Annette, you 've gone quite mad.

ANNETTE. No — not mad — I 'm so happy.

LUCIE. What is it, little girl?

ANNETTE [*in tears*] I 'm happy! I 'm happy!

LUCIE. Why, what 's the matter with the child?

ANNETTE. No, no. It 's all right — don't speak to me. I shall soon be better. It 's nervous. [*She laughs and cries at the same time*]. I tell you I 'm happy — only — only — How stupid it is to cry like this. I can't help it. [*She puts her arms round Lucie's neck*]. Oh, little mother, I love you — I *do* love you. [*She kisses Lucie: another little sob*]. Oh, I *am* silly. There now, it 's all right — I 've done. [*She wipes her eyes*] There: now I 'm going to tell you. [*With great joy and emotion, and very simply*] I am going to be married. Monsieur and Madame Bernin are coming to see you about it.

LUCIE. Why?

ANNETTE. Because Jacques has told them to.

LUCIE. Jacques!

ANNETTE [*very fast, tumbling out the words*] Yes, it was when I was practising with Gabrielle. He had guessed — it happened this way — practising — he sings a little — oh, nothing very grand — once — [*she laughs*] but I 'll tell you about that afterwards — it 's because of that — we shall be married soon. [*Fresh tears. Then she says gravely, embracing Lucy*] I *do* love him so, and if he had n't asked me to marry him — You don't understand?

LUCIE [*laughing*] I guess a little.

ANNETTE. Do you want me to tell you all about it, from the beginning?

LUCIE. Yes.

ANNETTE. I want to so much. If it won't bore you. It would make me so happy.

LUCIE. Go on.

ANNETTE. Well, when I was playing duets with
Gabrielle — I must tell you that I began by detesting
him because he will make fun of everybody. But he's
most kind, *really*. For instance —

LUCIE. Now keep to the point. When you played
duets —

ANNETTE. Yes, I was telling you. When I played
duets with Gabrielle he used to come and listen to us.
He stood behind us to turn over the leaves: once he put
his hand upon my shoulder —

LUCIE. You let him?

ANNETTE. He had his other hand on Gabrielle's
shoulder — it would have been priggish to say anything.

LUCIE. Yes, but with Gabrielle it's different.

ANNETTE. That's what I was going to say. My
heart began beating so — I got so red, and I had no idea
what I was playing. And then, another time — he
could n't see the music — he stooped right down. But
that's all nothing. We love each other, that's the whole
thing.

LUCIE. And has he told you that he loves you?

ANNETTE [*gravely*] Yes.

LUCIE. And you hid all that from me? I'm sorry,
Annette.

ANNETTE. I'm so, *so* sorry. But it all came so gradually. I can hardly tell now exactly when it began. I
even thought I was mistaken. And then — then — when
we first dared to speak to one another about what we had
never spoken of, though we both knew it so well — I
knew I'd done wrong. But I was *so* ashamed I *could n't*
tell you about it then.

LUCIE [*tenderly*] All the same it was very naughty
of you, darling.

ANNETTE. Oh, don't scold me! Please, please don't
scold me. If you only knew how I've repented — how
unhappy I've been. Have n't you noticed?

LUCIE. Yes. Then he's spoken to his father and mother?

ANNETTE. Some time ago.

LUCIE. And they consent?

ANNETTE. They are coming this afternoon.

LUCIE. Why did n't they come sooner?

ANNETTE. Well — Jacques begged them to, but they did n't want it at first. They wanted Gabrielle to be married first. It was even arranged that I should pretend I did n't know they had been told. Then, to-day, I met Jacques in the street —

LUCIE. In the street?

ANNETTE. Yes. Lately he has not been coming to our practices — so I meet him —

LUCIE. In the street!

ANNETTE. Generally we only bow to one another, and that's all. But to-day he said to me as he passed, " My mother is going to your house. She's there behind me." Then I hurried in to tell you. [*With a happy smile*] He was quite pale. Please don't scold me, I am so happy. Forgive me.

LUCIE [*kissing her*] Yes: I forgive you. Then you 're going away from me, you bad thing.

ANNETTE. Yes, I am *bad*. Bad and ungrateful. That's true.

LUCIE. Marriage is a serious thing. Are you sure you will suit one another?

ANNETTE. Oh, I 'm certain of it. We 've quarrelled already.

LUCIE. What about?

ANNETTE. About a book he lent me.

LUCIE. What book?

ANNETTE. Anna Karénina. He liked Vronsky better than Peter Levin. He talked nonsense. He said he did n't believe in Madame Karénina's suicide. You remember, she throws herself under the wheels of the train

Vronsky is going away in. Don't you remember? It
does n't matter.

Lucie. And then?

Annette.   And   then — there 's   a   ring — perhaps
that 's the Bernins.

A silence. Catherine appears with a card.

Lucie. Yes. It 's Madame Bernin.

Annette. Oh! [*Going to her room*] You 'll come
and fetch me presently.

Lucie. Yes. [*To Catherine*] Show the lady in.

Annette. Don't be long.

She goes out. Lucie tidies herself before a glass. Madame Bernin comes in.

Mme. B. How do you do, Madame Brignac?

Lucie. How do you do, madame?

Mme. B. Are you quite well?

Lucie. Very well, madame. And you?

Mme. B. I need not ask after M. Brignac.

Lucie. And M. Bernin?

Mme. B. He 's very well, thank you.

Lucie. Won't you sit down?

Mme. B. Thank you. [*Sits*] What lovely weather.

Lucie. Yes, is n't it? How lucky you are to be able
to get into the country. Annette is so looking forward
to her visit to you.

Mme. B. Well, I came to-day — first of all to have
the pleasure of seeing you — and then to have a chat
with you about that very matter.

Lucie. And about another matter, too, I think.

Mme. B. Another matter?

Lucie. Not about another?

Mme. B. No, I don't quite understand —

Lucie. Oh, then I beg your pardon. Tell me what
it is about Annette's visit.

Mme. B. My daughter has just got an invitation to
spend some time with her cousins the Guibals, and we

can't possibly refuse to let Gabrielle go to them. So I 've come to beg you to excuse us, because — as Gabrielle won't be there —

LUCIE. Oh, of course, madame. Will Mademoiselle Gabrielle make a long stay with her cousins?

MME. B. Well, that 's just what 's so annoying. We don't know exactly: it might be a week, or it might be a month. And she *may* stay there all the time we are away from Châteauneuf.

LUCIE. Poor little Annette!

MME. B. But I thought you were going away somewhere yourselves this Easter?

LUCIE. Yes.

MME. B. [*kindly*] That relieves my mind a little, and I hope it will make up to Mademoiselle Annette for the disappointment I am obliged to cause her — to my very great regret.

LUCIE [*after a silence*] Will you excuse me, madame. [*Hesitating*] Perhaps this is indiscreet.

MME. B. Oh, I am sure not, Madame Brignac.

LUCIE. I only wanted to ask you if it is long since Mademoiselle Gabrielle got this invitation from her cousins?

MME. B. About a week.

LUCIE. A week!

MME. B. Why does that surprise you?

LUCIE. Because she did not mention it to Annette.

MME. B. She was afraid of disappointing her.

LUCIE. Only yesterday Annette was telling me about all sorts of excursions your daughter was planning for them both. Madame, this invitation is an excuse: please tell me the whole truth. Annette is only my sister, but I love her as if she was my own child, and I speak as a mother to a mother. I 'm not going to try to be clever or stand on my dignity. This is how it is: Annette believes your son loves her, and when you were announced just now she thought you came to arrange her marriage with him. Now you know all that I know. Tell me the truth, and let us do what we can to prevent unhappiness.

MME. B. As you speak so simply and feelingly I will tell you candidly exactly what is in my mind. As a matter of fact this invitation to Gabrielle is only a device of ours to prevent Jacques and Annette seeing any more of one another.

LUCIE. Then you don't want them to see any more of one another?

MME. B. No, because I don't want them to marry.

LUCIE. Because Annette is poor?

MME. B. [*after some hesitation*] Well — since we 're speaking plainly — yes, because she is poor. Ah, dear Madame Brignac, we have both been very much to blame for not foreseeing what has happened.

LUCIE. *We* have been to blame?

MME. B. I know Annette, and I like her very much. I know you too, better than you think, and I have the greatest respect and esteem for you; it has never even occurred to me that in seeking our acquaintance you had any other motive than friendship. But you ought to have feared and foreseen what has happened.

LUCIE. What should I fear? Annette went to see Gabrielle. How could I know that you let your son be with them? You knew it because it happened at your house, and it is you who have been wanting in prudence and foresight. You invited this poor child, you exposed her to danger, you let her take a fancy to your son, you allowed them to fall in love with one another, and you come to-day and calmly tell me that this marriage is impossible, and you are going off to the country leaving it to me to break the poor child's heart.

MME. B. How do you know I foresaw nothing? And how can one tell the right moment to interfere to prevent playmates becoming lovers? While I was uncertain did n't I run the risk of causing the very thing I was anxious to prevent, by separating them without a good reason? When I really felt sure there was danger I spoke to Jacques. I said to him, "Annette is not a suitable match for you: you must be very careful how you behave to her: don't forget to treat this girl as a sister."

LUCIE. And he said " It is too late: we love each other."

MME. B. On the contrary, he said: " You need n't worry, mother. I have been thinking the same thing myself, and I am a man of honor. Besides, though Annette is charming, she 's not the sort of woman I mean to marry."

LUCIE. How long ago did he tell you that?

MME. B. About two months ago.

LUCIE. Well, at that time he had already spoken of marriage to Annette; or at least he had spoken of love, which from him to her is the same thing.

MME. B. I can only tell you what I know.

LUCIE. Well, madame, all this is beside the question. You are opposed to this marriage?

MME. B. Yes.

LUCIE. Finally? Irrevocably?

MME. B. Finally. Irrevocably.

LUCIE. Because Annette has no money?

MME. B. Yes.

LUCIE. Your son knew she had no money when he made her love him.

MME. B. Believe me, he did n't mean to do the harm he has done. A young girl of his own age was his sister's constant companion, and at first he treated her as he treated his sister. At first, I 'm sure, it was without any special intention that he saw so much of her. Afterwards probably he made some pretty speeches to your little Annette, and no doubt he was greatly taken with her. As Annette is more innocent and simple and affectionate, and of course more ignorant than he is, she has been more quickly and more deeply touched. But my son is not the worthless fellow you think him, and the proof of that is that he himself came and told me all about it.

Lucie. And when you told him he must give up Annette, he agreed?

Mme. B. Yes, he agreed. He 's reasonable and sensible, and he saw the force of my arguments. He saw that this parting, though it will be painful, was an absolute necessity. He will certainly suffer; but they are both so young. At that age love troubles don't last.

Lucie. I understand. In a week your son will have forgotten all about it. But Annette —

Mme. B. She will soon forget it, too.

Lucie. I don't know — I don't know. Oh, my poor darling! If you had seen her just now when she came to tell me about it! It 's not for joy she will cry now. Oh! — [she begins to cry].

Mme. B. [moved] Don't cry — oh, don't cry. I assure you I am most deeply sorry. Oh, if it were only possible, how happy it would make me that my boy should marry Annette. The girl he is engaged to is an affected little thing who annoys me, and I really love your sister.

Lucie. But if that is true you can afford to let your son marry a girl without fortune.

Mme. B. No: we 're not so well off as people think. There 's Gabrielle to be provided for. There will be next to nothing left for Jacques.

Lucie. But he might work.

Mme. B. He has not been brought up to that.

Lucie. That was a mistake.

Mme. B. The professions are overcrowded. Would

you have him go into an office and get 200 francs a month? They would n't be able to keep a servant.

Lucie.   He could earn more than that.

Mme. B.   If he got 500 — could he keep up his position? Could he remain in his present set? It would be a come-down for him; a come-down he would owe to his wife; and sooner or later he would reproach her for it. And think of their children! They would have just enough to send their son to a public school, and make their daughter a post office clerk. And even then they would have to pinch and screw to provide for her until she got in.

Lucie.   It 's true.

Mme. B.   You see that I 'm right. I can't say I 'm proud of having to say such things — of belonging to a society that forces one to do such things. But we 're not in a land of romance. We live among vain, selfish, hard-headed people.

Lucie.   You despise them, and yet you sacrifice everything to their opinion.

Mme. B.   Yes: because everything depends upon their opinion. Social position depends upon it. One must be a very exceptional person to be able to defy public opinion. And Jacques is not exceptional.

Lucie.   That 's nothing to be proud of. If he was exceptional, I mean if he was different to all these people about, he would find his love would prevent him from troubling about the sneers of worthless idlers.

Mme. B.   His love! Love goes: poverty stays: it is a proverb. Beauty passes: want remains.

Lucie.   But you, madame, yourself — you and your husband are a proof that one can marry poor and make a fortune. Your story is well known. Your husband began in an office, then he started his own business; and if riches make happiness, you are happy now — you and he — are n't you?

MME. B. No, no, *no;* we are not happy, because we
have worn ourselves out hunting after happiness. We
wanted to " get on," and we got on. But *what* a price
we paid for it! First, when we were both earning wages,
our life was one long drudgery of petty economy and
meanness. When we set up on our own account we lived
in an atmosphere of trickery, of enmity, of lying; flattering the customers, and always in terror of bankruptcy.
Oh, I know the road to fortune! It means tears, lies,
envy, hate; one suffers — and one makes other people
suffer. I 've had to go through it: my children shan't.
We 've only had two children: we meant only to have
one. Having two we had to be doubly hard upon ourselves. Instead of a husband and wife helping one another, we have been partners spying upon one another;
calling one another to account for every little expenditure
or stupidity; and on our very pillows disputing about
our business. That 's how we got rich; and now we
can't enjoy our money because we don't know how to use
it; and we are n't happy because our old age is made
bitter by the memories and the rancor left from the old
bad days: because we have suffered too much and hated
too much. My children shall not go through this. I endured it that they might be spared. Good-bye, madame.

LUCIE. Good-bye.

*Madame Bernin goes out. After a moment Lucie goes
slowly to Annette's door and opens it.*

ANNETTE [*coming in*] You 've been crying! It 's
because I 'm going away, is n't it? Not because there 's
anything in the way of — [*with increasing trouble*] Tell
me, Lucie!

LUCIE. You love him so much then?

ANNETTE. If we were not to be married — I should
die.

LUCIE. No, you would n't die. Think of all the girls
who have said that: did they die?

ANNETTE. Is there anything to prevent?

LUCIE. No, no.

ANNETTE. And when is it to be? Did you talk about that?

LUCIE. What a state of excitement you are in! Annette, dear, you must try to control yourself a little.

ANNETTE [*making an effort*] Yes. You're right. I'm a little off my head.

LUCIE. You are really.

ANNETTE [*still controlling herself*] Well, tell me. What did Madame Bernin say?

LUCIE. What a hurry you are in to leave me! You don't care for me any more, then?

ANNETTE [*gravely*] Ah, my dear! If I had n't you what would become of me! [*A silence*] But you're telling me *nothing*. You don't seem to be telling me the truth — you're hiding something from me — there *is* some difficulty, I'm certain of it. If there was n't you'd say there was n't, you would n't put me off — you'd tell me what Madame Bernin said.

LUCIE. Well — there is something.

ANNETTE [*bursting into tears*] Oh, my God!

LUCIE. You are both very young. It would be better to wait a little — a year — perhaps more.

ANNETTE [*crying*] Wait — a year!

LUCIE. Come, come, stop crying. There's really no reason for all this. I am not quite pleased with you, Annette. You're barely nineteen. If you waited to marry until you are twenty it would be no harm.

ANNETTE. It's not possible!

LUCIE. Not possible? [*She looks searchingly at her*]. Annette, you frighten me. If it was n't you — [*tenderly and gravely*] Have I been wrong to trust you?

ANNETTE. No! No! What can you be thinking of — Oh, indeed —

LUCIE. What is it, then?

ANNETTE. Well, I 've been such a fool as to tell some friends I was engaged.

LUCIE. Before speaking to me about it?

ANNETTE [*confused*] Don't, please, ask me any more questions.

LUCIE. Annette, I must scold you a little. You 've hurt me very much by keeping me in the dark about all this. Nothing would have made me believe that you 'd do such a thing. I thought you were too fond of me not to tell me at once about anybody — any man — you were interested in. I find I was mistaken. We see one another every day, we are never parted, and yet you have managed to conceal from me the one thing your heart was full of. You ought to have told me. Not because I am your elder sister, but because I take mother's place towards you. And for a better reason still — because I am your friend. It 's been a kind of treason. A little more, and I should have heard that you were engaged from strangers and not from you. Well, my dear, you 've been wrong: these people are not worth crying about. Now be brave and remember your self-respect: I am going to tell you the whole truth. They don't want you, my poor little girl: you are not rich enough for them.

ANNETTE [*staring blindly at her sister*] They don't want me! They don't want me! But Jacques! Jacques! Does *he* know?

LUCIE. Yes, he knows.

ANNETTE. He means to give me up if they tell him to?

LUCIE. Yes.

ANNETTE [*beside herself*] I must see him. I will write to him. I *must* see him. If they don't want me there is nothing left but to kill myself.

LUCIE [*obliging Annette to look her in the face*] Annette, look at me. [*Silence. Then tenderly and gravely*] I think you have something to tell me.

ANNETTE. [*tearing herself away*] Don't ask me —
don't [*very low*] or I shall die of shame.

*Lucie forces her to sit down beside her and takes her
in her arms.*

LUCIE. Come — into my arms. Put your head on my
shoulder as you used when you were little. There now,
tell me what the trouble is. [*Speaking low*]. My darling — my little darling — I 'm afraid you 're most unhappy. Try and think that it 's mother.

ANNETTE [*very low, crying piteously*] Oh, mother!
If you knew what I have done!

LUCIE [*rocking her gently*] There — tell me. Whisper it to me. Whisper —

*Annette whispers. Lucie rises and separates herself
from her sister. She hides her face in her hands.*

LUCIE. Oh, Annette! *You!*

ANNETTE [*kneeling and stretching out her arms*] Forgive me! Forgive me! Forgive me! I deserve it all.
But I 'm almost mad.

LUCIE. You, Annette! *You!*

ANNETTE. Are you going to make me sorry I did n't
kill myself before I told you! Forgive me —

LUCIE. Get up. It 's too awful. I must forgive you.
[*She sits down*].

ANNETTE [*still kneeling*] I did n't know — I understood nothing. He took me by surprise. I had loved
him for a long time. When he was with his regiment I
used to look forward for weeks to his coming home on
leave. Just the thought of seeing him used to make me
tremble. Before I even knew myself that I was in love
with him, he guessed it. He made me tell him so when
he asked me to marry him. Then one day — his father
and mother were away, and someone came and called
Gabrielle, I don't know why. When we were alone —
I did n't understand — I thought he had suddenly gone
mad. But when he kissed me like that I was stunned —

I could n't do anything — happy, and afraid, and ashamed. That was three months ago. The next day I met him in the street. I was in such a state that he said, quite of himself, " I shall speak at once to my people about our marriage." I know he meant it, because really he is honest and good. Only, I suppose he had n't courage. Then, when I found they were going away so soon, I said to him yesterday, " You *must* speak." And now they don't want me!

LUCIE. And he knows that —?

ANNETTE. No. No. Since that day — O, that day! — I 've never been alone with him. We say " monsieur " and " mademoiselle " when we meet and [*in an awe-struck tone*] he is the father of my child.

LUCIE [*after a silence*] It 's not a question now of a girl not to be married because she is poor. It 's a question of atoning for a crime. Julien must speak to M. Bernin.

ANNETTE. You 're going to tell him?

LUCIE. I must. Go back to your room. You 're in no fit state to come to dinner. [*She looks at the clock*] I have only just time to dress. Directly the people are gone I shall speak to Jules. When do they go away?

ANNETTE. In a fortnight.

LUCIE. It 's no matter. Jules shall see M. Bernin to-morrow.

ANNETTE. He won't. He 'll have nothing more to do with me.

LUCIE. No. He will do all he can to save you.

ANNETTE. I don't think so. Dearest, you are mistaken.

LUCIE. No, I 'm not mistaken. I am *certain*. Go. [*Annette goes out*]. I 'm *not* mistaken. But if I were! If there were no one but me to defend this child and her baby! [*A knock at the office door*]. Come in. [*The clerk enters*] What is it?

CLERK [*laying a paper on the table*] It is the circular from the Minister of the Interior. M. le sous-préfet told me to put it here.

ACT II

Same scene.

Lucie, the colonel, Madame Chevillot, Chevillot, the sous-intendant, Brignac, Jacques Poiret, Pierre Poiret, and Laurent. The last three are provincial mayors.

Lucie and Madame Chevillot are in smart evening gowns; the colonel and the sous-intendant in uniform; Chevillot and Brignac are in evening dress; Jacques Poiret in a frock coat, and Laurent and Pierre Poiret in morning coats.

It is after dinner. They are drinking coffee.

Pierre [*a tall, thin peasant, embarrassed by his coffee cup, speaks aside to Laurent in a strong provincial accent*] A fine thing, ain't it, to be so rich and not have enough tables to go round.

Laurent [*formerly a working man, to Pierre Poiret*] At lunch 't was just the same.

Jacques [*a crafty farmer, putting his cup down upon the centre table, and speaking generally*] As for me, I —

Laurent [*passing his cup to Jacques*] M. le maire, would you mind?

Pierre [*the same*] M. le maire, would you —?

They get rid of their cups, passing them from one to the other.

Brignac [*to the mayors*] Will you take liqueurs? [*He points to a bottle and small glasses on a tray*].

All Three [*making too much fuss about it*] Thank you, thank you, M. le sous-préfet.

30

BRIGNAC.   Delighted.   [*He passes behind the centre table and pours out liqueur*].

SOUS-IN.   [*He is small and thin and wears spectacles: a professor disguised as a soldier*]   Yes, ladies: it is an eccentricity.   I acknowledge it and beg you to excuse it: I am a collector.   But you must confess that I have not bored you with it.

COLONEL   [*very much the fine gentleman*]   Indeed, no, it was I who let out the secret.   But I said also that you are a learnèd man.

SOUS-IN.   A dabbler only, colonel.

BRIGNAC [*pretending to find upon the table the circular mentioned in the first act*]   Hullo!   what's this?   [*No one hears him.   He puts the circular back again upon the table*].

LUCIE   [*to the sous-intendant*]   And are you also a literary man?

SOUS-IN.   The Intelligence Department is the literary section of the army.

LAURENT   [*to Jacques Poiret, passing him his glass*]   M. le maire —?

PIERRE   [*same thing*]   M. le maire —?

BRIGNAC   [*again taking up the circular: in a louder voice*]   Hullo!   What's this?   [*They all look at him*].   It's that very circular I was talking about at dinner: the one from the Minister of the Interior.

COL.   About the decline of the population?

BRIGNAC.   Yes, colonel.   This is an important official document.   It came to-day, and I have been carefully considering what can be done to advance this movement in my own humble sphere of influence.   [*To Chevillot*]   As I said to you a short time ago, M. le maire of Château-neuf, the Minister desires to see the whole of France covered with associations having the increase of the population for their object; I am certain that you will desire that this town of Châteauneuf, of which you are

the chief magistrate and in which I am the representative of the Republic, should have the honor of being
among the first to set out upon the road indicated to us.

CHEV. I 'm with you. I am a manufacturer: I am all
for large populations.

BRIGNAC. You are the very man to be president of
the Châteauneuf association.

COL. I am a soldier: I also am for large populations.

LUCIE. And you, M. l'intendant?

SOUS-IN. I, madame, am a bachelor.

COL. [*joking*] More shame for you!

BRIGNAC [*also joking*] It 's a scandal, monsieur, a
perfect scandal.

MME. CHEV. You don't regret it?

SOUS-IN. Ah, I don't say that, madame.

BRIGNAC [*to the three mayors*] You have heard, mes-
sieurs les maires: commerce and the army require the
increase of the population, and the Government com-
mands you, therefore, to further this end to the best of
your ability, each one of you in his own commune.

*The three mayors seem annoyed. They look at one
another.*

PIERRE [*nervelessly*] All right, M. le sous-préfet.

LAUR. [*in the same tone*] I 'll mention it.

JACQUES [*the same*] I 'll think it over.

BRIGNAC. Oh, but gentlemen, I want something more
definite than that. I am a man of action: I am not to be
put off with words. "Acta non verba." May I depend
on you to set to work?

LAUR. You see, M. le sous-préfet, this 'll take a bit
of thinking over.

JACQUES. Don't be in a hurry.

BRIGNAC. We must be men of action. M. Pierre Poiret, now is your chance, won't you give them a lead?

PIERRE. *Me* — M. le sous-préfet?

BRIGNAC. Yes, *you*, M. le maire!

PIERRE. No — oh, no — not *me*. If you knew — no — not me. [*Pointing to his neighbor*] My brother, Jacques Poiret: he's your man. Ask Jacques, M. le sous-préfet, he can't refuse. But *me* — not me!

BRIGNAC. Then it is to be you, M. Jacques Poiret?

JACQUES. If they want to start an association in my commune, M. le sous-préfet, they must get Thierry to see to it.

BRIGNAC. Who is Thierry?

JACQUES. My opponent at the next election.

BRIGNAC. Why?

JACQUES. Why — if he goes in for this I'm certain to get in. But about the next commune, I can't understand why my brother Pierre won't.

PIERRE. Me?

JACQUES. Yes, you're the very man.

BRIGNAC. Why?

JACQUES. Why? Because he has eight children.

BRIGNAC. You, M. Pierre Poiret, you have eight children, and you said nothing about it! Let these ladies congratulate you.

PIERRE [*resisting*] It's not civil, M. le sous-préfet, it's not civil.

BRIGNAC. What d' you mean?

PIERRE. When you ask people to dinner it's not to make fun of them.

BRIGNAC. But I'm not making fun of you.

PIERRE. You'd be the first that did n't. *I* can't help it! It's real bad luck, that's what it is. But it's no reason why I should always be made fun of.

BRIGNAC. But —

PIERRE. Yes, it's always the same. In my commune —

BRIGNAC [*interrupting*] But I assure you —

PIERRE. In my commune they're always joking about me. They say "Hey, Pierre Poiret, there's a prize for the twelfth!" Or they say "Pierre Poiret"—and there is n't a single day they don't say it, and everyone thinks it 's funny, and they split with laughing—they say "Pierre Poiret"—only—hum—not before the ladies. [*Jacques Poiret is holding his sides*] Just look at that fool! I 'm sure he brought the talk round to that a' purpose.

BRIGNAC. No, no.

PIERRE. I bet you he did. Whenever we 're in company it 's the same thing. I won't go about with him any more.

BRIGNAC. But your position is most honorable.

PIERRE. And the worst of it is that he 's right. I call myself a fool myself when I 'm alone. [*Jacques Poiret goes on laughing*] Look at him—grinning—look!—because he 's only got two. [*To his brother*] You puppy!

COL. [*to Pierre Poiret*] You deserve the greatest credit, M. Pierre Poiret.

BRIGNAC. You do.

CHEV. You do, indeed, monsieur.

COL. [*to Pierre Poiret*] In comparing your conduct with your brother's all men of real worth will blame him and congratulate you, as I do, most sincerely. [*He shakes him by the hand*].

CHEV. [*to Pierre Poiret*] Bravo, monsieur! You are helping us in our great work. [*He shakes him by the hand*].

JACQUES [*looking at his brother*] They *seem* as if they meant it!

BRIGNAC [*to Jacques Poiret*] You, monsieur, have chosen the easier and more agreeable life; don't be surprised if we look upon your brother as the more meritorious, though you may be cleverer.

PIERRE [*striking his thigh*] That 's the talk. [*To his brother*] Put that in your pipe, M. Jacques.

JACQUES. All right. You are the most meritorious.
Is that what you 're going to pay your baker with?

PIERRE. Shut up! I 'm the best citizen! I 'm the
most meritorious!

JACQUES. H'm — yes. What does that bring you in?

SOUS-IN. *I* will tell you that, monsieur. It brings in
to your brother, as the poet says, " The joy of duty
done."

JACQUES. H'm. *That* won't put butter on his bread.

SOUS-IN. That is true. But one can't have everything.

PIERRE [*to Brignac, pointing to his brother*] He 's
right, monsieur. For the once that I 've been compli-
mented, I 've had to go through some bad times.

BRIGNAC. You must n't think of that.

PIERRE. Oh — must n't I? Go along! *He 's* right.

BRIGNAC. He 's not.

PIERRE. Yes, he is.

CHEV. and COL. No, no.

PIERRE. Yes, he is.

BRIGNAC. No. It 's possible that some people might
think so now; but in ten years the tables will be turned.
He may die lonely, while you will have a happy old age
with your children and your grandchildren.

PIERRE. Perhaps it was like that once; but nowadays
as soon as the children can get along by themselves, off
they go!

CHEV. Even so they will send you help if you need it.

JACQUES. They could n't help him, even if they
wanted to.

COL. Why not?

JACQUES. Because as there were eight he could n't do
anything for them, so they 'll only be struggling, hand-
to-mouth creatures; not earning enough to keep themselves, much less help him.

PIERRE. And he 's been able to bring up his well.

He 's only one girl: he gave her a fortune and she made a fine marriage. He 's only one boy: he was able to send him to Grignon and he 'll earn big money like his father. No: it 's no use your talking. They 're right when they say " Well, Poiret," — h'm — not before the ladies.

He goes to the table, pours himself out a glass of cognac, and drinks it.

Col. I regret to say we have become too farseeing a nation. Everyone thinks of his own future: no one thinks of the good of the community.

Brignac. In former times people troubled less about the future. They had faith, and remembered the words of the Scriptures, " Consider the lilies of the field, how they grow; they toil not, neither do they spin: and yet I say unto you, that even Solomon in all his glory was not arrayed like one of these."

Lucie. And yet there are little children going about in rags.

Sous-In. God must be less interested in them than in the lilies of the field.

Col. [*to Jacques Poiret*] But, monsieur, you need hands, too, in harvest-time.

Jacques. I have a cutting-and-binding machine. It does the work of twelve men, and only cost a thousand francs. A child costs more.

Chev. We must have workmen to make machines.

Jacques. We buy the machines ready-made in America much cheaper than w. can make them in France.

Chev. If there were a greater number of workmen we might cut down wages and produce at lower prices.

Jacques. Cut down wages! The workmen are complaining already that they can't live on their wages.

Chev. Bah! give them twenty francs a day, and they 'll still complain.

Sous-In. You have not tried that yet.

Col. My dear fellow, remember that, as a bachelor, you are out of this discussion.

Sous-In. I withdraw.

Chev. I did n't mean that for you, Laurent. [*To the Colonel*] M. Laurent, the mayor of Ste. Geneviève, was formerly a workman of mine, but he came into a little money, and went back to his native place. [*To Laurent*] No — I did n't mean it for you; but they 're not all like you, you know.

Brignac [*to Laurent*] So you refuse to form an association too?

Laur. Refuse, M. le sous-préfet? No.

Brignac. At last! Here 's a mayor who understands his duties. He 'll start the thing among his people, and before long we shall have the commune of Ste. Geneviève setting an example to the whole of France.

Laur. Don't get that into your head, monsieur; you 'll be disappointed.

Brignac. No, no.

Laur. Whether you form your association or don't form your association, the people at home are too sensible to have more children than they 've cradles for. They know too well they must put a bit by.

Brignac. If you think that an association will make no difference why do you agree to form one?

Laur. Because I want you to get me what you promised me.

Brignac. What was that?

Laur. You know.

Brignac. No, I don't.

Laurent touches his buttonhole.

Brignac [*angrily*] Is that what we 've come to? We were speaking of the good of the community.

Chev. [*the same*] It 's most discouraging. We point out to you that the trade of the country is in danger.

Brignac. And you only think of yourself.

CHEV. You only think of yourself.

BRIGNAC. What a want of public spirit!

CHEV. Bad citizenship!

LAUR. [*getting excited*] Oh, yes! Making the poor do everything! Go and talk to the middle classes, who 've money enough to rear children by the dozen, and who 've fewer than the workmen. Here 's M. Chevillot: he has twenty thousand francs a year, I have two thousand. When he has ten children, then I 'll have one. That 'll be fair and square, won't it now?

CHEV. These personalities —

LAUR. Is it true that you 've only one son?

CHEV. It 's true. But if I had several my works would have to be sold at my death, and —

LAUR. There we are. These gentlemen are too precious careful about the fortunes they leave their own children; but when it 's a question of the workmen's children, they think it don't matter if there ain't enough victuals to go round.

CHEV. It is to the interest of the workmen that my works should be prosperous.

LAUR. But you only take unmarried men.

CHEV. I beg your pardon — I —

LAUR. Is it true?

CHEV. It 's because of the Employers' Liability Bill. Let me explain — [*Laurent turns his back on him. He addresses himself to Brignac*] Allow me to — [*Brignac does not listen. To the sous-intendant*] If I was allowed to explain you would understand. I 'm perfectly consistent.

LAUR. Are we to do as you say, or are we to do as you do? If you believed what you say you 'd act accordingly.

CHEV. But —

BRIGNAC. We should n't indulge in these personalities. We must look higher. Lift up your hearts. Sursum corda. You have just heard, gentlemen, that commerce and the army protest against the decline of the population. And I, the representative of the Government of this country, tell you, in concert with commerce and the army, that there must be more births.

LAUR. And what's the Government doing?

BRIGNAC. What is it doing! — well — and this circular?

SOUS-IN. We must be just. Besides this circular, the Government has appointed a Commission to enquire into the matter.

BRIGNAC. Various measures are being brought up.

LAUR. When they're passed — we'll see.

BRIGNAC. Those who have a large family will be exempted from taxation.

LAUR. From what taxes?

BRIGNAC. What taxes! The taxes you pay to the collector, of course.

LAUR. Listen, M. le sous-préfet. The poor pay next to nothing of those taxes. They pay the *real* taxes: the taxes upon bread, wine, salt, tobacco: and they'll go on paying them. The more children you have, the more money the State takes from you.

SOUS-IN. Pray do not forget that the State proposes to confer a decoration upon every mother of seven children.

PIERRE [*to Laurent*] There you are!

JACQUES. M. le sous-préfet, we must be off. We've a long way to go.

BRIGNAC [*to Jacques*] Good-night, M. le maire.

PIERRE [*tipsy*] I'm all right here. Why go 'way?

LAUR. I'm a fool, M. Brignac. I'm afraid I've been setting you against me. I'll start an association — trust me. Good-night. Good-night, madame.

JACQUES. Good-night, madame.

LUCIE. Good-night, good-night.

PIERRE. Good-night, ladies, gents, and — hic — the company.

They go out, accompanied by Brignac.

COL. [*to Lucie and Madame Chevillot*] I'm afraid we've bored you, ladies, with our discussion.

LUCIE. Not at all.

COL. I notice that women are usually a little impatient if we talk of these questions.

SOUS-IN. As impatient as we should be if they discussed the recruiting laws without consulting us.

MME. CHEV. Precisely.

COL. [*to Lucie*] Perhaps, too, you don't agree with us.

LUCIE. You'll never make women understand why children must be created to be killed in your battles.

COL. [*to the sous-intendant*] There, that's how the military ruin of a country is brought about.

SOUS-IN. You're right, colonel, if it be true that power is a function of number.

COL. Well, is n't it?

SOUS-IN. Those who believe the contrary say "There is no evidence in history that supremacy, even military supremacy, has ever belonged to the most numerous peoples." I quote M. de Varigny. General von der Gotz shares this opinion, and our own General Serval says, "All great military operations have been performed by small armies."

Brignac comes in.

COL. Oh, ho, Mr. Bachelor, you've got all the arguments on your side at your finger-ends.

BRIGNAC. We shall make laws against you and your like, M. le sous-intendant. We shall make it impossible for you to receive money by will, as the Romans did. We shall make you pay fines, as the Greeks did. And we'll invent something new, if necessary.

SOUS-IN. Compulsory paternity!

Col. One may fairly ask whether people have the right to shirk these obligations.

Sous-In. Some people think it is their duty.

Brignac. Their duty!

Sous-In. Are you sure that all men who don't marry are bachelors from pure selfishness?

Col. Of course, we're not speaking of you personally.

Sous-In. Do so, by all means. It was not out of mere lightness of heart that I deprived myself of the tenderness of a wife and the caresses of a child. When I was young I was poor and sickly. I did not choose to bring children into the world when I had nothing to leave them but my bad constitution. I said, in the words of a great poet:

> Remain
> In the elusive realm of might-have-been,
> O son more loved than any ever born!

I thought it better to be lonely than let the stock go from bad to worse. I believe it is a crime to bring a child into the world if one cannot give it health and bring it up well. We saw one hundred conscripts this morning, colonel, and we passed sixty. Would it not have been better if there had only been eighty and we could have passed them all?

Col. Perhaps you are right. I said what I said because I've heard it so constantly repeated.

Sous-In. When there are healthy houses and food and clothing for everyone it will be time to think of adding to the number.

Lucie. That is very true.

Chev. You evidently don't share M. Brignac's ideas, madame.

Brignac. Oh, indeed she does. Madame Brignac and I have three children, and we don't mean to stop there: so my wife may qualify for that decoration some day.

Lucie [to Chevillot] As far as I can see, M. le

maire, when children are born now society does not
always make them welcome.

BRIGNAC.   I think, my dear, that you had better
leave the discussion of this important question to the
gentlemen.

LUCIE.   But surely it has some interest for us women!
I hear everyone else consulted about it — political people
and business people — but nobody ever thinks of consulting us.

BRIGNAC.   Far from not welcoming the children that
are born, society —

LUCIE [to Brignac]   Stop! Do you remember what
happened lately, not a hundred miles from here? I mean
about the servant who was turned out into the street
because she was going to have a baby. She will have
to go to some hospital for her confinement. And after
that what will happen to her and her child?

BRIGNAC [to the others]   Madame Brignac speaks of
something which took place recently in a most respectable family. The incident has nothing whatever to do
with the principles we are defending. It is clear that
one cannot have a servant in that condition in a well-
kept house. And there are higher considerations which
will always prevent a respectable citizen from even appearing to condone immorality by sheltering it. One
must not offer a premium to evil-doing.

CHEV.   Very true.

LUCIE.   And the unfortunate girl, who is very likely
only the victim of another person, is condemned by
everyone.

BRIGNAC [timidly]   No, no, I don't say that. I myself
am very liberal, and I confess that in — exceptional
circumstances — one should be indulgent to her.

LUCIE.   Very well. Don't forget you have said that.

COL.   Good-night, madame. I must be going. Thank
you for a charming evening.

CHEV. I also, madame — charming.

BRIGNAC [*pointing to the door into his office*] This way. As you go out I want to show you a diagram I have had done, by which you can make yourself acquainted at a single glance with the political conditions of the division. There is an arrangement of pins — [*They hesitate*] One minute. It will only take a minute. You can go out through the office. One minute — while you are putting on your coats. The coats are in there. I 'm going out with you to a reception at the club. You 'll see — it 's rather curious. [*To Lucie, aside*] You come too. [*Aloud*] I think the idea is ingenious.

He talks them all off. When they are gone there is a short pause, and then Catherine opens the door at the back and steps forward.

CATHERINE [*to Annette, who has come into the ante-room*] Yes, mademoiselle, they are all gone.

Annette comes in. She takes off her hat and cloak and hands them to Catherine, who takes them into the anteroom and comes back to turn out the principal electric lights and to take away the tray. Annette, with fixed, staring eyes, sits rigidly upon the couch. Lucie comes in.

LUCIE. Annette! Where have you been?

ANNETTE. I have been to see Jacques Bernin.

LUCIE. You have seen him? You have spoken to him?

ANNETTE. I went to his father's house.

LUCIE. Well?

ANNETTE. There is no hope.

LUCIE. What did they say to you?

ANNETTE. I ought n't ever to tell anyone about the two hours I have just lived through. It 's too shameful. Too vile. What I can't believe is that all that really happened to *me*, and that I am alive still.

LUCIE [*tenderly*] Tell me all about it.

ANNETTE. What 's the good of my telling you? It 's

all over. There's nothing left. He didn't love me: he never loved me. He's gone. He's going to marry another woman.

LUCIE. He's *gone?*

ANNETTE. He went this evening. They all went. M. and Madame Bernin and Gabrielle dined at the station; Jacques dined at a restaurant with some friends. I went there. I sent up for him. From where I was standing, in the vestibule, I heard their jokes when the waiter gave him my message.

LUCIE [*in gentle reproach*] Annette!

ANNETTE. I wanted to know. I was certain his people were taking him away by force, and I was making excuses for him. I was certain he loved me. I should have laughed if anyone had told me he would n't be horrified when he heard what had happened to me. I thought that when he knew, he'd take my hand, and go with me to his people, and say "Whether you wish it or not, here is my wife." As I was sure it would end like that, I thought it was better it should be over at once. I expected to come back here to beg your pardon — to kiss you and comfort you.

LUCIE. And what did he say?

ANNETTE [*without listening*] I think I've gone mad. All *that* happened, and I'm here. I'm quiet: I'm not crying: it's as if I was paralyzed.

LUCIE. You said you sent a message to him at the restaurant?

ANNETTE. Yes.

LUCIE. Did he come?

ANNETTE. Yes. He said he thought some chorus-girl wanted him.

LUCIE. Oh! And when he found it was you?

ANNETTE. He took me out into the street for fear I should be recognized, and I had to explain it to him in the street. [*A pause*] People passing by stared at us,

and some of them laughed.   [*With passion and pain*]
Oh! if I only had no memory!

Lucie.   Tell me, darling, tell me.

Annette [*with violence*]   Oh, I 'll tell you.   You 'll
despise me a little more; but what can that matter to me
now?   First he pretended not to understand me: he
forced me to say it quite plainly: he did it on purpose —
either to torture me, or to give himself time to think.
You 'll never guess what he said — that it was n't true.

Lucie.   Oh!

Annette.   Yes, that it was n't true.   He got angry,
and he began to abuse me.   He said he guessed what I
was up to; that I wanted to make a scandal to force
him to marry me — oh, he spared me nothing — to force
him to marry me because he was rich.   And when that
made me furious, he threatened to call the police!   I
ought to have left him, run away, come home, ought n't
I?   But I could n't believe it of him all at once, like that!
And I could n't go away while I had any hope.   You see,
as long as I was with him, nothing was settled: as long
as I was holding to his arm it was as if I was engaged.
When he was gone I should only be a miserable ruined
girl, like dozens of others.   Then — I was afraid of
making him angry: my life was at stake: and to save
myself I went down into the very lowest depths of vile-
ness and cowardice.   I cried, I implored.   I lost all
shame and I offered to go with him to a doctor to-morrow
to prove that what I told him was true.   And what he
said then I cannot tell you — not even you — it was too
much — *too* much — I did n't understand at first.   It
was only afterwards, coming back, going over all his
words, that I made out what he meant.   He did n't believe what he said.   He *could n't* have believed what he
said.   At any rate he knows that I am not a girl out of
the streets.   But at first I did n't understand.   Then —
where was I?   I don't remember —   At last he looked at

his watch and said he had only just time to catch the train. He said good-bye and started off at a great pace to the station. I followed him imploring and crying. I was so ashamed of my cowardice. It was horrible and absurd! I could n't believe it was the end of everything. I was all out of breath — almost running — and I prayed him for the sake of his child, for the sake of my love, of my misery, of my very life; and I took hold of his arm to keep him back. My God! what must I have looked like! At the station entrance he said, "Let go your hold of me." I said, "You shall *not* go." Then he rushed to the train, and jumped into a carriage, and almost crushed my fingers in the door; and he went and hid behind his mother, and she threatened too to have me arrested. And Gabrielle sat there looking white and pretending not to know me. I came back. I have n't had courage enough to kill myself, but I wish I was dead! [*Breaking into sobs, and in a voice of earnest supplication*] Lucie, dear, I don't want to go through all that 's coming — I 'm too little, I 'm too weak, I 'm too young to bear it. Really, I have n't the strength.

LUCIE. Annette — don't say that. Hush, my darling, hush. In the first place, everything has n't been tried. You have entreated these people; now we must threaten.

ANNETTE. It 'll be no use.

LUCIE. It *will* be of use. The way they 're hurrying away shows how afraid they are of scandal. As soon as my husband comes in I will tell him all about it.

ANNETTE. Oh, my God!

LUCIE. He will go down and see them. He will threaten them with an action. They will give in.

ANNETTE. We can't bring an action against them. He told me so.

LUCIE. Then there are other ways of defending you. Believe me, I 'm sure of it.

ANNETTE. There are *not*.

LUCIE. There are. And even if there were n't, you must n't talk of dying at your age. Am I not here? Annette, Annette, my little one, I will help you through this trouble! You believe me, don't you? You know how I love you? You know that mother left you in my care? I 'll help you and comfort you and love you so well that you 'll forget.

ANNETTE. Forget!

LUCIE. Yes, yes; people forget. If it were n't for that no one would be alive.

ANNETTE. I feel as if I had lived a hundred years. Life is hard, hard; too hard.

LUCIE. Life is hard for all women.

ANNETTE. It 's worse for me than for anyone else.

LUCIE. Oh, Annette! If you only knew!

ANNETTE. When I 've seen mothers with their little children I 've had such dreams.

LUCIE. If you only knew! Those mothers had their own troubles. Nearly every woman carries about with her the corpse of the woman she might have been.

ANNETTE. Ah, Lucie, dear, it 's easy for you to talk.

LUCIE. Darling, you must n't think you 're alone in your sorrow. I seem to you to be happy with my children and my husband, and you think my happiness makes light of your distress. But you 're wrong. Your misery makes me so weak, I must tell you what I wanted always to hide from you. My husband does not love me. I don't love him. Can you realize the loneliness of that? If you knew what it means to live with an enemy and to have to endure his caresses!

ANNETTE. My poor dear!

LUCIE. So you see, Annette, you must n't think about dying, because perhaps I shall want your help as much as you want mine. I heard the door shut. It 's Julien.

ANNETTE. Don't tell him: please don't. Spare me the shame.

LUCIE. Go away, now.

ANNETTE. You 've given me back a little hope. Dearest sister help me, I have nobody else.

LUCIE. Go!

She goes: Brignac comes in.

BRIGNAC [*making for the door of his office*] Not gone to bed yet? I had a stroke of luck at the club. I met the editor of the ' Independent ' and I promised to write him an article about the minister's circular for to-morrow's paper. An official's day is sometimes pretty full, eh?

LUCIE. Julien, I have something very important to tell you. A great misfortune has happened to us.

BRIGNAC. Good heavens, what is it? The children?

LUCIE. No, it has to do with Annette.

BRIGNAC. You said she did n't come to dinner because of a headache. Have you been concealing something?

LUCIE. She is not ill, but she is cruelly and grievously unhappy.

BRIGNAC. Nonsense! Unhappiness at her age! A love affair. Some marriage she had set her heart on.

LUCIE. Yes, a marriage she had set her heart on.

BRIGNAC. Ouf! I breathe again. What a fright you gave me! *That 's* not of much consequence.

LUCIE. Yes, it 's of the greatest consequence. Julien, I appeal to your heart, to your kindliness, to your best feelings.

BRIGNAC. But what 's the matter?

LUCIE. Annette made the mistake of trusting entirely to the man she loved, who had promised to marry her. He took advantage of the child's innocent love. She has been seduced. [*In a low voice*] Understand me, Julien, she 's going to have a baby in six months.

BRIGNAC. Annette!

LUCIE. Annette.

BRIGNAC. It 's impossible. It 's —

LUCIE. She is certain of it. She told me about it herself.

BRIGNAC [*after a silence*] Who is it?

LUCIE. Jacques Bernin.

BRIGNAC [*furious*] Jacques Bernin! Well, *this* is a nice piece of work! She goes it, this little sister of yours, with her innocent airs!

LUCIE. Don't accuse her. Don't.

BRIGNAC. I really cannot compliment her! I'm nicely repaid for all I've done for her, and you may thank her from me for her gratitude.

LUCIE. Oh, don't be angry.

BRIGNAC. Well, if you are able to hear news like this perfectly calmly, you are certainly endowed with unusual self-control.

LUCIE. It was the child's innocence that made the thing possible.

BRIGNAC. I daresay. Go and tell that to the Châteauneuf people! Besides, if she was so innocent, why did n't you look after her better?

LUCIE. But it was *you* who were always urging her to go to the Bernins.

BRIGNAC. In another minute it's going to be all my fault! I was glad she should go to their house because I thought old Bernin might be useful to us. How should I know that the girl could n't behave herself?

LUCIE. [*indignantly*] Oh, hush! I tell you Annette is the victim of this wretch. If you are going to do nothing but insult her, we had better stop discussing the matter.

BRIGNAC. I'm in a nice fix now! There's nothing left for us but to pack our trunks and be off. I'm done for, ruined! smashed!

LUCIE. You exaggerate.

BRIGNAC. I exaggerate! I tell you if she was caught red-handed *stealing*, the wreck would n't be more complete. I even think that would have been better. I should be less definitely compromised, and less disqualified.

Lucie. You can abuse her by and by: the business now is to save her. The Bernins have gone away this evening; find them to-morrow; and, if you speak to them as you ought, they'll understand that their son *must* marry Annette.

Brignac. But Jacques Bernin is engaged.

Lucie. He must break it off, that's all.

Brignac. He won't break it off, because it means lots and lots of money, and because he is the most ferocious little fortune-hunter I ever met. Yes, he is; I know him, I see him at the club. I've heard him holding forth about women and money; his opinions are edifying. By the way, has Annette any letters from him connecting him with this business?

Lucie. No.

Brignac. He's not such a fool as to compromise himself. He'll deny everything.

Lucie. You must threaten them with a scandal.

Brignac. We should be the first to suffer from that.

Lucie. But we must do something. We must bring an action.

Brignac. There is no affiliation law in France.

Lucie. You refuse to go and see what can be done with the Bernins?

Brignac. Not at all. I say that it would be a useless journey.

Lucie. Then what are we to do?

Brignac. Not a soul in Châteauneuf must know what has happened. Fortunately we have a little time.

Lucie. What are you going to do?

Brignac. We'll see. We'll think it over. One doesn't come to a decision of this importance in ten minutes.

LUCIE. I want to know what you are going to do. Your point of view surprises me so much that I wish to understand it completely.

BRIGNAC. Understand this, then: if the matter is kept secret, it is only our misfortune; if it becomes public, it will be a scandal.

LUCIE. How can it be kept secret?

BRIGNAC. We must pack Annette off before anyone suspects.

LUCIE. Where is she to go?

BRIGNAC. Ah! that 's the devil. Where — where? If only we had some friends we could trust, in some out-of-the-way place, far away. But we have n't. Still, we *must* send her somewhere.

LUCIE. Oh, my God! [*She sobs*].

BRIGNAC [*irritated*] For Heaven's sake don't cry like that. That does n't mend matters. We must make some excuse. We 'll invent an aunt or a cousin who 's invited her to stay. I will find a decent house in Paris for her to go to. She 'll be all right there. When the time comes she can put the child out to nurse in the country, and come back to us. I shall certainly have got my promotion by that time: we shall have left this place, and the situation will be saved — as far as it can be saved.

LUCIE. You propose that to me and you think I shall consent to it!

BRIGNAC. Why not?

LUCIE. You 've not stopped to think. That 's your only excuse.

BRIGNAC. I must say, I don't see —

LUCIE. You seriously propose to send that poor child to Paris, where she does n't know a soul?

BRIGNAC. What do you mean by that? I will go to Paris myself, if necessary. There are special boarding-houses: very respectable ones. I 'll inquire: of course without letting out that it is for anyone I know. And

I 'll pay what is necessary. What more can you want?
We shall be sure of keeping the thing quiet that way.
I believe there are houses in Paris subsidized by the
State, and the people who stay in them need not even
give their names.

LUCIE. I tell you, you 've not stopped to think. Just
when the child is most in need of every care, you propose
to send her off alone; *alone*, do you understand, alone!
To tear her away from here, put her into a train, and
send her off to Paris, like a sick animal you want to
get rid of. It would be enough to make her kill
herself.

BRIGNAC. Can you think of anything better?

LUCIE. Everything is better than that. If I consented to that I should feel that I was as bad as the man
who seduced her. Be honest, Julien: remember it is
in our interest you propose to sacrifice her. We shall
gain peace and quiet at the price of her loneliness and
despair. To save ourselves trouble — serious trouble,
I admit — we are to abandon this child to strangers.
She does not know the meaning of harshness or unkind-
ness; and we are to drive her away now — now, of all
times! Away from all love and care and comfort, without a friend to put kind arms round her and let her sob
her grief away. I implore you, Julien, I entreat you,
for our children's sake, don't keep me from her, don't
ask me to do this shameful thing. I will *not* do it! We
must do something else. Make *me* suffer if you like, but
don't add abandonment and loneliness to the misery of
my poor little helpless sister.

BRIGNAC. There would have been no question of misery if she had behaved herself.

LUCIE. She is this man's victim! But she won't go.
You 'll have to drive her out as you drove out the servant.
Have you the courage? Just think of what her life will
be. Try to realize the long months of waiting in that

dreadful house: the slow development of the poor little creature that she will know beforehand is condemned to all the risks children run when they are separated from their mothers. And when she is torn with tortures, and cries out in that fearful anguish I know so well, and jealous death seems to be hovering over the bed of martyrdom, waiting for mother and child; just when one is overcome by the terror and amazement of the mystery accomplished in oneself; then, then — there 'll be only strangers with her. And if her poor anguished eyes look round for an answering look, perhaps the last; if she feels for a hand to cling to, she will see round her bed only men doing a duty, and women going through a routine. And then — after *that* — she 's to let her child go; to stifle her strongest instinct; to silence the cry of love that consoles us all for the tortures we have to go through; to turn away her eyes and say " Take him away, I don't want him." And at *that* price she 's to be forgiven for another person's crime!

BRIGNAC. But what can I do? I can't alter the world, can I? The world is made like that. If Annette was ten times more innocent she could n't stay here.

LUCIE. I —

BRIGNAC [*violently*] And I don't choose that she shall stay here. Do you understand? I 'm sorry she has to go by herself to Paris. But once more, if she had behaved respectably she would n't be obliged to do it.

LUCIE. Oh!

BRIGNAC. Can't you understand that she would suffer much more here, surrounded by people who know her, than she would there, where she would be unknown? Here she could n't so much as go down the street without exposing herself to insult. Why, if she even went to mass or to a concert after her condition became evident, it would be a kind of provocation; people would avoid her as if she had the plague. Mothers would sneer and tell their daughters not to look at her, and men would smile in a way that would be an outrage.

LUCIE. If necessary she can stay at home.

BRIGNAC. Stay at home! Rubbish! What would be the good of that? Servants would talk, and the scandal would be all the greater. And you have n't reflected that the consequences would fall upon me. You have n't troubled to consider me, or to remember the drawback this will be to me. I am not alluding to the imbecile jokes people are sure to make about the apostle of re-population. But our respectability will be called in question. People will remark that there are families in which such things don't happen. Political hatred and social prejudice will help them to invent all sorts of tales. And the allusions, the suggestions, the pretended pity! There would be nothing left for me but to send in my resignation!

LUCIE. Send it in.

BRIGNAC. Yes, and what should we live upon then?

LUCIE [after a silence] Then that is society's welcome to the newborn child!

BRIGNAC. To the child born outside marriage, yes. If it was n't for that there would soon be nothing but illegitimate births. It is to preserve the family that society condemns the natural child.

LUCIE. If there is guilt two people are guilty. Why do you only punish the mother?

BRIGNAC. What am I to say to you? Because it 's easier.

LUCIE. And that 's your justice! The truth is, you all uphold the conventions of society. You do. And the proof is that if Annette stayed here in the town to have her baby, you 'd all cry shame upon her; but if she goes to Paris and has it secretly and gets rid of it, nobody will blame her. Let 's be honest, and call things by their names: it is not immorality that is condemned, but motherhood. You say you want a larger number of births, and at the same time you say to women "No motherhood without marriage, and no marriage without money." As long as you 've not changed *that* all your circulars will be met with shouts of derision — half from hate, half from pity!

BRIGNAC. Possibly. Good-night. I 'm going to work.

LUCIE. Listen — Then you drive Annette from your house?

BRIGNAC. I don't drive her from my house. I beg her to go elsewhere.

LUCIE. I shall go with her.

BRIGNAC. You mean, leave me?

LUCIE. Yes.

BRIGNAC. Then you don't love me.

LUCIE. No.

BRIGNAC. Ah! Here 's another story. Since when?

LUCIE. I never loved you.

BRIGNAC. You married me.

LUCIE. Not for love.

BRIGNAC. This is most interesting. Go on.

LUCIE. You 're another victim of the state of society you are defending.

BRIGNAC. I don't understand.

LUCIE. I was a penniless girl, and so I had no offers of marriage. When you proposed to me I was tired of waiting, and I did n't want to be an old maid. I accepted you, but I knew you only came to me because the women with money would n't have you. I made up my mind to love you and be loyal.

BRIGNAC. Well?

LUCIE. But when my first baby came you deceived me. Since then I have only endured you, and you owe my submission to my cowardice. It was only my first child I wanted, the others you forced upon me, and when each was coming you left me. It 's true I was unattractive, but that was not my fault. You left me day after day in my ugliness and loneliness, and when you came back to me from those other women, you were full of false solicitude about my health. I begged for a rest after nursing. I asked to be allowed to live a little for myself, to be a mother only with my own consent. You laughed at me in a vain, foolish way. You did not consider the future of your children or the life of your wife, but you forced upon me the danger and the suffering of bringing another child into the world. What was it to you? Just the satisfaction of your vanity. You could jest with your friends and make coarse witticisms about it. Fool!

BRIGNAC. That's enough, thank you. You're my wife —

LUCIE. I'll not be your wife any longer, and I won't have another child.

BRIGNAC. Why?

LUCIE. Because I've just found out what the future of my poor, penniless little girls is to be. It's to be Annette's fate, or mine. Oh, to think I've been cruel enough to bring three of them into the world already!

BRIGNAC. You're mad. And be good enough not to put on these independent airs. They're perfectly useless.

LUCIE. You think so?

BRIGNAC. I am sure of it. If you have had enough of me, get a divorce.

LUCIE. But you would keep the children?

BRIGNAC. Naturally. And let me tell you that as long as you are my wife before the world, you'll be my wife really.

LUCIE. And you will force me to have a child whenever you please?

BRIGNAC. Most certainly.

LUCIE. My God! They think a woman's body is like the clay of the fields; they want to drag harvest after harvest from it until it is worn out and done for! I refuse this slavery, and I shall leave you if you turn out my sister.

BRIGNAC. And your children?

LUCIE. I will take them with me.

BRIGNAC. And their food?

LUCIE. I will work.

BRIGNAC. Don't talk nonsense. You could n't earn enough to keep them from starving. It 's late: go to bed.

LUCIE [*her teeth clenched*] And wait for you?

BRIGNAC. And wait for me. Precisely. [*He goes out*].

LUCIE [*rushing to the door on the left*] Annette! Oh, Annette! There 's nobody to help us!

ACT III

A court house, of which only two sides are visible. The footlights would almost correspond with a line drawn from one angle to the opposite one. On the left, to the front, is the raised seat of the public Minister. Further back, to the left, the court. Facing the audience, successively, counsels' bench; the defendants' bench, a little raised; and the police bench.

In the centre, facing the table on which lie the " pièces à conviction," is the witness-box.

To the extreme right are three or four benches, of which a part only is visible, reserved for the public. The jury, which is not visible, would be in the prompter's place.

There are present the advocate-general; the president of the court and his assessors; also the counsel for the defence and some junior barristers. In the dock are Madame Thomas, Marie Caubert, Tupin, Madame Tupin, and several policemen. Madame Chevillot is among the public.

PRESIDENT [*authoritatively, to the counsel for the defence*] Maître Verdier, you cannot speak now. I see what line you propose to take for the defence, and I give you fair warning that I shall use my whole power and authority to prevent you from making light of the criminal acts attributed to the defendants.

COUNSEL FOR THE DEFENCE. You are mistaken, M. le président. I have no intention of making light of them. On the contrary, I declare definitely that in my eyes abortion is a crime, because it deprives of life a creature already living; and to condone it would lead to condoning infanticide also. But what I propose to demonstrate is that in not permitting affiliation and in not respecting all motherhood, whatever its origin may be, society has lost its right to condemn a crime rendered excusable by the hypocrisy of custom and the indifference of the laws.

PRES. This is not the time for your address. Let the woman Thomas stand up. [*To Madame Thomas*] So you hunted up your clients in the provinces?

MME. THOMAS. No, M. le président. They came and found me.

PRES. We shall see. Usher, bring forward the witness — [*he hunts for the name in his notes*] — Madame Lucie Brignac.

MME. CHEV. [*among the audience, to her neighbor*] Must n't Brignac be in a hurry to get his divorce!

Lucie has approached the witness-bar. She is thinner and older.

PRES. [*to the usher*] Has the witness been sworn?

USHER. Yes, M. le président.

PRES. [*to Lucie*] Was it of her own free will that your sister, the unfortunate Annette Jarras, in consequence of whose death the defendants have been arrested, came to Paris and placed herself in the hands of this woman?

LUCIE. Yes, M. le président.

PRES. Very well. Go and sit down. I will call you again presently. [*Lucie retires to her place, sobbing*] Marie Caubert, come forward. [*A small, thin woman rises*]. Your name is Marie Caubert? How old are you?

SCHOOLMISTRESS. Twenty-seven.

PRES. Profession?

Sch. Schoolmistress.

Pres. You have come from the country, too: do you know what you are accused of?

Sch. Yes, M. le président.

Pres. What have you to say in your defence?

Sch. I did not know I was doing wrong.

Pres. Your levity amazes me. You are a school-mistress, and you do not realize that the sacred mission with which you are entrusted, the mission of preparing citizens and citizenesses for the glories of the future, demands that your life should be exemplary. You are appointed to give the elementary course of lessons in civic morality: is it thus that you practise that morality? You have no answer? According to the notes I have here you insisted upon nursing your two children yourself. Do you love them?

Sch. It was just because I love them.

Pres. But you decided that two were enough. You ventured to limit the work of the Creator.

Sch. I should have liked nothing better than to have four or five children.

Pres. Indeed! Then allow me to inform you that you 've not taken the best means for arriving at that desirable result. [*He laughs, turning to his assessor on the right, who laughs also*].

Sch. One must have money enough to bring them up.

Pres. Ah! Stop a moment. If some people were to make that bad excuse I might understand it. But from you, who enjoy the inestimable advantage of being under the protection of the State, I do not understand it. You are never out of work.

Sch. I earn 83 francs a month, and my husband, who teaches too, earns the same. That makes 166 francs a month to live on and to rear two children. When there were four of us we could just scrape along, but with five we could n't have managed it.

PRES. You forget to mention that when your children are coming you have a right to a month's holiday on full salary.

SCH. Yes, at one time, M. le président, but not now. In 1900 a ministerial circular announced to us that there was not enough money, and we could practically only have holidays at half salary. To get the whole salary we must have a certificate from the inspector, giving reasons. One has to petition for it.

PRES. Well, then one petitions.

SCH. It's hard to seem like a beggar simply because one has children.

PRES. Oho! You're proud.

SCH. That's not illegal.

PRES. And that's why you went to the woman Thomas?

SCH. Yes, monsieur. My husband and I had arranged our expenses carefully. On the evening of the day we were paid our salary we used to divide the money into little portions and put them away. So much for rent, so much for food, so much for clothing. We just managed to get along by being most careful; and several times we cut down expenses it did n't seem possible to cut down. A third child coming upset everything. We could n't have lived. We should all have starved. Besides, the inspectors and directresses don't like us to have many children, especially if we nurse them ourselves. They told me to hide myself when I was suckling the last one. I only had ten minutes to do it in, at the recreations at ten o'clock and at two o'clock; and when my mother brought baby to me I had to shut myself up with him in a dark closet.

PRES. All that's irrelevant.

COUN. DEF. No, M. le président, it ought to be known here how the State, which preaches increase of the population, treats its employés when they have children.

PRES. [*furious*] You have no right to speak. [*To the schoolmistress*] Have you anything more to say?

SCH. No, M. le président.

PRES. Then sit down. Tupin, stand up.

TUPIN [*a working man, mean and wretched*] After you, Calvon.

PRES. What! *What* did you say?

TUPIN. I said "After you, Calvon." Calvon's your name, is n't it?

PRES. I warn you I shall not stand any insolence from you.

TUPIN. I say to you "After you, Calvon," as you say to me "Tupin, stand up." If that's insolence, I did n't begin it.

PRES. I shall have you turned out of the court. Stand up.

TUPIN [*standing*] There: I'm very glad to. It'll take the stiffness out of my legs.

PRES. Your profession?

TUPIN. Electrician.

PRES. You were once. It is a long time since you worked regularly.

TUPIN. I can't get work.

PRES. Because you look for it in the public house. The police reports about you are the most unfavorable.

TUPIN. I never liked the police: I'm not surprised they don't like me. [*Laughter from the audience*]

PRES. Silence! or I shall clear the court. [*To Tupin*] The name of your wife, Eugénie Tupin, has been found in the papers of the woman Thomas. Where is the woman Tupin? Stand up. [*To Tupin*] That will do, sit down. You attempted to conceal her from the police.

TUPIN. I thought they were not good company for her.

PRES. [*pretending not to hear and consulting his*

notes] You gave yourself up and declared that you yourself took her to this woman's house.

TUPIN. You speak like a book.

PRES. You persistently accused yourself. Did you want to go to prison?

TUPIN. It's not a bad place. One's warm, and there's food at every meal.

PRES. It is true that prison diet is better than your everyday fare.

TUPIN. Now you're talking.

PRES. [*consulting his notes*] When you were arrested you were both completely destitute. What remained of your furniture had been sold, and you were entering upon a state of complete vagabondage. No doubt you also will accuse society. You are an unruly person. You frequent Socialist clubs; and when you don't affect a cynical carelessness in your language, as you are doing now, you like to repeat the empty phrases you have picked up from the propagandist pamphlets which are poisoning the minds of the working classes. But we know all about you; and if you are a victim, you are the victim of your vices. You drink.

TUPIN. I have taken to it lately. That's true.

PRES. You confess it. Most extraordinary.

MME. TUPIN. What does that prove?

PRES. Your eldest daughter is on the streets and one of your sons has been sent to prison for a year for theft. Is that true?

TUPIN. Possibly.

PRES. Not quite so insolent now. I congratulate you. We will proceed. You took your wife to an abortionist. Why?

TUPIN. Because I considered that bringing seven miserable little devils into the world was enough.

PRES. If you had continued to be the honest and laborious workman that you once were you might have had another child, without that child being necessarily a miserable little devil.

Mme. Tupin. That is n't true.

Tupin. No, monsieur. After four it 's impossible.

Pres. I don't understand you.

Tupin. What I say is that a workman's family, however hard they work and screw, can't get along when there are five children.

Pres. If that is true there are — and this society you despise. may be proud of it — there are, I say, many charities on the watch, so to speak, for the destitute; and they make it a point of honor to leave none without relief.

Tupin [*indignant*] Oh, and that seems all right to you, does it? You say it 's a workman's duty to work and to have a lot of children, and when he does it, fair and square, and it makes a beggar of him, it seems to you all right!

Pres. Ah, ha! Here 's the orator of the public house parlor. In the first place, we have only your assertion that a workman's family cannot live when there are five children. But, thank God, there are more than one or two in that condition who have recourse neither to charity nor to an abortionist.

Mme. Tupin. That 's not true.

Tupin. Shall I prove to you that you 're wrong?

Pres. That has nothing to do with the charge against you.

Mme. Tupin. Yes, it has.

Tupin. I beg your pardon. If I prove it that will explain how I came to do what I did.

Mme. Tupin. I should think so!

Pres. Very well, but cut it short.

Tupin. I gave my lawyer the month's account. Please let him read it to you.

Pres. Very well.

The counsel for the defence rises.

COUN.   Here it is.

PRES.   Stop. You 're not Tupin's counsel.

COUN.   No, M. le président. But my learned friends, with a confidence which honors me, and for which I thank them, have begged me to take over the conduct of the case as a whole, reserving to themselves the right to discuss important matters affecting their several clients.

PRES.   Then I give you permission just to read this document. But do not attempt to address the court. This is not the time. You can read the paper and that is all. Do you understand?

COUN.   I perfectly understand, M. le président. [*He reads*].[1]

DAILY EXPENSES

For the Mother and Children	f.	c.
Breakfast.		
Milk, 20c., bread, 10c.	0	30
Dinner.		
Bread	0	70
Wine	0	20
Vegetables and dripping for soup	0	20
Meat	0	60
A relish for the children	0	25
Supper for all the Family		
Stew	0	90
Potatoes, etc.	0	20
Wine	0	40
For the Husband		
Tramway return fare	0	30
Tobacco	0	15
Dinner (out)	1	25
Total for the Day	5	45

Comes to 1989f. 25c. per annum

[1] A shorter version of this document, for the theatre, will be found in a note at the end.

YEARLY EXPENSES

Rent, 300f.

Dress.— Three skirts at 5f.; three bodices at 3f.; sixteen pairs of boots for the children at 4f. 50c. the pair; four for the parents at 8f. Two hats at 2f. Underclothes for the mother, 5f.; for the father, 15f.; for the children, 30f. Bedding and linen, 10f. Clothes of the father, 120f. Total, 312f.

The expenses are therefore 2,600f. a year. Tupin, who was a capable workman, earned 175f. a month, or 2,100f. a year. There was therefore an annual deficit of 500f. As I promised, I abstain from comment. [*He sits down*]

MME. CHEV. [*to her neighbor*] There were three sous a day for tobacco that he might very well have saved.

COUN. Perhaps this document might be formally put in evidence.

PRES. It is quite useless. [*To Tupin*] I am not going to dispute your figures. I admit them, and I repeat there are charities.

TUPIN. And I repeat that I 'm not a beggar.

PRES. You prefer to commit what is almost infanticide. A man who has a daughter on the streets and a son a thief may accept charity without degradation.

MME. TUPIN [*outraged*] Oh!

TUPIN [*indignant*] In those days they were not what they are now. If they fell so low it was because I had too many children and I could n't look after my boy; and because my girl was deserted and starving. But you must be made of stone to throw that in my teeth.

And if you took to drinking it 's not your fault either, I suppose?

TUPIN. I want to explain about that. When we began to get short in the house my wife and I started to quarrel. Every time a child came we were mad at making it worse for the others. And so — I need n't make a long story of it — I ended up in the saloon. It 's warm there, and you can't hear the children crying nor the mother complaining. And besides, when you 've drink in you you forget.

MME. TUPIN. It 's the sort of thing that it 's good to forget.

TUPIN. And that 's how we got poorer and poorer. My fault if you like.

PRES. And the last child, what about that?

MME. TUPIN. Oh, the last.

TUPIN. The last? *He* cost us nothing.

PRES. [*carelessly*] Eh?

MME. TUPIN. No.

TUPIN. No, he was a cripple. He was born in starvation, and his mother was worn out.

PRES. And his father was a drunkard.

TUPIN. Maybe. Anyway that one, the sickly fellow, wanted for nothing. They took him into the hospital. They would n't let me take him away.

MME. TUPIN. He was a curiosity for the doctors.

TUPIN. And they nursed him and they nursed him and they nursed him. They did n't leave him a minute. They made him live in spite of himself. And they let the other children — the strong ones — go to the bad. With half the money and the fuss they wasted on the cripple they could have made fine fellows of all the others.

PRES. And was that the reason you did away with the next?

MME. TUPIN. For all the good he 'd have got out of this world he might thank me for not letting him come into it.

PRES. He should never have been created.

TUPIN. That 's true.

PRES. If everyone was like you the country would soon go to the dogs. But you don't trouble yourself much about the country, I expect.

Tupin. Someone said "A man's country is the place where he's well off." I'm badly off everywhere.

Pres. You are perfectly indifferent to the good of humanity.

Tupin. Humanity had better come to an end if it can't get on without a set of miserable wretches like me.

Pres. The jury thoroughly appreciate your moral sense. You can sit down.

Evening has come. The ushers bring lamps.

Pres. [*to Madame Tupin*] Have you anything more to say?

Mme. Tupin. I have to say that all this is not my fault. My husband and I worked like beasts; we did without every kind of pleasure to try and bring up our children. If we had wanted to slave more I declare to you we could n't have done it. And now that we've given our lives for them, the oldest is in hospital ruined and done for because he worked in a "dangerous trade" as they call it!

Pres. Why did n't you put him into something else?

Mme. Tupin. Because there's no work anywhere else. They're full up everywhere else. There are too many people in the world. My little girl is a woman now like lots of others in Paris. She had to choose between that and starving. She chose that. I'm only a poor woman, and I know what it means to have nothing to eat, so I forgave her. The worst of it is that sometimes she's hungry all the same.

Tupin. And they say God blesses large families!

Pres. [*from his notes*] Two others of your children are dead. The two youngest are out at nurse.

Mme. Tupin. Yes. They were taken away as soon as they were born. All I know about them is the post-office order I send every month to the woman who's bringing them up. Oh, it's cruel! It's cruel! It's cruel! [*She sits down*]

PRES. We have now only to examine the case of Annette Jarras. Let the woman Thomas stand up. [*To
Madame Thomas*] This was your victim. She was nineteen, quite young, and in perfect health. Now she is in
her grave. What have you to say?

MME. THOMAS [*quietly*] Nothing.

PRES. You don't excite yourself. Oh, we know you
are not easily moved.

MME. THOMAS. If I told you that it was pity made me
do it, you would n't believe me.

PRES. Probably not. But at any rate you might try.
Every accused person has a right to say whatever he can
in his own defence: of course under the control of the
president of the court.

MME. THOMAS. It is n't worth while.

PRES. Oh, yes. Let us hear. The gentlemen of the
jury are listening.

MME. THOMAS [*after a sign from her counsel*] A girl
came to me one day; she was a servant. She had been
seduced by her master. I refused to do what she asked
me to do: she went and drowned herself. Another I
refused to help was brought up before you here for infanticide. Then when the others came, I said Yes. I 've
prevented many a suicide and many a crime.

PRES. So that 's your line of defence. It is in pity,
in charity, that you have acted. The prosecution will
answer that you have never failed to exact payment for
your services, and a high payment.

MME. THOMAS. And you? Don't they pay you for
condemning other people?

PRES. Those you condemn to death and execute yourself are all innocent.

MME. THOMAS. You prosecute *me*, but you decorate
the surgeons who trade in sterility.

PRES. Be silent. Sit down. Madame Lucie Brignac.
[*Lucie comes forward, in great emotion*] Calm your-

self, madame, and tell us what you know.   You are called
for the defence.

LUCIE.   It was I, monsieur, who asked to be heard.

PRES.   Speak up, madame, I cannot hear what you say.

LUCIE [*louder*]   It was I, monsieur, who asked to be
heard.   I wanted to defend the memory of my little one.
I fear now I shall not have the strength.   [*She controls
herself*]   Annette was seduced by the man who had promised to marry her.   She lived with us.   When my husband knew that my sister was in a certain condition, he
wished to send her away.   I was indignant, and I left his
house with her and my children.   We went to Bordeaux.
We had a few hundred francs, and we thought we could
work for our living.   [*She stops*]

PRES.   Well?

LUCIE.   Our money was soon spent.   Annette was giving some music lessons; they guessed her condition and
they sent her away.   I did some sewing.

PRES.   And earned some money?

LUCIE.   I could n't always get work.   When I got it, I
was paid fifteen cents for twelve hours.   I was not
a skilled worker.   Some people get twenty-six cents.
We were in despair, thinking of the child that was
coming.

PRES.   That was not a reason for leading your sister
and her child to their deaths!   [*Lucie is seized with a
nervous trembling and does not answer*]   Answer!

COUN. DEF.   Give her a moment to recover, M. le
président.

LUCIE [*controlling herself*]   I wanted to get her into
a hospital, but they only take them at the end.   It seems
there are homes one can go to in Paris, but not in the
provinces.

PRES.   You could have applied for charity.

LUCIE.   Six months' residence was necessary.   And
then, what should we have done with the child?

PRES. As it was impossible for you to bring it up, your sister could have taken it to a foundling hospital.

LUCIE. Abandon it — yes, we thought of that. We made inquiries.

COUN. DEF. It is necessary to get a certificate of indigence, and then make an application to the board of admission. They inquire into the case and admit or reject. The child may die meanwhile.

LUCIE. And they make a condition that the mother shall not know where her child is. That she shall never see it or hear of it again. Only once a month she will be told if it is alive or dead. Nothing more.

PRES. Proceed, madame.

LUCIE. Then I brought my children back to my husband, because we had nothing left. I went to see the parents of the young man, who is the cause of everything. They practically turned me out of doors. The young man is going to be married.

COUN. DEF. May I say a word, M. le président?

PRES. You are sure it is only a word?

COUN. DEF. Yes, M. le président. All the guilty are not in court. I look in vain for the seducer of this poor girl. He is waiting anxiously in the provinces to hear the result of this trial, fearing his name may come out. I have received from him and from his family an imploring letter, entreating me to spare him and not to mention him by name during the proceedings. Until now, as a matter of fact his name has not been mentioned, and we are at the end of the trial. Well, I am going to make it known at once. I shall have no more pity for the family and the intended wife of this criminal, than he had for the woman who is dead, and for the woman whose life he has ruined. If there is no law in the Code of this country which can reach him, there will be at least indignation enough in the hearts of all honest people to prevent Jacques Bernin from enjoying in peace the happiness he has stolen! [*Prolonged applause*]

PRES. [*to Lucie*] Proceed, madame. [*Pause*] Kindly conclude your evidence.

LUCIE. I implored my husband to take us back, Annette and me. He would n't. We came to Paris with a little money he gave me. It was too soon for them to take Annette into one hospital: in another, where they would have taken her, there was no room. My husband filed a petition for divorce.

PRES. Kindly tell us about what concerns the woman Thomas.

LUCIE [*with growing emotion*] Yes, monsieur. Annette was always reproaching herself with having accepted what she called my sacrifice. She kept saying she was the cause of all my troubles. [*A silence*] One day they came to fetch me, and I found her dead at this woman's house. [*In a burst of sobs, which become hysterical, she cries out*] My little sister, my poor little sister!

PRES. [*kindly, to the usher*] Take her back to her place, or, if necessary, take her outside and do all you can for her. [*To the defendants*] Then none of you has any more to say in your defence?

TUPIN [*excited*] Oh, if we said all we 've got to say we should be here until to-morrow morning!

MME. TUPIN [*the same*] *That* we should!

TUPIN [*shouting*] We should never stop!

PRES. I call upon the counsel for the prosecution for his speech.

SCH. But, monsieur, you are not going to condemn me? It 's not possible. I have n't said everything.

TUPIN. *We 're* not the guilty ones.

SCH. I 'm afraid of getting a bad name. And we had n't the means to bring up another.

MME. TUPIN [*violently, much excited*] Shut up! As

it 's like that — as that 's what they do to our children —
as men have found nothing to change that — we must
do it — the women must do it.   We must start the great
strike — *the* strike — the strike of the mothers.

>   *Cries in the audience, " Yes, yes."*

PRES.   Silence.

MME. TUPIN [*shouting*]   Why should we kill ourselves
to get wage-slaves and harlots for other people?

TUPIN.   *We 're* not the guilty ones.

PRES.   I did not —

MME. THOMAS.   And all the men that seduced the girls
I saved — have you punished *them?*

PRES.   Sit down.

TUPIN.   The guilty ones are the people that tell us to
have more children when the ones we have are starving.

COUN. DEF.   The seducers are the guilty ones; and
social hypocrisy.

*During the proceedings, anger, which rapidly becomes
fury, has taken possession of the defendants.   They are
all on their feet except the schoolmistress, who goes on
sobbing and murmuring to herself unintelligibly.   The
president, also standing, strikes his desk with a paper-
knife, trying to impose silence.   He shouts, but cannot
make himself heard.   The tumult increases until the curtain falls.   The voices of the counsel for the defence and
the defendants drown those of the president and the
counsel for the prosecution.*

MME. THOMAS.   The fine gentlemen that get hold of
them and humbug them!

PRES.   I will have you taken back to prison.

MME. THOMAS.   And the rich young man, and the old
satyrs — and the men!   The men!   All the men!

COUNSEL FOR THE PROSECUTION.   Police, can't you
silence these lunatics?

COUN. DEF.   You have no right to insult the defendants.

TUPIN. They 've been doing nothing else the whole time.

COUN. PROS. Keep his rabble quiet! The defendants must respect the law.

COUN. DEF. And you, sir, must respect justice.

COUN. PROS. You sympathize with their crime. I am outraged by it.

COUN. DEF. They are right. They are not guilty. You must respect —

COUN. PROS. I demand —

COUN. DEF. Our customs are guilty, which denounce the unmarried mother!

AUDIENCE. Bravo! Hear, hear!

COUN. PROS. I demand that the counsel for the defence —

COUN. DEF. Every woman with child should be respected, no matter what the circumstances are. [*Applause*]

PRES. Maître Verdier, by article forty-three of the regulations —

COUN. DEF. Their crime is not an individual crime, it is a social crime.

COUN. PROS. It is a crime against nature.

COUN. DEF. It is *not* a crime against nature. It is a revolt against nature.

PRES. Police, remove the defendants. [*The police do not understand or do not hear*] Maître Verdier, must we employ force? [*Tumult in the whole court*]

COUN. DEF. [*rhetorically*] It *is* a revolt against nature! And with all the warmth of a heart melted by pity, with all the indignation of my outraged reason, I look for that glorious hour of liberation when some master mind shall discover for us the means of having only the children we need and desire, release us for ever from the prison of hypocrisy and absolve us from the profanation of love. That would indeed be a conquest of nature —

savage nature — which pours out life with culpable profusion, and sees it disappear with indifference.   But,
until then —

The tumult recommences.

Pres.   Police, clear the court!   Police — police, remove the defendants.   The sitting is suspended.   [*The
magistrates cover their heads and rise*].

Mme. Thomas.   It's not I who massacre the innocents!   *I'm* not the guilty one!

Sch.   Mercy, monsieur, mercy!

Mme. Tupin.   *She's* not the guilty one!

Tupin.   She's right.   She's *not!*

Mme. Thomas.   It's the men!   the men!   *all* the men!

*The magistrates go out by the narrow door reserved
for them, the backs of their red robes disappearing
slowly during the last words.*

TUPIN'S BUDGET (Condensed).

The daily food of the mother and the five children consists of a loaf
of bread, soup made of dripping and vegetables, and a stew.
Total cost, 3f. 75c.

The husband's expenses are: carfare, 30c.; tobacco, 15c.; lunch,
1f. 25c.

General expenses of the family: rent, 300f.; clothing, linen, boots
(sixteen pairs for the children at 4f. 50c. the pair, four for the
parents at 8f.), are again 300f.

Annual total, 2,600f.

THE THREE DAUGHTERS
OF M. DUPONT

[Les Trois Filles de M. Dupont]

Translated by

ST. JOHN HANKIN

Cast of the original production before the Stage Society at the King's Hall, London, on March 12, 13 and 14, 1905.

MME. DUPONT........................Kate Bishop
COURTHEZON.........................Leon M. Lion
CAROLINE............................Italia Conti
JULIE...............................Ethel Irving
M. DUPONT..........................O. B. Clarence
JUSTINE............................Lois Crampton
M. MAIRAUT.........................Arthur Chesney
MME. MAIRAUT.......................Agnes Thomas
ANTONIN MAIRAUT................Charles V. France
LIGNOL.............................Lewis Carson
M. POUCHELET.......................G. M. Graham
MME. POUCHELET.....................Dora Barton
FRANÇOISE..........................Florence Adale
ANGÈLE.............................Gertrude Burnett

ACT I

A very undistinguished room in a house in a French country town. The time is February. There is in the centre of the room a table, with chairs round it; a fireplace on the left, and window on the right; a piano; lamps; a bronze statuette of Gutenberg; holland covers on the furniture. There are doors to right and left and at the back.

Madame Dupont is discovered alone, darning stockings. After a moment or two Courthezon comes in, with some papers in his hand.

COURTHEZON. Why, you 're all alone, Madame Dupont?

MME. DUPONT. Yes, M. Courthezon.

COURTHEZON. Your young ladies are listening to the band?

MME. DUPONT. No: Julie has gone to pay a call, and Caroline is at Benediction. She goes every Sunday.

COURTHEZON. Oh, yes, of course.

MME. DUPONT. On Sunday we never see her, except at déjeûner. The rest of the day she 's at church. I believe she never misses a service. And now she is one of the Enfants de Marie. At her age, too!

COURTHEZON. How old is she?

MME. DUPONT. Thirty-three.

COURTHEZON. And still very religious?

MME. DUPONT. Very.

COURTHEZON. [*nodding*] Her mother was just the same.

79

MME. DUPONT. You remember my husband's first wife?

COURTHEZON. Yes. I came to the printing office two years before she died. [*Pause*] M. Dupont is at his game at the Café du Commerce, no doubt? I should be there myself if I could afford it.

MME. DUPONT. You have your savings.

COURTHEZON. Precisely; and I don't want to lose them. But you are working, Madame Dupont?

MME. DUPONT. Mending some stockings. One must find something to do.

COURTHEZON. I've been hard at it, too, all day.

MME. DUPONT. Still at your invention?

COURTHEZON. Yes. I tell you it's splendid. I've been downstairs to the printing office to see if there were any orders.

MME. DUPONT. Were there any?

COURTHEZON [*looking through papers in his hand*] Three hundred visiting cards, a price list, and an announcement.

MME. DUPONT [*stopping her work*] Death? Birth?

COURTHEZON. Neither. A marriage.

MME. DUPONT. Give it me. [*Reads paper which Courthezon gives her*] M. Jacquemin! M. Jacquemin! And who is this Mlle. Martha Violet whom he is marrying?

COURTHEZON. One of the Violets of the Rue du Pré.

MME. DUPONT. Oh, yes, of course. [*To Courthezon, who makes as if to take back the paper*] Leave it with me. I will send it down to you. I want to show it to Julie. So you are pleased with your invention?

COURTHEZON [*sitting down*] I am delighted with it. Delighted! I've been working at it twenty years! And now it's finished. What do you think of that?

Enter Caroline. She is tall, stringy, not pretty, not attractive, but not absurd. She has a prayer-book in her hand.

MME. DUPONT [*carelessly, to Courthezon, who has stopped*] Go on. It's only Caroline. [*Interested*] And you still won't tell us what it is?

COURTHEZON. Not yet. [*Rising, bowing to Caroline*] Good-day, Mlle. Caroline.

CAROLINE [*half returning his bow*] Good-day, M. Courthezon.

MME. DUPONT. I can imagine how pleased you are.

COURTHEZON. Of course I am.

CAROLINE. You have finished your invention?

COURTHEZON. Yes. How did you guess?

CAROLINE [*a little confused*] Oh, only —

COURTHEZON. Only?

CAROLINE [*in a lower voice*] Only that I knew it.

COURTHEZON. You knew it?

CAROLINE [*confused*] Yes. But never mind about that.

MME. DUPONT [*to Courthezon*] And now you will become a rich man, eh, M. Courthezon?

COURTHEZON. Not all at once. I must first find someone who will buy my invention, or who will advance me money to push it for myself. But there's plenty of time to think of all that: and whether I succeed or not, I am glad to have given twenty years of my life to inventing something that will make life a little easier for those who will come after me. And now I am going downstairs to the office to do a little work. You'll send down that announcement, won't you?

MME. DUPONT. I won't forget.

COURTHEZON. Good-evening, Madame Dupont. Good-evening, Mlle. Caroline.

CAROLINE and MME. DUPONT. Good-evening, M. Courthezon.

Courthezon goes out.

MME. DUPONT. Why were you so sure he had completed his invention?

CAROLINE [*confused, after a moment's silence*] You won't tell anyone, mother?

MME. DUPONT. No.

CAROLINE. Because I prayed for it.

MME. DUPONT [*not spitefully, but with a slight shrug of the shoulders*] I see.

Julie comes in.

JULIE. Here I am, maman [*she kisses her*]. You here, Caro? [*She does not kiss her*].

MME. DUPONT. Ah, Julie! Sit down, dear, and tell me what you have been doing and whom you have seen. [*Her warm greeting to Julie contrasts markedly with the cold reception she previously gave to Caroline*].

JULIE. I went to see Madame Leseigneur.

MME. DUPONT. I might have guessed that.

JULIE. Why?

MME. DUPONT. You only go to houses where there are children. And as Madame Leseigneur has six —

JULIE. I wish I were in her place. Only think: André, the youngest, you know, the one who is only six months old?

MME. DUPONT. Yes.

JULIE. He *recognized* me. There never *was* such a baby for taking notice.

MME. DUPONT. You talk as if you were a mother yourself.

JULIE. Jean laughed till he cried when he saw what I had brought him. Charles and Pierre were in disgrace because they 'd been fighting. But I got their mother to forgive them, so that was all right. To-morrow I shall go to Madame Durand to hear how Jacques is going on. I hear he has the whooping-cough.

MME. DUPONT [*laughing*] You ought to have been a nurse.

JULIE [*seriously*] No, no. I should have died when I had to leave the first child I had nursed.

MME. DUPONT. Then you should marry.

JULIE. Yes. [*Pause*].

MME. DUPONT [*to Caroline*] Well, Caroline, what are you doing there with your mouth open?

CAROLINE. I was listening.

MME. DUPONT. Have you finished your painting?

CAROLINE. No. I still have six of the Marie Antoinette figures to do, and a dozen china Cupids to finish.

JULIE. How funny it is to think of Caro painting Cupids!

CAROLINE. Why?

MME. DUPONT [*to Caroline*] And you have to send all those off by twelve o'clock to-morrow?

CAROLINE. Yes.

MME. DUPONT. You will never have them ready.

CAROLINE. I shall manage.

MME. DUPONT. You might do a little at them now, before dinner, instead of sitting there twiddling your fingers.

CAROLINE. I shall get up early to-morrow.

MME. DUPONT. Even if you *do* get up early —

CAROLINE. I shall begin at six, as soon as it is light.

MME. DUPONT. Still, you might do some work on them now.

CAROLINE. I would rather not.

MME. DUPONT. Because it 's Sunday, I suppose; and one must n't work on Sunday.

CAROLINE. Yes. [*Pause*] Why should *you* mind, mother, if I —

MME. DUPONT. I? Not the least in the world. Do as you please. You are old enough to decide for yourself.

JULIE [*who has been reading one of the papers*] Is Courthezon down in the office? I should like the next part of this.

MME. DUPONT. You know quite well your father does n't like you to read the proofs of the stories he has to print.

JULIE. I have no others. Listen to this: is n't it too bad to have to stop there? [*Reads*] " Solange was still in Robert's arms. At this moment the Count entered, menacing, terrible, his revolver in his hand." I do so want to know what happened next!

CAROLINE. The Count will kill them, of course. It is his right.

JULIE. I wonder.

CAROLINE. According to law.

JULIE. That 's no reason. I want to read over again where Robert comes in. It 's lovely. And the meeting with Solange in Italy, one evening in May. Where is it? Ah, here! [*Reads*] " Under the deep blue of the sky, picked out by stars, by the shore of the calm sea that a perfumed breeze just ruffled, and in which were reflected with the stars above the many distant lights of Mentone and of Monte Carlo — "

MME. DUPONT [*smiling*] And your father imagines he has cured you of all such foolishness!

JULIE. I am doing no harm.

MME. DUPONT. No matter. I would rather you did n't read any more novels.

JULIE. Why? Berthe Paillant reads all the stories that come out, and she 's younger than I am.

MME. DUPONT. Berthe Paillant is married.

JULIE. There it is! If one is not to remain a child to the end of one's days one must marry. I am twenty-four, and I may n't read the books which Berthe can read at eighteen.

MME. DUPONT. There 's my thread broken again. I believe you bought it at Lagnier's, Caroline.

CAROLINE. Yes.

MME. DUPONT. Why did n't you go to Laurent's?

CAROLINE. I thought we ought to deal with those who believe as we do.

MME. DUPONT. If only one could find a good Catholic who sold good wool!

CAROLINE. There is n't one in the town.

JULIE [*with a sigh*] Heigho! You don't know of a husband for me, do you, Caro?

CAROLINE. What sort of one do you want?

JULIE [*seriously*] I am getting to the time of life when a woman accepts the first man who offers himself. Choose whatever sort you think best for me [*laughing*]. What would be your ideal? Someone in business? A captain in the army? Tell me.

CAROLINE. No.

JULIE. Why not?

CAROLINE. If I were to marry, I should choose a worker, a man with a noble aim, a man who would be ready to sacrifice himself to make life a little easier for those who will come after him.

MME. DUPONT. Oh, don't talk like a sentimental novel, Caroline.

CAROLINE. I was not.

MME. DUPONT. Well, I 'm sure I 've read that some-where. Besides, at your age one does n't speak of those things any longer.

JULIE. Talking of that, you know Henriette Longuet?

MME. DUPONT. Yes.

JULIE. She is going to be married.

MME. DUPONT. Indeed?

JULIE. Yes. [*Thoughtfully*] I 'm the last to go.

MME. DUPONT. The last go off best. What a week this is for marriages! Courthezon brought me an announcement just now which I kept to show you. Where is it? Ah, here it is. [*Hands it to her*].

JULIE [*after looking at it, sadly*] That finishes it!

MME. DUPONT. What do you mean?

CAROLINE. What is it, Julie?

JULIE. Nothing.

MME. DUPONT. Were *you* thinking of M. Jacquemin?

JULIE. How do I know? He has never said anything to me, of course, but I fancied he had noticed me. I did n't care much about him, but he was better than nothing. Better than nothing! [*Sighs*] It's a stupid sort of world for girls nowadays.

Dupont comes in.

DUPONT [*brimming over with excitement and importance*] Ah! Here are the children. Run away, my dears, for a few minutes. I'll call you when I want you.

JULIE [*going with Caroline*] Caroline! Do you think it is —?

CAROLINE [*thoughtfully*] It does look like it.

They go out together.

MME. DUPONT. Well, what is it?

DUPONT [*with an air of importance*] M. and Madame Mairaut will be here in an hour, at six o'clock.

MME. DUPONT. Yes?

DUPONT [*craftily*] And do you know why they are coming?

MME. DUPONT. No.

DUPONT. To ask for Julie's hand in marriage. That's all!

MME. DUPONT. For their son?

DUPONT. Well, my dear, it's not for the Sultan of Turkey.

MME. DUPONT. M. Mairaut, the banker.

DUPONT. M. Mairaut, head of the Banque de l'Univers, 14 Rue des Trois-Chapeaux, second floor.

MME. DUPONT. Yes; but —

DUPONT. Now, now, don't excite yourself. Don't lose your head. The thing is n't done yet. Listen. For the last fortnight, at the Merchants' Club, Mairaut has been taking me aside and talking about Julie — asking me this, that, and the other. As you may suppose, I let him run on. To-day we were talking together about the difficulty of marrying one's children. " I know something of that," said he. " So do I," I said. Then he grinned at me and said: " Supposing Madame Mairaut and I were to come in one of these days to discuss the question with you and Madame Dupont? " You may imagine my delight. I simply let myself go. But no, when I say I let myself go, I do myself an injustice. I kept a hand over myself all the time. " One of these days? Next week, perhaps? " I said, carelessly, just like that. " Why not to-day? " said he. " As you please," said I. " Six o'clock? "   " Six o'clock." What do you think of that?

MME. DUPONT. But M. Mairaut — the son, I mean — Monsieur — what is his Christian name?

DUPONT. Antonin, Antonin Mairaut.

MME. DUPONT. Antonin, of course. I was wondering. Is M. Antonin Mairaut quite the husband we should choose for Julie?

DUPONT. I know what you mean. His life is n't all that it should be. There 's that woman —

MME. DUPONT. So people say.

DUPONT. But we need n't bother about that. There 's another matter, however, that *is* worth considering — though, of course, you have n't thought of it. Women never do think of the really important things.

MME. DUPONT. You mean money? The Mairauts have n't any. They only keep a couple of clerks altogether in their bank. They may have to put up the shutters any day.

DUPONT. Yes: but there 's someone else who may put his shutters up first. Antonin's uncle. The old buffer may die. And he has two hundred thousand francs, and never spends a penny.

MME. DUPONT. True. But —

DUPONT. But — But — There you go. You 're determined never to see anything that is more than an inch before your nose. I don't blame you for it. Women are like that.

MME. DUPONT. But suppose he disinherits Antonin?

DUPONT. You forget I shall be there. I flatter myself I shall know how to prevent Uncle Maréchal from disinheriting his nephew. Besides, what is Uncle Maréchal?

MME. DUPONT. Antonin's uncle.

DUPONT. You don't understand. I ask you what he *is*. What is his position, I mean?

MME. DUPONT. He 's head clerk at the Préfecture.

DUPONT. Exactly. And he could get me the contract for all the printing work at his office. Thirty thousand francs a year! How much profit does that mean?

MME. DUPONT. Five thousand francs.

DUPONT. Five thousand? Ten thousand! If one is only to make the ordinary trade profit, what 's the good of Government contracts?

MME. DUPONT. I 'm afraid young M. Mairaut's character —

DUPONT. His character! We know nothing about his character. He has one virtue which nothing can take away from him: he is his uncle's nephew. And his uncle can get me work that will bring in ten thousand francs a year, besides being as rich as Crœsus.

MME. DUPONT. Still, are you sure that he is the right sort of husband for Julie?

DUPONT. He is the right sort of husband for Julie, and the right sort of son-in-law for me.

MME. DUPONT [*dubiously*] Well, you know more of these things than I do.

DUPONT [*looks at his watch*] Ten minutes past five. Now listen to me. We have very little time, but I feel the ideas surging through my brain with extraordinary clearness. It 's only in moments of emergency that I feel myself master of all my faculties, though I flatter myself I'm not altogether a fool at the worst of times. [*He sits upon a chair, his hands leaning upon the back of it*] I will explain everything to you, so that you may make as few blunders as possible. We must get old Mairaut to agree that all the money, Julie's and Antonin's, shall be the joint property of them both.

MME. DUPONT. But there will be Julie's dot.

DUPONT [*pettishly*] If you keep interrupting we shall never be done. The joint property of them both, on account of Uncle Maréchal's money. Do you understand?

MME. DUPONT. Yes.

DUPONT. That's a blessing. Well, then we shall ask for —

MME. DUPONT. No settlements. I understand.

DUPONT. On the contrary, we shall ask for the strictest settlements on both sides.

MME. DUPONT. But —

DUPONT. You are out of your depth. Better simply listen without trying to understand. [*He rises, replaces his chair, and taps her knowingly on the shoulder*] In these cases one should never ask for the thing one wants. One must know how to get the other side to offer it, and be quite pleased to get it accepted. Well, then, I am giving Julie fifty thousand francs as her dot.

MME. DUPONT. Fifty thousand! But Julie has only twenty-five thousand.

DUPONT. That is so. I shall give her twenty-five thousand down and promise the rest for next year.

MME. DUPONT. You can't mean that. You will never be able to keep such a promise. [*She rises*]

DUPONT. Who knows? If I get the contract from the Préfecture.

MME. DUPONT. We ought to ask Julie what she thinks of this marriage.

DUPONT. We have n't much time, then. Still, call her; and take off these covers [*pointing to the chairs*].

MME. DUPONT [*she goes towards the door on the right; then returns*] But have you thought —

DUPONT. I have thought of everything.

MME. DUPONT. Of everything? What about Angèle and her story?

DUPONT [*pompously*] Angèle is no longer my daughter.

MME. DUPONT. Still, we shall have to tell them.

DUPONT. Naturally. Since they know it already.

MME. DUPONT. I am nearly sure it was she I met last time I was in Paris.

DUPONT. You were mistaken.

MME. DUPONT. I don't think so.

DUPONT. In any case, in acting as I did I was doing my duty. I can hold my head up and fear nothing. Call Julie. She will help you to put the room tidy. [*Madame Dupont goes out*].

DUPONT [*rubbing his hands*] I think I've managed things pretty well this time! I *think* so!

Julie and Madame Dupont come in.

JULIE. Father, is it someone who wants to marry me?

DUPONT. It is. [*To Madame Dupont, pointing to the chairs*] Take off those covers. [*To Julie*] You know young M. Mairaut — M. Antonin Mairaut? [*He sits down*] You have danced together several times.

JULIE. Yes.

DUPONT. What do you think of him?

JULIE. As a husband?

DUPONT. As a husband. Don't answer in a hurry. Take off that cover from the chair you are sitting on and give it to your mother.

JULIE [*obeying*] Have his parents formally proposed for him?

MME. DUPONT. No. But if they should do so your father and I wish to know —

DUPONT [*to Madame Dupont, giving her the last chair cover, which he has taken off himself*] Take all these away. [*Madame Dupont goes out*] The formal offer has not been made, but it will be soon, in less than an hour.

JULIE. Is that why you are taking all this trouble? [*She points to the chairs*].

DUPONT. Precisely. We must n't appear to be paupers or people without social position. [*He seizes a bowl in which there are some visiting cards*] Very old, these cards. Very yellow. And the names, too, common rather. I must put that right. [*To his wife, who returns*] Go down to the printing office and ask Courthezon to give you some printed specimens of our new visiting cards at three francs — no, three francs fifty. And then put that Wagner opera on the piano which someone left to be bound. [*Madame Dupont goes. To Julie*] I have no desire to influence you, my dear.

JULIE. Still —

DUPONT [*going to the mantelpiece*] Still what? Wait until I light the lamp. [*He strikes a match*].

JULIE. Why, it 's still quite light.

DUPONT. When one receives visitors one does n't wait till it is dark before — You are old enough to know — what the deuce is the matter with the oil? — old enough to know what you are about. Damn the lamps! When they are never lighted it is the devil's own job to make them burn. Yes, as I was saying, it is for you to weigh the pros and the cons. Marriage — There! [*He looks round him*] Is there anything else to be done to make things look better? What is that over there? That great stupid Caroline's hat!

MME. DUPONT [*coming in and bringing visiting cards and a piano score of an opera*] Here are the cards and the music book.

Dupont. Thanks. [*He gives Caroline's hat to Madame Dupont*] Take this thing away. And these stockings. Hide them somewhere. You don't want to appear to do your own darning, confound it! It's extraordinary you should n't have thought of that. [*Madame Dupont goes out, returning in a moment. Dupont continues mechanically to Julie*] It is for you to weigh the pros and cons. This is better. Vicomte de Liverolles; M. L'Abbé Candar, Honorary Canon; Ange Nitron, Ex-Municipal Councillor. That will look well enough. The Wagner score on the piano, open, of course. That's right. There's something else I want, though. Julie, the box of cigars which M. Gueroult sent me when he was elected to the Chamber.

Julie [*bringing a box*] Here it is.

Dupont. Give it me.

Julie. You have n't begun it yet.

Dupont. Wait. [*He rummages in his pocket and takes out a knife, which he opens*] We must show them that other people besides deputies smoke cigars at five sous. [*He opens the box*] Without being proud, one has one's dignity to keep up. There! [*He takes a handful of cigars and gives them to his daughter*] Put those in the drawer so that the box may n't seem to have been opened on purpose for them. [*He arranges the box on the table*] A fashion paper? Excellent! And for myself [*to Mme. Dupont*] Léontine, give me a fresh ribbon of my Order of Christ. This one is faded. [*To his daughter*] He is twenty-eight. He is good looking and distinguished. He passed his law examination at Bordeaux. [*He puts a fresh ribbon in his coat, and looks at himself for a considerable time in the glass*] In a town where I was not known this would be as good as the Legion of Honor. [*He turns round*] Well? Have you made up your mind?

Julie. I should like more time to think it over.

DUPONT. You have still a quarter of an hour.

MME. DUPONT. She would like a few days, perhaps.

DUPONT. That's it. Shilly shally! We are to have the story of that great stupid Caroline over again, are we? No! Your sister, whom you see now an old maid, who will never be married, unless her aunt in Calcutta leaves her some money — your sister, too, had her chance one day. She hum'd and ha'd; she wanted to think it over. And you see the result. That's what thinking it over leads to. Here she is, still on my hands!

MME. DUPONT. You must n't say that. She earns her own living.

DUPONT. She earns her own living, perhaps; but she remains on my hands all the same. By the way, we had better not say anything to the Mairauts about Caroline's working for money.

MME. DUPONT. They are sure to know.

DUPONT. Not they. What was I saying? Oh, yes. She remains on my hands all the same. And one old maid is quite enough in the family. Two would be intolerable. Remember, my child, you have no dot — at least, none worth mentioning. And as things go nowadays, when one has no dot, one must n't be too particular.

JULIE. To marry nowadays, then, a girl has to buy her husband?

DUPONT [shrugs] Well —

JULIE. And there's nothing but misery for girls who have no money.

DUPONT. It's not quite as bad as that. But obviously there is a better choice for those who have a good fortune.

JULIE [bitterly] And the others must be content with damaged goods, much reduced in price!

DUPONT. There are exceptions, of course. But, as a rule, husbands are like anything else. If you want a good article, you must be prepared to pay for it.

MME. DUPONT. And, even so, one is often cheated.

DUPONT. Possibly. But M. Antonin Mairaut is a very eligible young man. No? What do you want, then, in Heaven's name? If you are waiting for a royal prince, say so. Are you waiting for a prince? Answer me. Come, my child, this is an opportunity you may never see again: a young man, well brought up, with an uncle who is head clerk at the Préfecture and can double my profits by putting the contract for printing in my way, not to speak of other things. And you raise difficulties!

MME. DUPONT. Think, dear. You are four-and-twenty.

DUPONT. And you have had the astonishing good luck to captivate this young fellow — at a ball, it seems.

JULIE. I believe so. He wanted to kiss me in one of the passages. I had to put him in his place.

MME. DUPONT. You were quite right.

DUPONT. I don't say she wasn't — that is, if she didn't overdo it. In his case I'm sure it was only playfulness.

MME. DUPONT. Oh, of course.

JULIE. I only half like him, father.

DUPONT. Well, if you half like him, that's always something. Plenty of people marry without even that.

MME. DUPONT. You don't dislike him, do you, Julie?

JULIE. No.

DUPONT [*triumphantly*] Well, then!

JULIE. That's hardly enough, is it?

DUPONT. Come, come, my dear, we must talk seriously. As a child you were full of romantic notions. Thank Heaven, I cured you of that weakness. You know well enough that unhappy marriages are, more often than not, love marriages.

JULIE [*unconvinced*] I know, I know. Still, I want to have a husband who loves me.

DUPONT. But he *does* love you, does n't he, since you 've only just told us that he wanted to kiss you at a ball.

JULIE. I want to be something more than my husband's plaything.

DUPONT. You 'll lead your husband by the nose, never fear.

JULIE. How do you know?

DUPONT. Never you mind. I know it. And now really we have had enough of this. You think that a whim of yours is to upset all my plans, prevent me from increasing my printing business and retiring next year, as we intended, your mother and I. You think we have n't — I have n't — worked enough, I suppose. You don't wish us to have a little rest before we die? You think I have not earned that rest, perhaps? Answer me! You think I have not earned it?

JULIE. Of course you have, father.

DUPONT [*mollified*] Very well, then. Still, I don't want to make you uncomfortable. I don't press you for a definite answer to-day. All I ask is that you won't be obstinate, or refuse to let us present Antonin to you as a possible husband, if his parents make any advances. That is all. You will, then, talk with him, ask him questions. Naturally, you must get to know each other.

MME. DUPONT. Think carefully, my child.

DUPONT. Make up your mind whether you wish to follow the example of that great stupid Caroline.

MME. DUPONT. You are quite old enough to be married. [*A pause*].

DUPONT. Answer. Are n't you old enough to be married?

JULIE. Quite, father.

DUPONT. Have you any other offers?

MME. DUPONT. Have you any choice?

JULIE. No.

Dupont. You see!

Mme. Dupont. You see!

Dupont. Well, then, it's all settled. [*He looks at his watch*] And only just in time! M. Mairaut is punctuality itself. It's five minutes to six. In five minutes he will be here. [*Julie is silent, gazing through the open window. The laughter of children is heard outside. To Madame Dupont, irritably*] What's she looking out of that window for?

Mme. Dupont. It's Madame Brichot. She is just going in with her children.

Julie [*to herself, with a smile of great sweetness, recalling a word which she has just caught while dreaming*] Maman!

Dupont. Well?

Julie. I will do as you wish.

Dupont. Ouf! Now go and change your dress.

Julie. Change my dress?

Mme. Dupont. Of course. You will be supposed to know nothing; but you must be tidy.

Julie. What am I to put on?

Mme. Dupont [*reflecting*] Let me see. [*A sudden inspiration*] I know. Isn't there a dance at the Gontiers' to-night?

Julie. But we said we would n't go.

Mme. Dupont [*rising, briskly*] We are going all the same. Put on your ball dress.

Julie. Before dinner? Is he marrying my clothes?

Mme. Dupont. No. But you look best in your ball dress. Do as I tell you, dear.

Julie. Very well. [*She goes out*].

Dupont. Are you really going to this ball?

Mme. Dupont. Certainly not.

Dupont. Well, then?

Mme. Dupont. M. Antonin is coming.

Dupont [*understanding*] And Julie looks far better

when she is — you are quite right. [*A bell rings*] There they are! Come into the next room, quick!

MME. DUPONT. Why?

DUPONT. We must keep them waiting a little. It creates an impression. [*To the maid, who passes to go to open the door, in an undertone*] Ask them to wait a moment.

MAID. Yes, monsieur.

DUPONT. Now, then. [*He bustles Madame Dupont out of the room. After a moment M. and Madame Mairaut enter, followed by the maid. Their faces wear a genial smile, which freezes as soon as they see that the room is empty*].

MAIRAUT. They are not here?

MAID. I will tell madame. [*She goes out*].

MME. MAIRAUT. Tell madame! [*To her husband*] They saw us coming.

MAIRAUT. You think so?

MME. MAIRAUT. Of course. Why was that lamp lighted? Not for an empty room, I imagine! I don't think much of their furniture. Very poor. Very poor. [*Lifts up a piece of stuff from the back of an armchair*] This chair has been re-covered.

MAIRAUT [*at the bowl with the visiting cards*] They know some good people.

MME. MAIRAUT. Let me see. [*She looks at the bowl*]. Those cards were put there expressly for us not an hour ago.

MAIRAUT. Oh, come!

MME. MAIRAUT. Look! The top ones are all new. The underneath ones are quite yellow.

MAIRAUT. Because the underneath ones are older.

MME. MAIRAUT. Because the underneath ones have been left out ever since New Year's Day, while these are just printed. We must be careful. Above all things, don't *you* make a fool of yourself.

MAIRAUT. All right.

MME. MAIRAUT. Don't let them think you're set on this marriage.

MAIRAUT. I understand.

MME. MAIRAUT. Get them to offer that all moneys shall be held jointly.

MAIRAUT. Yes.

MME. MAIRAUT. And to work this, insist on separate settlements.

MAIRAUT. Yes.

MME. MAIRAUT. For the rest, do as you usually do. Say as little as possible.

MAIRAUT. But —

MME. MAIRAUT. You know well enough that's the only way you ever do succeed with things.

MAIRAUT. But there's something I want to say to you.

MME. MAIRAUT. Then it's sure to be something stupid. However, we have nothing better to do. Go on.

MAIRAUT. It's what I spoke to you about before. It's been worrying me a good deal. If the Duponts give us their daughter, who has probably a dot of twenty-five thousand francs —

MME. MAIRAUT. Twenty or twenty-five thousand, I expect.

MAIRAUT. Well, if they give her to us, who have nothing but the bank, it must be because they don't know that Uncle Maréchal is ruined.

MME. MAIRAUT. Obviously. Nobody knows.

MAIRAUT. It isn't honest not to tell them.

MME. MAIRAUT. Why?

MAIRAUT. Surely, my dear —

MME. MAIRAUT. If you're going to tell them that, we may as well be off at once.

MAIRAUT. You see!

MME. MAIRAUT. I see that we ought to hold our

tongues. Oh, yes, we ought. For if you have scruples
about injuring the Duponts I have scruples about injuring Uncle Maréchal.

MAIRAUT. What do you mean?

MME. MAIRAUT. We have no right to betray a secret.
I'm sorry you should n't have seen that I am quite as
particular as you are; only I put my duty to my family
before my duty to strangers. If I am wrong, say so.

MAIRAUT. But if they ask us point blank?

MME. MAIRAUT. Then we must consult Uncle Maréchal, since he is the principal person concerned.

MAIRAUT. In spite of all you say it seems to me —
[*He hesitates. A pause*]

MME. MAIRAUT. Well, my dear, which is it to be?
If you want us to go, let us go. You are the master. I
have never forgotten it. Shall we go?

MAIRAUT [*giving in, after a moment of painful in-
decision*] Now that we are here, what would the Duponts think of us?

MME. MAIRAUT. And then we must remember that
the eldest Dupont girl got into trouble and is now living
a disreputable life in Paris. That will make them less
difficult.

MAIRAUT. Hush!

*Madame Dupont and Dupont enter the room. Gen-
eral greetings. " How do you do, dear madame? How
are you? How good of you to call! Sit down," etc.
All sit. Silence.*

MME. MAIRAUT. My dear Madame Dupont, I will
come straight to the point. The object of our visit is
this: M. Mairaut and I think we have observed that
mademoiselle, your daughter, has made an impression —
how shall I put it? A certain impression on our
son.

MAIRAUT. A certain impression. Yes.

MME. MAIRAUT. Antonin will join us here immediately, but of course we have said nothing to him about this.

Dupont.   Julie, of course, has not the least idea —

Mme. Dupont.   She is dressing.   We are going to the ball at the Gontiers' to-night, and the dear child asked if she might dress before dinner.

Dupont.   Not that she is vain.

Mme. Dupont.   Not the least in the world.

Dupont [*to his wife, in an off-hand tone*]   She makes her own dresses, does n't she?

Mme. Dupont.   Of course.   In this house we don't know what it is to have a bill from the dressmaker.

Dupont.   Yet with all her other occupations she 's an excellent musician.

Mme. Dupont.   Quite excellent.   She has a passion for really good music.   She knows Wagner thoroughly.

Mme. Mairaut.   Wagner!   Good Heavens!

Mme. Dupont.   To talk about, I mean.

Mme. Mairaut.   I know your daughter is charming.

Mme. Dupont.   And good, too.   You would never believe how responsive that poor child is to affection!

Dupont [*to Mairaut, offering the box*]   Have a cigar?

Mairaut.   No, thanks.   I never smoke before dinner.

Dupont.   Take one, all the same.   You can smoke it afterwards.   They are my usual brand, but pretty fair.

Mairaut [*taking one*]   Thank you.

Mme. Mairaut.   If Antonin is not married already it is because his father and I wished him to find a wife who is worthy of him.   The question of money, with us, is of secondary importance.

Mme. Dupont.   And with us.   I 'm so glad we agree about that.

Mme. Mairaut.   Antonin might have made quite a number of good matches.

Dupont.   It is just the same with Julie.   In spite of that unfortunate affair in the family.

MAIRAUT. Yes, we know.

MME. MAIRAUT. Unfortunate affair? We have heard nothing of any unfortunate affair. What are you saying, my dear?

MAIRAUT [*mumbling confusedly*] I was saying — nothing — I was saying — No, I was n't saying anything.

MME. MAIRAUT [*to Madame Dupont*] Then there has been some unfortunate affair in your family?

DUPONT. Yes. By my first marriage I had two daughters. One, that great fool of a Caroline whom you know.

MME. MAIRAUT. Quite well. She remains unmarried, does she not?

DUPONT. She prefers it. That's the only reason. The other was called Angèle. When she was seventeen she was guilty of an indiscretion which it became impossible to hide. I turned her out of my house [*Quite sincerely*] I was deeply distressed at having to do it.

MME. DUPONT. For three days he refused to eat anything.

DUPONT. Yes, I was terribly distressed. But I knew my duty as a man of honor, and I did it.

MME. MAIRAUT. It was noble of you! [*She shakes him warmly by the hand*].

MAIRAUT. Since you were so fond of her, perhaps it would have been better to keep her with you.

MME. MAIRAUT. My dear, you are speaking without thinking. [*To Dupont*] And what has become of her?

DUPONT [*lying fluently*] She's in India.

MME. DUPONT. In India?

DUPONT [*to Madame Dupont*] Yes, with her aunt, a sister of my first wife's. I have had news of her from time to time. [*To Madame Mairaut*] Indirectly, of course.

MME. MAIRAUT. I repeat, M. Dupont, all this does you honor. [*Thoughtfully*] Still, some people might feel — However, I don't think this discovery need make us abandon our project at once. Not at once. [*To Mairaut*] What do you think, my dear?

MAIRAUT. I?

MME. MAIRAUT. You think, as I do, that we must take time to consider, do you not? [*A pause*] Without any definite promise on either side, but merely in order to get rid of all money questions, which are most distasteful to me, will you allow me to ask you one question, M. Dupont?

DUPONT. Certainly, Madame Mairaut.

MME. MAIRAUT. Have you ever considered [*she hesitates*] what you would give your daughter?

DUPONT. Oh, yes — roughly, you know.

MAIRAUT. Just so.

MME. MAIRAUT. And the sum is — roughly?

DUPONT. Fifty thousand francs.

MME. MAIRAUT. Fifty thousand francs. [*To her husband*] You hear, dear, M. Dupont will give his daughter only fifty thousand francs.

MAIRAUT. Yes. [*A pause*].

MME. MAIRAUT. In cash, of course.

DUPONT. Twenty-five thousand at once. Twenty-five thousand in six months.

MME. MAIRAUT [*to Mairaut*] You hear?

MAIRAUT. Yes.

MME. MAIRAUT. For practical purposes that is only twenty-five thousand francs and a promise.

DUPONT [*with dignity*]. Twenty-five thousand francs and my word.

MME. MAIRAUT. Precisely. That is what I said [*looking at her husband*]. Under these circumstances, we regret very much, but M. Mairaut must decline. It really is not enough.

DUPONT. How much are you giving M. Antonin?

MME. MAIRAUT. Not a sou! On that point we are

quite decided and quite frank. As soon as he marries his
father will take him into partnership, and his wife's dot
will be the capital which he will put into the business.

MAIRAUT. That is the exact position.

MME. MAIRAUT. Antonin will have nothing except
what may come to him after our death.

MME. DUPONT. And I am glad to think you are both
in excellent health.

MME. MAIRAUT [*modestly*] That is so.

MME. DUPONT [*meditatively*] Has n't your son an
uncle, by the way?

MME. MAIRAUT. Yes, madame.

MAIRAUT. Uncle Maréchal.

DUPONT. People say M. Maréchal has a great affection for M. Antonin.

MME. MAIRAUT. Yes.

MAIRAUT. Very great.

DUPONT. He is rich, too, people say.

MME. MAIRAUT. So they say.

MAIRAUT. However, we have n't taken him into account, have we?

MME. DUPONT. Still, M. Maréchal would naturally
leave everything to his nephew.

MAIRAUT and MME. MAIRAUT [*together*] Oh, certainly. We can promise that. He will leave him everything he has.

MME. DUPONT. M. Maréchal has considerable influence at the Préfecture, has he not?

MME. MAIRAUT. No doubt. But all this is really
beside the mark. At twenty-five thousand francs we
could not —

DUPONT. I am sorry.

MME. MAIRAUT. We are sorry, too. [*She rises, saying
to her husband*] Come, my dear, we must be taking our
leave.

DUPONT. I might, perhaps, go to thirty thousand.

Mme. Mairaut. I am afraid fifty thousand is the lowest.

Dupont. Let us split the difference. Thirty thousand and my country house at St. Laurent.

Mme. Mairaut. But it is flooded two months out of the twelve.

Dupont. Flooded! Never.

Mme. Mairaut [*to her husband*] Well, my dear, what do you think?

Mairaut. Antonin is much attached to Mlle. Julie.

Mme. Mairaut. Ah, yes, if it were not for that! [*Seats herself*] My poor boy! [*She weeps*].

Mme. Dupont. My poor little Julie! [*She weeps*].

Mairaut [*to Dupont*] You must excuse her. After all, it is her son.

Dupont. My dear sir, I quite understand.

Mme. Mairaut [*wiping her eyes*] And, of course, there would be the other twenty-five thousand in six months.

Mme. Dupont. Of course.

Mme. Mairaut. Have you any views as to settlements?

Dupont. On that point I have very definite ideas.

Mairaut. So have I.

Dupont. The money on each side must be strictly settled.

Mairaut. Strictly settled? [*A silence of astonishment*].

Dupont. Yes.

Mairaut. His and hers?

Dupont. Certainly. You agree?

Mairaut. Oh, yes, I agree, I agree. Unless you preferred —

Dupont. That all moneys should be held jointly?

Mairaut. Perhaps that would be —

Dupont. Perhaps so. There is something distasteful, I might almost say sordid, about strict settlements.

MAIRAUT. That's it. Something sordid.

DUPONT. They imply a certain distrust.

MAIRAUT. Yes, don't they? Well, that's agreed, then?

DUPONT. Quite. The moneys to be held jointly. All moneys, that is, that may come to them in the future. The first twenty-five thousand, of course, will be settled on Julie. They will form the dot.

MME. MAIRAUT. The second twenty-five thousand, which you will pay over in six months, to be held jointly.

DUPONT. Yes. We will draw up a little agreement.

MAIRAUT. Quite so.

Antonin Mairaut comes in. He is a handsome youth of twenty-eight, very correct in manner. Greetings are exchanged.

MME. MAIRAUT. Antonin. [*To Dupont and Madame Dupont*] You allow me?

MME. DUPONT. By all means.

MME. MAIRAUT [*she draws Antonin aside and says to him in a low voice*] It's settled.

ANTONIN. How much?

MME. MAIRAUT. Thirty thousand, the house, and twenty-five thousand in six months.

ANTONIN. Good.

MME. MAIRAUT. Now you've only the girl to deal with.

ANTONIN. Is she romantic or matter of fact? I don't quite know.

MME. MAIRAUT. Romantic. Raves about Wagner.

ANTONIN. Good Heavens!

MME. MAIRAUT. So I said. But once she's married and has children to look after —

ANTONIN. Children! Don't go too fast. Children come pretty expensive nowadays. Troublesome, too.

MME. MAIRAUT. Never mind. Don't cross her now. Later on, of course, you'll be master.

ANTONIN. I rather think so.

MME. MAIRAUT [*returning to Madame Dupont*] My dear madame —

MME. DUPONT. Yes?

MME. MAIRAUT. He is afraid he may not please Mlle. Julie.

DUPONT. Absurd!

MME. MAIRAUT. The amount of the dot, too —

DUPONT. It is my last word. [*To his wife*] But what is Julie about? [*He rings*].

MME. DUPONT [*rises*] I will go and find her.

A maid enters.

DUPONT. Wait! [*To the maid*] Ask Mlle. Julie to come here if she is ready.

The maid goes out.

ANTONIN. I must tell you, monsieur and madame, how flattered I am to find that the preliminaries have been settled between you and my parents on this important question. I do not know what will be the issue, but —

MME. DUPONT. It is we, monsieur, who are flattered. But you 'll see Julie in a moment. Of course she knows nothing.

MME. MAIRAUT. We might leave them to talk a little together, perhaps?

MME. DUPONT. By all means. We are going to the ball at the Gontiers'. She asked to be allowed — Here she is. [*Julie comes in. Madame Dupont advances to meet her*] There is a crease in your dress, dear. [*She takes her apart, saying to the Mairauts*] Will you excuse me?

JULIE [*in a low tone*] Well?

MME. DUPONT. It rests entirely with you. We are going to leave you to talk together. Remember, it may be your last chance. Don't throw it away.

JULIE. I have thought it over and I don't intend to

do as Caroline did.   So if, after we have had a
talk —

Mme. Dupont.   You'll have to manage him a little.
He has a great eye for business.   If you could make him
think you would be useful in the bank.

Julie.   But I hate figures.

Mme. Dupont.   Once married you will do as you
please.   Tuck in that lace a bit.   It's a little soiled.
[*She tucks in the lace of Julie's corsage*]   And remember, between lovers there may be little things which he
considers himself entitled to.

Julie.   I understand.   They can see you whispering.
Go to them.   [*Madame Dupont goes back to Madame
Mairaut*].

Mme. Mairaut.   What did she say?

Mme. Dupont.   She has not the least suspicion at
present.

Mme. Mairaut.   Let us leave them together.   [*Aloud*]
My dear M. Dupont, I have long wished to go over a
printing office.   May we?

Dupont [*delighted*]   If you will kindly come this way.

Mairaut.   Thank you.

Mme. Mairaut.   But there really are too many of us.
[*Carelessly*]   The children might stay here, don't you
think, madame?

Mme. Dupont.   By all means.

They go out.

Antonin [*looking at the music on the piano*]   You
are fond of Wagner, mademoiselle?

Julie.   I adore him.

Antonin.   So do I.

Julie.   What a genius he is.

Antonin.   Wonderful.

Julie.   For me he is the only composer.

Antonin.   The greatest, certainly.

Julie.   No: the only one.

ANTONIN. Perhaps so. How nice it is we should have the same tastes in art! [*Pause*] Er — they have told you nothing, I understand?

JULIE. About what?

ANTONIN. Your parents, I mean. Mine have said nothing, either.

JULIE. They have said nothing, of course, but I guessed.

ANTONIN. So did I. Then I may consider myself engaged to you?

JULIE. Oh, not yet. We must know each other better first.

ANTONIN. We have often danced together.

JULIE. Yes. But that's hardly enough.

ANTONIN. It's enough for me. Ever since the first time I saw you at the ball at the Préfecture.

JULIE. No. It was at the band, one Sunday, that your mother first introduced you to me.

ANTONIN. Was it? I forgot.

JULIE. I should like to know more about you. Will you — will you let me ask you some questions? It is not usual, perhaps, but —

ANTONIN. Certainly. Pray ask them.

JULIE. Are you fond of children?

ANTONIN. Passionately.

JULIE. Really and truly?

ANTONIN. Really and truly.

JULIE. I am quite crazy about them. For me children mean happiness. They are the one thing worth living for [*wistfully*]. But I think I have a higher idea of marriage than most girls. I want to have my mind satisfied as well as my heart.

ANTONIN. So do I.

JULIE. A marriage that is a mere business partnership seems to me horrible.

ANTONIN. Horrible! That's just the word.

JULIE. And tell me, are you very fond of society?

ANTONIN. Not particularly. Are you?

JULIE. No.

ANTONIN. I am delighted to hear it. The fact is I am sick to death of parties and balls. Still, if it were necessary for business reasons: if it would help to get business for the bank, you would n't mind?

JULIE. Of course not. What kind of business do you do at your bank?

ANTONIN. Oh, the usual kind.

JULIE. I have often read what is put up on the wall: Current Accounts, Bourse Quotations.

ANTONIN. Coupons cashed.

JULIE. That must be very interesting.

ANTONIN. Would you take an interest in all that?

JULIE. Of course. When I was little my father used to make me help him with his books.

ANTONIN. But now?

JULIE. Now, unfortunately, he has a clerk. I am sorry.

ANTONIN. Do you know that you are charming?

JULIE. So you told me once before.

ANTONIN. Yes: at that ball. You had on a dress just like this one. You are beautiful! Beautiful! [*He seizes her hand*].

JULIE [*a little troubled*] Please!

ANTONIN. Come! We are engaged, as good as married. Give me one kiss.

JULIE. No! No!

ANTONIN. Won't you?

JULIE [*frightened*] No, I tell you.

ANTONIN. What beautiful arms you have. [*He draws her towards him*] You remember how I adored you when we were dancing.

JULIE. Let me go.

ANTONIN [*greatly excited, in a low voice*] Don't move. You are entrancing. [*He kisses her upon the arm; she pulls it away sharply*].

JULIE. Monsieur!

ANTONIN [*angry*] I beg your pardon, mademoiselle.
                    A very long silence.

JULIE [*after looking at him for some time*] I have vexed you?

ANTONIN. Well, when I see that you positively dislike me. [*Julie, after a short inward struggle, goes to him*].

JULIE [*putting her arm to his lips with a resigned sadness, which she hides from him*] Antonin!

ANTONIN [*kissing her arm*] Oh, I love you! I love you!

JULIE. Hush! They are coming back.
        The Mairauts and Duponts come in again.

DUPONT. And when I have the contract from the Préfecture, I shall double my business.

MAIRAUT. Excellent! Excellent!

MME. MAIRAUT. We must be going, dear madame. We have stayed far too long already. Are you coming, Antonin?

ANTONIN [*to Julie, aloud, bowing profoundly*] Mademoiselle. [*In a low voice*] My beloved Julie. [*To his mother*] She's charming. I was charming, too, by the way. Wagner — children — every kind of romantic idiocy. And she believed me. [*Aloud to Dupont*] M. and Madame Dupont, my parents will have the honor of calling upon you to-morrow to ask on my behalf for the hand of Mlle. Julie.

DUPONT. Till to-morrow, then. Till to-morrow. [*To Antonin*] All sorts of messages to your uncle, if you see him.

ANTONIN. I shall not fail. [*He bows. The Mairauts take their leave*].

Dupont [*to Julie*] That's all right, then?

Julie. Yes. I really do like him. I think I managed him pretty well too. Wagner — the bank — He thinks I 've a perfect passion for banking.

Dupont [*laughing*] Good. You 're my own daughter. Kiss me. And your father? He managed pretty well, I think. I have arranged that all moneys except your dot shall be held by you both jointly; so that if you are divorced, or if you die after Uncle Maréchal, your dot will come back to us, and half whatever he leaves. I call that a good day's work. And at dessert we 'll drink a bottle of the best to the health of Madame Antonin Mairaut.

Mme. Dupont [*embracing her*] My poor little daughter.

Dupont. Poor, indeed! She 's a very lucky girl. I wonder where that great stupid Caroline has got to. [*He calls*] Caroline! She is never here when one wants her. [*He calls again*] Caroline! She is hard at work painting Cupids on plates, I bet. [*Caroline appears*] Here she is. Great news. Your sister is engaged to be married.

Caroline. Julie! Is it true?

Julie. Yes.

Caroline. Ah!

Dupont. Is that all you have to say?

Caroline. I am very glad, very glad. [*She bursts into tears*].

Dupont [*astonished*] What 's wrong with her? Crying! And she 's not even asked who he is. She 's to marry M. Antonin Mairaut, nephew of M. Maréchal.

Mme. Dupont. Don't cry like that, my dear.

Julie. Caroline!

Caroline [*trying to restrain her sobs*] Don't mind me. It is only because I love you, dear. Now you at least will be happy.

JULIE [*musing*] Yes.

DUPONT [*to himself*] The moral of all this is that that little affair of Angèle's is costing me an extra five thousand francs and my house at St. Laurent.

ACT II

The salon of a house in the country. A July night. At the back, through glass doors, you see the garden brilliantly lighted by the moon. As you look out you have two doors on your right-hand side, and to your left, in a cross-wall, the door of the bedroom, inside which part of the bed is visible. The fireplace is to your right. When the curtain rises Antonin, Courthezon, and Caroline are on the stage; Caroline is doing up a parcel.

ANTONIN. That's settled, then, M. Courthezon. I'll write to the Bordeaux people about your invention this evening.

COURTHEZON. I am greatly obliged to you, M. Antonin. You'll write this evening without fail, won't you? M. Smith is leaving to-morrow.

ANTONIN. Without fail.

COURTHEZON. Shall I post the letter for you on my way through the town?

ANTONIN. Well — it's rather a difficult letter to write. It'll take a little time. Lignol, whom you met at dinner out in the garden, has to go back to-night. He'll take it.

COURTHEZON. It's very good of you.

ANTONIN. And now let's go and have our coffee.

COURTHEZON. Not for me, thanks. I'm afraid I ought to go by the 8.9 train. I shall be taking some china for Mlle. Caroline and the drawings.

ANTONIN. As you please. Good-bye, then.

COURTHEZON. Good-bye, M. Antonin. Thank you again. [*Antonin goes out*].

CAROLINE. I shall not keep you a moment. The parcel is just ready.

COURTHEZON. There is no hurry, mademoiselle. I can take the next train. It's of no importance. Indeed I prefer it. It carries third-class passengers. The fact is I didn't want to go back to the others. M. and Madame Mairaut, M. Lignol, all those people frighten me. Besides, I'm so happy just now I can think of nothing else.

CAROLINE. M. Antonin is going to do something about your invention?

COURTHEZON. Yes. I have begun negotiations with a business house at Bordeaux. M. Antonin knows the heads of the firm, and he has been kind enough to say he will write to them about me. But M. Smith goes away to-morrow. That was why I was so anxious the letter should go to-night.

CAROLINE [*giving him the parcel which she has just finished*] It's very kind of you to take charge of this. I have put the china in it and the drawings they asked for. You will make my apologies to the firm, won't you? I have not been very well.

COURTHEZON. Not well?

CAROLINE. Nothing serious. But the doctor said a little country air would be good for me, so Julie and her husband asked me here. They have been very kind. I have been with them a week, and I'm feeling ever so much better.

COURTHEZON. They would hardly have left you in your lodgings with no one to look after you. [*Pause*] What a strange idea it was of yours to go off and live by yourself like that!

CAROLINE. I thought it better. After Julie's marriage I preferred it.

COURTHEZON. It must cost more.

CAROLINE [*shrugs*] I dare say. [*Pause*] You are
going to have a lovely night for your journey. How
bright the moon is! One can see as clearly as if it were
broad daylight.

COURTHEZON [*suddenly remembering*] There now!
I was just going to forget! I brought a letter for M.
Dupont from the office. It came after he left. It's
about the printing contract for the Préfecture.

CAROLINE. For the Préfecture? He'll want to see
that directly he comes in.

COURTHEZON. And now I really must be off. Good-
bye, Mlle. Caro.

CAROLINE. Good-bye, M. Courthezon. [*He goes out*].
*After Courthezon's departure Caroline returns to her
seat. She makes a slight sign of the cross, closes her
eyes, and sits motionless, praying silently. After a few
seconds she again crosses herself, but does all this very
quietly. Lignol comes in through the glass doors, giving
his arm to Julie. Antonin and M. and Madame Mairaut
follow.*

ANTONIN. We shall be more comfortable here than in
the garden. It's getting rather chilly. [*To Lignol*]
You can smoke.

LIGNOL. We really could have stayed out quite well.

ANTONIN. And given Julie cold, eh?

JULIE. My dear, I assure you —

ANTONIN. Oh, yes, I know. But you are n't wrapped
up enough. [*He touches her arm*] In that thin dress
you've simply nothing on. Just feel, Lignol, feel.

JULIE [*protesting*] My dear!

MME. MAIRAUT. What a charming frock you have on,
my dear. Quite delightful.

JULIE. It came from Madame Raimond.

MME. MAIRAUT [*to Mairaut*] From Madame Raimond? I thought she made all her own dresses.

Lignol [*to Julie*]   You know, madame, that you have not convinced me yet.

Julie.   Admitting that I am wrong— [*They go towards the garden door with Antonin, talking*].

Mme. Mairaut. [*to Mairaut*] And *you* urged on that marriage.

Mairaut.   I !

Mme. Mairaut.   When she was at home she never went to a dressmaker.   And now!   It 's too much!   And we shall have the river in here before long.   That wall is bound to go.

Mairaut.   Do you think so?

Mme. Mairaut.   We shall have the whole house about our ears.   And that fool —

Mairaut.   What fool?

Mme. Mairaut.   Your son, of course, who has put in electric light.

Antonin [*from the garden door, to Lignol*]   You did n't know I 'd had electric light put in.   We have lots of water power, you see.   I ought to have turned it on before.   Look! [*He touches a button and turns up the light*].

Lignol.   That 's better. [*They talk on*].

Mme. Mairaut.   If the river rises another couple of inches, down will come four hundred feet of that wall.

Mairaut.   It 's not as bad as that.

Mme. Mairaut.   Oh, you have let yourself be nicely done.

Mairaut.   Come, come!

Mme. Mairaut.   The girl is utterly useless.   She can do nothing.   And the house will cost more in repairs than it is worth.   When I think I was idiot enough to listen to you. [*She listens*] What was that?

Mairaut.   I hear nothing.

Mme. Mairaut.   The wall!   Listen! [*They listen intently*].

JULIE [*coming forward with Lignol and Antonin*] Oh, yes, we 're comfortable enough here, as you see.

MME. MAIRAUT. Comfortable enough! [*To Mairaut*] Come with me. This way. I am certain the wall has fallen. If it has we must have a little talk with the Duponts; and I, for one, shan't mince matters. [*Turning to the others*] My husband finds the heat a little too much for him. We are going for another turn in the garden. Oh, it 's nothing, nothing at all.

MAIRAUT [*mumbling*] Nothing. Giddy, that 's all.

ANTONIN. Quite right. Get all the fresh air you can while you are in the country. Don't be long. We 're expecting visitors, you know.

MME. MAIRAUT. We 'll be back in time. [*Madame Mairaut and Mairaut go out into the garden*].

ANTONIN. Here, you see, is the staircase which leads to the upstairs rooms and down to the garden. [*He goes to the door on his left*] Here is our bedroom.

JULIE [*in a low voice, so as not to be noticed by Lignol*] Antonin!

ANTONIN [*aloud*] Nonsense, dear. Why not? [*He opens the door. To Lignol*] Look!

LIGNOL. Charming.

ANTONIN. A real nest, eh? A nest for love-birds. That 's what I call it. [*To his wife*] Kiss me, dear.

JULIE. But —

ANTONIN. Kiss me! Come!

JULIE [*gently*] But we 're not alone.

ANTONIN. Lignol won't mind. Eh, Lignol?

LIGNOL [*laughs*] Don't mention it. You were n't so shy at dinner.

ANTONIN [*to Julie, smiling*] Come! Wives must obey, you know. [*She kisses him*] And now go and see about that beer.

JULIE. May n't I send the servant?

Antonin. She does n't know where it is. It's not unpacked yet. [*To Lignol*] It's a wedding present. We are going to broach it to-night.

Lignol. Not for me. I must go in a moment.

Antonin. I was n't thinking of you, my dear fellow. You 're a friend. These formal entertainments are reserved for acquaintances. For the Pouchelets, in fact. M. Pouchelet has just been elected a Departmental Councillor. He and his wife are paying their first visit here to-night.

Lignol. So late?

Antonin. On their way back from the Préfet's. They are dining there, and we are near neighbors. They are very well off, very influential. Useful people altogether. What was I saying? [*To Julie*] Oh, yes, the beer: that girl will never be able to find it. Besides, I 'd rather you went. She would only break the bottles. [*Julie pouts*] Wives must obey, you know.

Julie. Very well. I shall be back before you go, M. Lignol. [*She goes out*].

Caroline [*to Antonin*] You won't forget the letter for M. Courthezon, will you, M. Antonin?

Antonin. Of course not.

Caroline. If you write I feel sure he will succeed.

Antonin. Yes, yes, I know.

Caroline. I will go to Julie.

Antonin. You 'd much better go and put on another dress or something. Just to smarten yourself up. The Pouchelets are coming. We must all look our best.

Caroline [*rather aghast, looking at her clothes*] But — [*A pause*] Very well. [*She goes out*].

Lignol. Who is that lady? She never spoke a word all through dinner.

Antonin [*carelessly*] A poor relation. The usual thing; an old maid, always at church. Awfully prim and proper, you know. [*Rather shamefaced*] In fact —

I don't mind telling *you* — she really works for her living.

LIGNOL.   Well, why not?   There's nothing dishonorable about that, is there?

ANTONIN.   I know.   But still —   She paints little Cupids and that kind of thing, on china.   [*He laughs loudly*].   Enough to make you split!   You don't see it? The other day someone offered her some work far better paid than what she's doing at present.   She refused. Guess why.

LIGNOL [*bored*]   Why?

ANTONIN [*giggling*]   Because the woman who kept the shop was divorced.   [*He laughs*].   But it is good to see you again, my dear chap.   [*He claps Lignol on the shoulder*].   Awfully good.

LIGNOL.   I've enjoyed coming immensely.   [*A pause*] Your wife is charming.

ANTONIN [*fatuously*]   Not bad, eh!

LIGNOL.   And she's clever, too.

ANTONIN.   Get out!

LIGNOL.   I'm quite serious.

ANTONIN.   Oh, yes, I dare say.   I know all about *that*. No use denying it.   Julie's stupid.   It was partly for that very reason I married her.

LIGNOL.   I don't think so.   She has read a lot.

ANTONIN.   Read!   Oh, yes, she's *read!*   She reads everything she comes across.   Before her marriage she read the proofs of everything her father printed.   Here she has unearthed a lot of books left behind by an old fool M. Dupont bought the house from.   She's read them all.

LIGNOL.   But then —

ANTONIN.   But she doesn't understand a word of what she reads.   Not a word!   The other day I looked at the author's name on the book in her hand.   It was Mill. You know, John Stuart Mill.

Lignol [*nods*] Yes, I know.

Antonin. So do I, by name. But I 've never read him, thank goodness. No, I tell you Julie 's stupid. But she 's pretty and she knows how to put on her clothes. I knew what I was about when I married her. With a little instruction from me she 'll learn to manage the house well enough. And that 's all I ask of a woman.

Lignol. Indeed! Well, my dear chap, if you imagine you 've married a stupid woman, you 're mistaken.

Antonin. How do you know?

Lignol. She and I have been talking while you were entertaining your inventor.

Antonin. You got her to talk, did you?

Lignol. Certainly.

Antonin. Wonders will never cease. When we 're alone she never has a word to say.

Lignol. And you?

Antonin. I have n't either.

Lignol. That 's awkward.

Antonin. I 'm always afraid of putting my foot in it. The fact is I don't understand Julie.

Lignol. And you 've been married five months.

Antonin. Four months and a week over. But then I 'm at business all the week. Every Saturday her parents and mine come down to spend Sunday with us. M. and Madame Dupont could n't get here in time for dinner to-night, but they 'll be here soon. When we are alone I try to find some subject of conversation, but I tell you it 's like walking on eggshells. Whew! And so —

Lignol. Well?

Antonin. And so I stop. And then I kiss her.

Lignol. You 're tremendously in love with her.

Antonin. Yes.

Lignol. And she?

Antonin. She 's just the same.

LIGNOL. Happy man!

ANTONIN. For the rest we can only wait and see how things turn out. She knows nothing of my tastes. I know nothing of hers.

LIGNOL. And what did you talk about while you were engaged?

ANTONIN. We were only engaged three weeks. Just long enough to get the money matters settled.

LIGNOL. You took good care about them, I bet.

ANTONIN. Rather. In fact it was a precious good stroke of business. [*He laughs*] If you only knew how we did the Duponts, maman and I! [*He laughs again*].

LIGNOL. Hush! Here's your wife. [*Julie comes in, and Lignol rises to go*] I am afraid I must be going, madame.

ANTONIN. But my letter for Courthezon. [*He looks at his watch*]. You've twenty minutes still.

LIGNOL. You're sure?

ANTONIN. Certain. Wait a second. I'll go and write it, and then I'll see you to the station. It's only a step. [*He goes out*].

JULIE. Thanks to you, M. Lignol, we have had a delightful evening.

LIGNOL. You flatter me, dear madame. I know quite well I have been in the way.

JULIE. On the contrary. I have not had such an evening's conversation since I married.

LIGNOL. Antonin isn't a great talker.

JULIE. You are old friends, aren't you?

LIGNOL. Yes. I've known him fifteen years. We are almost like brothers.

JULIE. Tell me! Is he what you would call a religious man?

LIGNOL. Antonin! [*Bursts out laughing*]. Why, he's a materialist. Not much idealism about him.

JULIE.   Indeed! Not much idealism! But he's fond of music? Good music, I mean: Wagner?

LIGNOL.   He likes a brass band or a comic opera. [*Julie shows surprise*] You are astonished? Oh, I forgot. He plays a little on the concertina. My dear madame, Antonin is a good chap but thoroughly matter of fact. Prosaic.

JULIE [*laughing*]   You are not very complimentary to your friends.

LIGNOL.   What annoys me is that he should possess a treasure like you and should seem quite unconscious of its value. Ah, when *I* marry —

JULIE.   You are going to marry soon?

LIGNOL.   I don't know. [*Musingly*] If I were to meet a woman like you, a woman with whom I could discuss everything in heaven and earth, everything that raises us, makes us higher, then —

JULIE.   Look for her. You'll find her easily enough.

LIGNOL.   And beautiful, too. Beautiful as you are. For you *are* beautiful, you know.

JULIE [*still rallying him*]   Are you making love to me by any chance, M. Lignol?

LIGNOL.   If making love to you means yielding to an overmastering attraction — to a fascination —

JULIE [*laughing*]   You certainly make the most of your time as friend of the family. But I shouldn't hurry if I were you. You will only be wasting a lot of pretty speeches which you could employ to greater advantage elsewhere. I have old-fashioned views on the subject of marriage.

LIGNOL.   Whatever they are I am sure they will be lofty and noble.

JULIE.   You are too good. But you are mistaken. My view is commonplace enough. All I ask of life is that I may love my children and love my husband.

Lignol.   Your children?

Julie [*quite simply, with a touch of emotion*]   Above everything my children. What I am going to say will sound absurd to you, but the day my first child is born will be the happiest day of my life. So you see, M. Lignol —

Lignol [*insinuatingly*]   Dear madame, we shall meet again.

Julie [*smiling*]   As soon as you please.

Antonin comes in.

Antonin.   Here's the letter. You'll slip it into the post-box, won't you? And now we've only just time.

Lignol.   I'm ready [*rising briskly*].   But don't let me drag you to the station. You'll be leaving madame alone.

Antonin.   That's all right. Come along. I can see if M. and Madame Dupont have arrived at the same time.

Lignol [*to Julie*]   Au revoir, madame. [*To Antonin*]   I am sorry not to say good-bye to mademoiselle. [*Antonin is puzzled*]   To the lady who dined with us.

Antonin.   Oh, Caro. I'll say it for you. No, here she is. [*Caroline comes in; and, as Lignol is saying good-bye to her, M. and Madame Dupont appear. Antonin hurriedly introduces*]   My friend Lignol. He has to catch this train.

Lignol.   So sorry. [*He goes out with Antonin*].

Dupont.   Ah, Caroline. There you are. I have good news for you. Your aunt is dead. Your aunt in India. She has left all her money to you and Angèle. Not much. Sixty thousand francs between you. I get nothing, of course. She never could endure me. My dear girl, what's the matter? Come, come, you're not going to cry because your aunt is dead! You've not seen her for five and twenty years. It's the greatest stroke of luck for you. And I shall have all the trouble, as usual! [*A

gesture of dissent from Caroline]. Oh, yes, I shall.
Your sister will have to come down from Paris.

MME. DUPONT. I thought you said she was in India.

DUPONT. In India! What are you talking about?
She is in Paris. She has never been anywhere except in
Paris. What should take her to India? [*To Caroline*]
Your sister Angèle will have to come down from Paris
because part of the money is in land. It will be sold, of
course, but still I shall have to see Angèle. And that
will set people talking. Lots of people don't even know
that I have three daughters. [*To Julie*] It's lucky for
you this did n't happen before your marriage, Julie.

CAROLINE. *Must* she come, father?

DUPONT. Certainly she must. You must both be
present at the lawyer's together to sign the documents.

CAROLINE. I will not go to the lawyer's.

DUPONT. If you refuse to go Angèle will not be
able to get her legacy, and she needs it.

CAROLINE. Well, perhaps I will go. I will think it
over and consult someone. I will give you my answer
to-morrow.

DUPONT. As you please. And not a word about this,
remember, either of you.

JULIE. Very well, father.

CAROLINE [*taking a letter from the mantelpiece*]
Courthezon brought this letter for you. It is about the
printing work for the Préfecture.

DUPONT [*he reads the letter*] Done, by Jove! Dumoulin gets the contract! Dumoulin! I expected this.
I expected it. Uncle Maréchal has done it on purpose,
curse him! [*To Julie*] How long have I been telling
you you ought to pay him a visit? Have you been? No!
And Antonin? Not he! Nor his father and mother!
The old fool is offended, and this is his revenge. And if
this goes on we shall never get a halfpenny of his money.
Why have n't you been to see him?

Julie. Antonin's parents did n't wish it.

Dupont. Ah! They did n't wish it! Well, I have a word or two to say to Antonin's parents, you 'll see. *I* do my duty. *I* go and call on Uncle Maréchal myself. *I* amuse the old idiot, though it 's not the pleasantest sort of job to have to do. They did n't wish it! I 'll show them the kind of man I am! And you — you were fool enough to do what they told you! I find a husband for you, a far better match than you could ever have hoped for. I *do* the Mairauts —

Mme. Dupont [*alarmed, looking round her*] Hush!

Dupont. Well, have n't I *done* the Mairauts?

Mme. Dupont. Yes, yes! But don't say it so loud.

Dupont. They are n't here. And if they were, Julie 's married now. [*Speaking lower, but with the same fury*] I *do* the Mairauts —

Mme. Dupont. Are you quite sure?

Dupont. Am I quite sure? Have n't I *done* them? I tell you I 've done them *brown!*

The maid-servant comes in.

Servant [*to Julie*] It 's about the beer, madame.

Julie. I 'm coming. Will you come, too, Caro? [*Julie and Caroline go out*].

Dupont [*fuming*] Brown, by Jove!

Mme. Dupont. Hush! Here they are.

Dupont. I 'm glad to hear it. Now you 'll see.

M. and Madame Mairaut come in.

Mme. Mairaut. Ah, you are here? Well, the wall has come down.

Dupont. I 'm not thinking about the wall.

Mme. Mairaut. Very likely. You have n't to pay for putting it up again.

Dupont. I 'm not thinking about the wall. I 'm thinking of something far more important. M. and Madame Mairaut, I regret to have to inform you that you are either deplorably unintelligent or else devoid of all sense of parental duty.

MME. MAIRAUT. Indeed! So it's you who propose to insult us just when —

DUPONT. I am a father and I love my children. When their interests are at stake I have the sense to keep on good terms with those who may be useful to them later on.

MME. MAIRAUT [*after a moment's thought*] I see. Uncle Maréchal?

DUPONT. You knew it? You did it on purpose?

MME. MAIRAUT. Uncle Maréchal! [*She bursts out laughing uproariously*].

MAIRAUT. Charlotte! My dear! Don't laugh like that.

MME. MAIRAUT. Why should n't I laugh? You are n't going to forbid me, I suppose [*looking full at Dupont and laughing more*], nor monsieur?

DUPONT. Well, since you take it like that, I propose to give you *my* view of the situation. Either you are hopelessly selfish or else you are hopelessly stupid.

MAIRAUT. Monsieur Dupont!

MME. MAIRAUT. You hold your tongue. Leave me to deal with him.

MME. DUPONT. My dear —

DUPONT. Be silent. Selfish or stupid? Which? [*Madame Mairaut shrugs her shoulders*] Is Uncle Maréchal a man with money to leave, or is he not?

MME. MAIRAUT [*decisively, after a moment's thought*] He is *not!*

DUPONT [*staggered*] He is not? But —

MME. MAIRAUT. I quite understand, and you have your answer. He is not.

DUPONT. He has not two hundred thousand francs?

MME. MAIRAUT. He had them. Somebody else has them now. He has lost them.

DUPONT. Lost them! If this is true —

MME. MAIRAUT. That is why we don't waste our time in going to see him.

DUPONT. But — I don't understand. [*A pause. He controls himself*] How long ago did this happen?

MME. MAIRAUT. More than six months ago.

DUPONT. More than six months? Then you knew?

MME. MAIRAUT. Yes, we knew.

DUPONT. And you never told me?

MME. MAIRAUT. You did n't ask us.

DUPONT. You ought to have informed me. It was dishonest.

MME. MAIRAUT. Monsieur!

DUPONT. You have swindled me.

MME. MAIRAUT. Swindled!

DUPONT. Yes! Swindled!

MME. MAIRAUT. Nonsense. We are as well off as you are, I hope. Our bank is worth as much as your printing business.

DUPONT. Most people would n't say so. As to that, by the way, I should like to ask you —

MME. MAIRAUT. No, monsieur. I have nothing further to say to you. And I am now going to inform my son how you have treated us.

MME. DUPONT. Madame Mairaut!

MME. MAIRAUT. Are you coming, Alfred?

Mairaut makes a gesture of regret and distress behind his wife's back, and then follows her out.

MME. DUPONT. This is terrible!

DUPONT. Eh? [*Pulling himself together*]. No! On reflection I 'm inclined to think it 's the best thing that could have happened. I regret nothing. Rather the contrary.

MME. DUPONT. I don't understand.

DUPONT. Naturally! You don't understand. You will later. [*Julie comes in*] We were just speaking of you. I hear your husband's business is shaky. Is it?

JULIE. I know nothing about it.

DUPONT. You know, I suppose, whether it is true that he got let in by the Bourdin failure?

JULIE. No.

DUPONT. Good Heavens! What on earth do you talk about at meals, and so on?

JULIE. We don't talk at all.

DUPONT. Still you must have noticed whether he was anxious and preoccupied, or whether he was in his usual spirits.

JULIE. I 've no idea what his usual spirits are. I 've only known him six months.

DUPONT. You 'd better ask him how things are going, at once.

JULIE. What 's the good?

DUPONT. You must ask him. You will have children some day, I suppose?

JULIE [*with a sigh*] If it were n't for that, I think I should go and drown myself.

DUPONT. That would be absurd. But we need n't discuss that now. Only, if you don't wish your children to be beggars, keep an eye on your husband's business affairs.

JULIE. Very well. I will.

Antonin comes in.

ANTONIN [*in a tone of mild reproach*] M. Dupont, this is very annoying. Here are my parents coming to me to complain that you have called them swindlers. I must say it 's pretty hard on me if I can't even spend a Sunday in the country in peace. From the moment you arrive on Saturday night you begin quarrelling. And now — swindlers! Come, come, M. Dupont, that 's not the sort of name one calls people, is it? They are very angry, and I don't blame them.

DUPONT. Oh, it was really nothing.

ANTONIN. Maman is furious.

DUPONT. That's absurd of her. You know what it is when people begin disputing; one word leads to another, and one says things one only half believes. However, to show how reasonable I am, I will go and make my apologies to Madame Mairaut. [*To Madame Dupont*] Come, my dear: you must do the talking.

ANTONIN. If you put yourself in my place, you will see how unpleasant this kind of thing is.

DUPONT [*with dignity*] Quite so. [*He and Madame Dupont turn towards the door*].

ANTONIN [*calling them back*] Here are M. and Madame Pouchelet. Wait! [*He goes to the door and calls to his parents*] Maman! They're here, and M. Dupont wants to apologize. It was a misunderstanding, and please don't let's have any quarrelling before visitors. [*To Julie*] Go and help them to get their things off.

Julie goes out to welcome the arrivals. M. and Madame Mairaut come in at the same moment as M. and Madame Pouchelet, Julie helping the latter to take off their wraps. M. Pouchelet is in evening dress, Madame Pouchelet in a ball dress.

JULIE. How good of you to come. My husband and I are so delighted.

POUCHELET. I promised your husband we would look in. Otherwise we should have gone straight home. The Préfet kept us longer than we wished, and we neither of us like late hours. We can only stay a moment.

MME. MAIRAUT [*pushing forward a chair for Madame Pouchelet*] Won't you sit down?

ANTONIN [*to Pouchelet*] Naturally the Préfet was only too glad to get you to come.

POUCHELET. Yes. There is a scheme on foot for reclassifying the roads in the Department.

ANTONIN [*with an assumption of great interest*] Really!

MME. MAIRAUT [*following suit*] Reclassifying the roads? Most interesting!

ANTONIN. It is a matter of the greatest importance. And you, of course, are the very man to give him the necessary information.

POUCHELET [*pompously*] I flatter myself I do know something of the subject.

DUPONT. It is a question I have also had a great deal to do with. Twelve years ago I printed —

POUCHELET. I intend to make —

DUPONT. No; it was thirteen —

MME. MAIRAUT [*to her husband*] Listen, dear: M. Pouchelet is speaking.

MAIRAUT. Yes, yes; I am listening.

POUCHELET. I intend to make an important speech on the subject at the Council. But you will read the report in the papers.

ANTONIN. I should think so. We must not miss that, Julie, must we?

POUCHELET. Oh, madame, I 'm afraid my speech is not likely to interest you.

ANTONIN. On the contrary. My wife only likes reading about serious subjects. Why the other day I found her reading — who was it? that English writer: what was his name, dearest?

JULIE. Never mind.

ANTONIN [*going over to Julie, summing up her points*] She 's a wonderful little woman, my wife. Are n't you, dearest? You are n't cold, are you? I am always telling you you don't wrap up enough. [*To Pouchelet*] She is charming, is n't she? And the most devoted wife! [*To Julie*] Are n't you a devoted wife, dear?

MME. MAIRAUT. Antonin, are n't you going to offer M. and Madame Pouchelet a little refreshment?

ANTONIN. Of course. [*To his wife*] Will you ring?

Julie rings the bell. The maid comes in almost at once with bottles of beer on a tray, and glasses.

JULIE [*to the maid*] Put it there.

ANTONIN [*to Madame Pouchelet*] My wife is a wonderful manager. We are really hardly settled in here. Yet everything is always ready directly one wants it. May I give you a glass of beer?

The glasses which Julie has poured out are handed round. Caroline comes in.

DUPONT. M. Pouchelet, allow me to present to you my second daughter, Caroline.

POUCHELET [*bows*] Madame.

ANTONIN [*correcting him*] Mademoiselle. Mlle. Caroline has always refused to marry. She prefers to devote her life to her art.

MME. POUCHELET. You are an artist, mademoiselle? How delightful. I adore artists.

CAROLINE. I only paint a little on china.

ANTONIN. And she does it most beautifully.

POUCHELET. You must send something to our local exhibition.

ANTONIN. Excellent! M. Pouchelet is right. Why have you never sent anything?

CAROLINE. I only paint china plates, knick-knacks, and so on.

ANTONIN. Just for your own amusement. [*To Pouchelet*] My sister-in-law just does it to amuse herself. But I am sure if she took the trouble —

CAROLINE. But I don't do it to amuse myself.

MME. MAIRAUT. Oh, yes, you do.

ANTONIN. Merely to amuse yourself.

DUPONT. Just for your own amusement.

ANTONIN. And the artist can put just as much of his art into small subjects. Look at Meissonier.

MME. POUCHELET. Of course. They give just as great scope for the imagination.

CAROLINE.   But I only copy what the people at the shop send me.

MME. MAIRAUT.   Another glass of beer, Madame Pouchelet?   It is French beer and can't —

MME. POUCHELET.   Not just now, thank you.   [*To Caroline*]   The shop people, mademoiselle?

CAROLINE.   Yes, madame, the people who keep the shop I work for.   They pay me quite good wages for what I do.

MME. POUCHELET.   I see.   [*A silence*].

ANTONIN   [*sotto voce, taking Caroline a glass of beer*]   Be silent, can't you?

CAROLINE   [*to him, puzzled*]   What is it?

ANTONIN   [*to Madame Pouchelet, leading her up to a picture*]   Madame Pouchelet, you understand pictures, I know.   What do you think of this?   I paid a long price for it.   [*They go on talking*].

CAROLINE   [*to Madame Mairaut, in a low voice*]   Have I done anything I should n't?

MME. MAIRAUT   [*drily*]   Oh, no!   Far from it!   [*She rises and goes over to Madame Pouchelet*].

MME. POUCHELET   [*coming down stage with Antonin*]   I don't care much about pictures unless they tell a story.   What is that one about?

JULIE.   It is an engraving of a picture by Gerard Dow.

MME. POUCHELET.   Never heard of him.

JULIE.   He was a Dutch painter.   Seventeenth century.

MME. POUCHELET.   Really!   But of course you know more about these things than I do.   A propos, M. Dupont, did you go to the lecture the other day on women's rights?

POUCHELET   [*laughing*]   Oh, yes; ha! ha!

MME. POUCHELET   [*to Julie*]   I should n't be surprised if you, madame, had some sympathy with such opinions?

JULIE [*evasively*] I don't know.

ANTONIN [*laughing*] Come, confess, my dear. Just a little, perhaps?

MME. MAIRAUT. Woman the equal of man!

JULIE [*mildly*] Why not?

MAIRAUT. There are some women who wouldn't gain much by that.

MME. DUPONT. But not all.

DUPONT. Women lawyers!

MME. POUCHELET. Women doctors!

POUCHELET. Women with votes!

ANTONIN [*laughing*] What a joke.

DUPONT [*laughing*] Women with votes!

POUCHELET. I call that rich. [*All three are convulsed with merriment*].

DUPONT. Think of it. Women in the Chamber of Deputies!

ANTONIN. Women Senators!

POUCHELET. Women in the Ministry!

DUPONT. In the Chamber they would want to keep their hats on.

POUCHELET. Yes [*to Julie*]. Eh, Madame Mairaut? They'd insist on keeping on their hats as they do at the theatres.

MME. POUCHELET. And at election times they'd go from house to house asking for votes. The modern women would enjoy that.

POUCHELET. And this parliament elected by women, what would it be like? [*More laughter*] A Chamber of Deputies chosen by women!

JULIE [*a little annoyed*] Really, gentlemen, judging by the results you've achieved so far by keeping the government to yourselves I don't think you need fear that women will do much worse. [*The laughter dies down uneasily*].

POUCHELET [*with pompous solemnity*] I know it is

the fashion nowadays to decry all our elective assemblies. But, as I am myself, in my humble way, one of the people's representatives, I cannot allow such views to pass without protest. [*An awful silence*].

JULIE [*apologizing*] I had no intention of saying anything that could wound you, M. Pouchelet.

MME. POUCHELET. We are sure of that, dear madame.

POUCHELET [*to his wife*] And now, my dear, it is time for us to be going.

ANTONIN. You must forgive my wife's little slip, dear monsieur.

POUCHELET. It is nothing — nothing at all.

ANTONIN. You must n't go like this. Another glass of beer?

MME. POUCHELET. You are very good. It has been so close to-day.

ANTONIN. Julie, a glass of beer for Madame Pouchelet. [*To her*] Yes; the heat this afternoon has been quite oppressive. [*To Julie*] Where 's that beer?

JULIE [*who has tried the various bottles, confused*] I will send for some more. These are empty.

ANTONIN. Really!

MME. POUCHELET. Oh, please don't trouble. Please! No; you really must not. We can have something when we get home. [*Going*] Our things are here, I think.

JULIE. Let me help you.

ANTONIN. I will come and put you on your way.

POUCHELET [*declining*] Thank you, monsieur. We know the way.

M. and Madame Pouchelet bow formally and coldly to each in turn and go out: Julie goes with them. There is a silence. Antonin paces the room irritably. Madame Mairaut grins.

DUPONT [*to his wife, in a low voice, after glancing at the others*] I think it 's time we went to bed.

MME. DUPONT. Very well, dear.

Formal bows, Monsieur, Madame, are exchanged. The Duponts go out and Julie returns.

ANTONIN [*his arms folded, sternly*] So there was no more beer?

JULIE. No, dear.

ANTONIN. It's intolerable.

JULIE. Here are the three bottles. You told me to buy three bottles. There they are.

ANTONIN. Nonsense! You make me ridiculous. I press Madame Pouchelet to have another glass and there isn't one. It's preposterous!

JULIE. It is not my fault.

ANTONIN. I suppose you think it's mine.

MME. MAIRAUT. Evidently.

ANTONIN. Besides, I have no recollection of saying three bottles.

JULIE. I assure you.

ANTONIN. I have no recollection whatever of it. On the contrary, I am certain I said buy four or five.

JULIE. No! Three!

ANTONIN. You make me look like a fool. These people will think I was laughing at them. You make me look like a fool, and that is a thing I won't have.

CAROLINE. M. Antonin, I was there when you spoke to Julie. You did say three bottles.

ANTONIN. My dear Caroline, I love you very much, but I can't help pointing out to you that the best possible way to aggravate a dispute between husband and wife is to interfere in it either on one side or on the other. If you don't realize that already, you may take it from me.

MME. MAIRAUT. If you spoke less, mademoiselle, it would certainly be better for all parties.

CAROLINE. Why? What have I said?

ANTONIN. Among other things you might refrain from proclaiming on the housetops that you are reduced to working for your living.

CAROLINE. There is nothing dishonorable in that.

MME. MAIRAUT. Very likely. But one does n't talk about it.

ANTONIN. I thought every moment you were going to ask M. Pouchelet for an order. Not very pleasant for us, that.

CAROLINE. I am sorry. I did n't mean to do anything wrong. [*She begins to cry*] But I 'm so unfortunate. I always make mistakes.

ANTONIN [*irritably*] Oh, for goodness' sake, my dear Caroline, don't begin to cry. There 's no earthly good in that.

MME. MAIRAUT. There 's really nothing to cry about.

JULIE [*going to her*] Caroline! Don't cry, dear. [*She takes her away*].

MME. MAIRAUT. Now, my son, we are going to say good-night.

ANTONIN. Good-night. [*He kisses her absently*].

MME. MAIRAUT. You 're not angry with us, dear, are you? You wanted to marry Julie, you know. Good-night.

M. and Madame Mairaut go out. Antonin, left alone, goes to the bell and rings it. The maid comes in.

ANTONIN [*to the servant*] Put out the lights. You can leave the two on the mantelpiece. Close those shutters. [*The maid does so and goes out. Julie returns*] I have something to say to you.

JULIE. I am listening.

ANTONIN. I do not wish Caroline to remain with us any longer.

JULIE. Why? What has she done?

ANTONIN. You know well enough.

JULIE. No, I do not.

ANTONIN. She gets on my nerves.

JULIE. Explain, please.

ANTONIN. It is not my business to give explanations.

I am the master in my own house. I shall be obliged if you will arrange with Caroline to bring her visit to a close on Monday.

JULIE. But she was to stay till the end of the month. She will want to know why. What am I to say to her?

ANTONIN. Whatever you please.

JULIE. She will be hurt.

ANTONIN. I don't care about that.

JULIE. But I do care.

ANTONIN. If you won't tell her, I will, in a way which won't admit of any misunderstanding.

JULIE. She will be angry.

ANTONIN. Let her.

JULIE. But if you two quarrel where shall I be able to see her? Here?

ANTONIN. No. I forbid you to do so.

JULIE. Have you the right to forbid me?

ANTONIN. Certainly.

JULIE. Why?

ANTONIN. Once more, because I am master here: because the husband is the master in his own house.

JULIE. That was not what you told me while we were engaged.

ANTONIN. I dare say.

JULIE. You have nothing more to say to me?

ANTONIN. Yes; I have.

JULIE. Well?

ANTONIN. When you have opinions of the outrageous description you gave vent to this evening, please keep them to yourself.

JULIE. Have n't I the right to have opinions?

ANTONIN. Nonsense! Once for all, I have made up my mind that you shall obey me and not spoil my prospects. M. and Madame Pouchelet are people of importance. They might be useful to me, and if you offend them with your absurdities you will be wanting in your duty. Marriage is a business partnership.

JULIE. Then I want to see the accounts. They say you are doing badly at the bank. Is that true?

ANTONIN. Women know nothing about such things. You look after your household and leave the rest to me. Under the terms of our marriage the management of our affairs is in my hands. I manage them to the best of my ability. That is all I have to say to you.

JULIE. In other words, I am a business partner who has to keep her eyes shut and say nothing.

ANTONIN. My dear, it's quite useless starting the lecture about women's rights all over again. I heard it the other evening. Leave that sort of thing to old maids with beards. If I were willing to listen to you, you'd reel off the whole catalogue of grievances against the laws which make women slaves. I know.

JULIE. No: it is not a question of law. It is a question of social usage. [*A pause*] What is wrong is not that there is such and such a provision in the Code. The real evil is that our parents married us as they did marry us.

ANTONIN. They did as most parents do.

JULIE. And so most marriages are unhappy.

ANTONIN. If you really loved me —

JULIE. But I don't love you. That is just the point. And you don't love me. And here we are chained to one another.

ANTONIN. Nonsense! I not love you?

JULIE. No, indeed. You don't love me.

ANTONIN. Come, come, you are talking foolishly. It's late. Let's go to bed. Things will be all right to-morrow morning. [*He goes into the bedroom*].

JULIE [*sits staring in front of her for awhile: then she says to herself*] No: things will never be all right. Never. Never.

ANTONIN [*calls*] Are you coming, Julie? [*Julie starts as if she had been dreaming. She looks round her in a dazed way*] Come along!

JULIE [*with a deep sigh, her face showing a mingled expression of profound disgust and sorrowful resignation*] I am coming. [*She goes slowly towards the door of the bedroom*].

ACT III

The scene is the same as in the first Act. It is September. Dupont and his wife are sitting together. There is a pile of account books on the table between them.

DUPONT [*to his wife, who is holding a paper*] You see what the accounts say. They are n't brilliant. [*To the maid who enters*] As soon as Mlle. Caroline comes in ask her to come here.

SERVANT. Yes, sir. [*The maid goes out*].

MME. DUPONT. The turnover is smaller than last year.

DUPONT. The profits are down to nothing. I 'm wrong. 112 francs 17. Splendid things, accounts!

MME. DUPONT. What 's to happen next?

DUPONT. I don't know. One thing is certain. Things can't go on like this.

MME. DUPONT. What are we to do, then?

DUPONT. Next year it will be worse, unless —

MME. DUPONT. Unless?

DUPONT. The fact is the business wants new plant. At present we are using an old machine worked by hand, which I inherited from my father. We have a gas engine not worth twopence. In fact, there 's only one hope for us.

MME DUPONT. What is that?

DUPONT. To get fresh capital somehow.

MME. DUPONT. That 's not very likely.

DUPONT. Who knows? It 's lucky for you your husband is no fool, my dear. I am going to see if I can get you out of this mess. [*Caroline comes in*] Here is Caroline. Go and find Julie. I shall want you both in a moment. I will call you.

Madame Dupont goes out.

DUPONT [*to Caroline*] My dear child, I have asked you to come here because I want to have a serious talk with you. After our long arguments you have at last come to see that it is your duty to accept the legacy from your aunt. Your sister Angèle is coming here.

CAROLINE. Coming here?

DUPONT. But that is another matter. We will discuss that in a moment with Julie and her mother. They are in the next room. At present I am speaking only of you. All difficulties are removed now — I had a lot of trouble over it, by the way — and to-morrow at four at the lawyer's you will receive the sum of thirty-one thousand three hundred and eighteen francs and a few centimes. Ahem! My dear Caroline, you are old enough to know what you are about. Still you are not one of those undutiful children who throw aside all obedience to their fathers as soon as they are of age. You continue, I am sure, to recognize my right at least to give you advice. I have lived longer than you, I am a man of business, and I can clearly be of use to you when you want to invest your money. Have you any plans as to this so far?

CAROLINE. I had some idea —

DUPONT. May I know what it is?

CAROLINE. I would rather not say.

DUPONT. Not say!

CAROLINE. Yes.

DUPONT. Indeed! Oh, in that case — [*shrug*]

CAROLINE. You don't mind, father?

DUPONT [*much put out, but endeavoring to control himself*] Not at all. By no means. Then there's nothing more to be said. I am a little surprised, of course; hurt even; greatly hurt, in fact.

CAROLINE. I am sorry, father.

DUPONT. No matter! No matter!

CAROLINE. You understand —

DUPONT. I understand that you do not trust your father. That is what I understand. But have your own way. I ask nothing.

CAROLINE. Are you vexed with me?

DUPONT. Oh, no. Not the least in the world. Only when you have given everything you possess to some religious community or other, I should like to know what you will have to live upon when you are old. I assume, of course, that it is some community you are thinking of. [*Caroline is silent*] You admit it?

CAROLINE. No. I would rather say nothing about it.

DUPONT. It is so, all the same?

CAROLINE. Please, father!

DUPONT. You won't give me any idea?

CAROLINE. No.

DUPONT. You refuse, then? You refuse absolutely?

CAROLINE. I have the right to do so, have I not?

DUPONT. Clearly. You are old enough.

CAROLINE. Don't let us talk about it any more.

DUPONT. Very well. [*After a moment, breaking into a passion*] So this is my reward! This is the result of having sacrificed my whole life for my daughters! You do not even trust me as much as you would trust any little attorney you consulted.

CAROLINE. Father! Of course I trust you.

DUPONT [*furiously*] Hold your tongue. You are heartless and undutiful. I did not expect this.

CAROLINE. Please don't be angry, father.

DUPONT. Angry? Yes, I am angry, and I have good reason. [*Striking the table*] Damnation! This is too much! To have lived to be sixty-two and be insulted like this [*He strides up and down the room*].

CAROLINE. I thought I could — I have only disposed of part of the money.

DUPONT [*stopping short*] What?

CAROLINE. I have only disposed of part of the money.

DUPONT [*mollified, becoming tenderly reproachful and coming to sit by her*] My dear child, why did n't you say so at once?

CAROLINE. You gave me no time.

DUPONT. How much is gone?

CAROLINE. Fifteen thousand francs.

DUPONT. Um! That is a large sum. But the sixteen thousand that remain?

CAROLINE. I meant to ask your advice about that.

DUPONT [*rising*] Ah, well, my dear, I have been thinking this over. Let 's consider what openings there are for capital. Suppose you invest it? Gilt-edged securities bring in two and a half per cent. If you take something rather more speculative, you may get four. Then there are the big industrial companies. But with them, too, there are risks to be faced. Foreign competition is more and more threatening. The struggles between labor and capital are reaching an acute phase.

CAROLINE. M. Antonin Mairaut has been to see me.

DUPONT. The scoundrel! I 'll bet he wanted you to invest the money in his bank.

CAROLINE. He did suggest it.

DUPONT. You see! I guessed as much. You sent him about his business, I hope?

CAROLINE. I said I would think about it.

DUPONT. That 's right. But what a fright you gave me. To invest your money in a bank. Nothing could be more risky. Well, as we were saying, — no public companies, no industrials, no shares in banks. What remains?

CAROLINE. I don't know.

DUPONT. There remains commercial enterprise, trade. But do you know anyone engaged in trade who will let you put capital into his business?

CAROLINE. I think not.

DUPONT. We must put our heads together. I confess I can think of no one. Madame Grandjean?

CAROLINE. Father! Madame Grandjean is divorced. You know quite well I refused even to accept employment from her.

DUPONT. That is true. More fool you, by the way. Still — M. Darbout?

CAROLINE. He is a Protestant.

DUPONT. Well, then, I don't see. There is no one, in fact.

CAROLINE. But you, father. If you would do it.

DUPONT. If I would do what? Manage it for you?

CAROLINE. Yes.

DUPONT. It is a great responsibility. I don't know whether — What interest would you expect?

CAROLINE. Whatever you thought right, father.

DUPONT. Well, I will speak to your mother about it. [*As if suddenly making up his mind*] No, I won't. I 'll do it. No one shall say I hesitated to do all I could for my daughter. Kiss me, my dear. I 'll do it.

CAROLINE. Thank you, father.

DUPONT. And you would still rather not tell me what you are doing with the other fifteen thousand.

CAROLINE. Please, father!

DUPONT. Very well. You are your own mistress. I 'll have the necessary documents prepared. Don't you worry about it. I will arrange everything beforehand. You will have nothing to do but sign. [*He looks at his watch*] Three o'clock. Now there is that other matter we have to talk of. [*He goes to the door and calls*] Come in, both of you. [*Julie and Madame Dupont enter*] Sit down [*When they are seated, he says*] My dears, I wanted you all to come here that we may decide how we are to receive Angèle. It is rather a diffi-

cult question. You know her life in Paris is — ahem! —
highly reprehensible. Ought we to let her come here?
Ought we to meet her, for instance, at the station?

JULIE. Papa, what has Angèle done? Now that I
am married surely I may know? People always stop
talking about her when I come in. I remember her quite
well.

MME. DUPONT. But you were only five when she went
away.

DUPONT. You understand, my children, how painful
this subject is both for you and for me. I will spare
you the details as far as possible. It is enough that you
should know, Julie, that when Angèle was seventeen she
was obliged to leave her home because — because —

MME. DUPONT [simply] Because she was about to
become a mother.

JULIE. She went away?

DUPONT. Yes.

JULIE. Of her own free will?

DUPONT. I sent her away.

JULIE. Ah!

DUPONT. As I said, the subject is a very painful one.
Let us get it over as quickly as possible. She is coming
here to-day. [He looks at his watch] She is on her way
now. Her train arrived five minutes ago. Now I hope
you will all of you behave with dignity, and neither be
too affectionate, which would be out of the question, nor
too cold, which would be unkind.

JULIE. Have you heard anything of her since she
left home?

DUPONT. Yes.

JULIE. And her behavior?

DUPONT. Far from what it should be, I 'm afraid.
Still —

CAROLINE. Father, you make too light of all this. We
have heard of her three times. First when her baby

died. Next we were told that she was singing at a music hall and was almost penniless. The third time we heard that she was rich, rich without working. When I think of it all I am sorry I consented to meet her.

JULIE. But she could n't get her share of the legacy unless you did. You could n't rob her of this money however you feel towards her.

CAROLINE. That was what decided me. But there is no reason why I should see her here.

DUPONT. I shall see her. Julie will see her. So will your mother. Why should you do differently from us?

MME. DUPONT. She was very fond of you, Caroline; and you were fond of her. Come, come, you must not be so hard. One should have compassion for those who have suffered as she has done.

CAROLINE [after a pause] Very well. I will do as you wish.

DUPONT. That's right. At the same time, I have no intention of going from one extreme to the other. There will be no question of asking her to stay, or even of inviting her to dinner. That is agreed, is it not?

CAROLINE. Yes. And now I am going downstairs to the office [She goes out].

DUPONT. You, Julie, had better go to your room. [She goes] In ten minutes she will be here.

MME. DUPONT. Well, I must say if she were my daughter, I should have been at the station long ago.

DUPONT. Do you suppose I have n't wanted to go?

MME. DUPONT. Why did n't you, then?

DUPONT. What would people say? Everyone knows me here. On the platform I should have met a dozen people who would have asked me whom I was meeting. And, besides, all things considered, it looks more dignified to receive her here. [Pondering] I 've been asking myself for the last fortnight what I should say when we do meet.

MME. DUPONT. Give her a kiss. The rest will come easily.

DUPONT. You think I should kiss her?

MME. DUPONT. Yes.

DUPONT. I think so, too. At the same time we must remember — how shall I put it? — her way of life. It is a difficult question. And then what am I to say to her? Ought I to refer to the past? I must not seem to be forgiving her, of course. I could n't do that. I could n't possibly. On the other hand, since she is coming, I can hardly — Confound it, it 's all extremely awkward. Eh?

MME. DUPONT. I can't advise you.

DUPONT [*still thinking it out*] Of course, she is my daughter. Still, I have not seen her for eighteen years. [*Peevishly*] I thought I should never set eyes on her again. In the early days, when she first went away, I was terribly distressed. But that could n't last, could it? And then, you understand — Well, well, you must advise me. I have prepared something to say, so as not to leave everything to the inspiration of the moment. If one does n't think things out beforehand, one always says too much or too little. So, as I said, I have prepared something. I even wrote it out, but I know it by heart. You can imagine how upset I am with all this. Here it is: " My child " — I think it best to say " my child." " Angèle " would be too familiar and " my daughter " too formal. " My child " — [*breaking off*] And what makes it all the harder is that I 've no idea what she will say to me. Her letters are very properly expressed, very properly. Still, will she cry? Will she break down? Will she faint? I don't know. It 's impossible to know. Dear me, I wish the next half hour were over. However: " My child, I thank you for having come." — The fact is I ought to tell you I have n't given Caroline quite a true account of how things stood. I thought it wiser not.

MME. DUPONT. What do you mean?

DUPONT. It 's this way. Caroline is the one who could not get her legacy without Angèle's signature. Not the other way about.

MME. DUPONT. But you said —

DUPONT. Yes; I did misrepresent matters a little. You see Caroline would never have agreed to meet Angèle if she had known that it was she who needed Angèle's presence, not Angèle hers. Angèle is the executor under the will. In fact, it is she who is doing us a service. But if we go into all that we shall never be done. Well, I say to her: " My child, I thank you for having come. Let us not speak of the past. I only wish to remember one thing, that you have not visited upon your sister Caroline the resentment which doubtless I inspire in you. I am grateful to you." What do you think of that? [*The maid comes in*] Good heavens, here she is! [*Pointing to the papers, account books, etc., which lie on the table*] And that fool Courthezon has never taken away the books. [*To the maid*] Wait a minute. [*To Madame Dupont*] Come! Come this way! You can tell me whether I ought to make any change. [*In a low voice to the maid*] Ask her to wait a moment. Say I am engaged. [*He goes out with Madame Dupont. The maid shows in Angèle. She is a woman of thirty-five, dressed in black, very quietly, but fashionably*].

MAID. Monsieur is engaged, but I don't think he will be long. Whom shall I say, madame?

ANGÈLE. Madame Angèle Dupont.

MAID. Madame has the same name as monsieur?

ANGÈLE. The same.

MAID. Will madame please be seated? [*She takes some books off a chair and goes out*].

ANGÈLE [*with a gesture of despondency, to herself*]
Nothing is as it used to be. Nothing.

Courthezon comes in.

COURTHEZON. M. Dupont asks you to be good enough
to wait five minutes, madame.

ANGÈLE. Certainly, monsieur. [*Courthezon collects
the books and papers, looking at Angèle the while out of
the corner of his eye. He makes as if to go*] You are
M. Courthezon, are you not?

COURTHEZON [*much embarrassed*] Yes, madame —
Mlle. Angèle. You remember me? You have a good
memory. Especially as I am not quite myself just now.
I have many things to worry me. But that is a long
story. [*He stands facing her, the books and papers
under his arm*] I recognized you at once. M. Dupont
told me.

ANGÈLE. My father is well in health?

COURTHEZON [*embarrassed*] Quite well. They are
all quite well. You, too, if I may judge by your looks?

ANGÈLE. Quite, thank you.

COURTHEZON. And you have come about this legacy?

ANGÈLE. Yes. [*A silence*].

COURTHEZON. You must find some changes down
here?

ANGÈLE. Very many. I hardly know the place.

COURTHEZON. We have moved since you went away.
The house where the press used to be was pulled down
when the Rue de l'Arbre-à-Poires was rebuilt.

ANGÈLE [*looking round her*] They have altered the
furniture in the drawing-room.

COURTHEZON. That was ten years ago.

ANGÈLE [*sadly*] If I had come here without warning,
I should n't have known I was in my father's house.

COURTHEZON. It is so long since you left. You must
feel it very much — the idea that you are to see him again?

ANGÈLE [*very slowly*] Yes. But less than I expected.

When I got my father's letter, I felt as if I should faint.
That was two months ago. Since then I have thought of
this moment every day. I have wondered so often what
my father would say to me and what I should answer
now that I no longer feel anything. That is strange, is
it not? Strange and sad. [*She sighs*] After all, M.
Courthezon, life is always more commonplace than we
expect; simpler, but less beautiful. [*A pause. Sadly*]
And besides, I have seen so much.

COURTHEZON. You have suffered, too?

ANGÈLE. A little.

COURTHEZON. Eighteen years, is it not?

ANGÈLE. Yes. Eighteen years.

COURTHEZON. I hear M. Dupont. I must be going.
Au revoir, madame.

*Courthezon goes out. A moment later the voice of Du-
pont is heard without through the half-open door, saying:
" Yes, yes; I want you to come with me." Then M. and
Madame Dupont come in. There is a long pause, and
finally Dupont says, with apparent calm.*

DUPONT. Good-morning, Angèle.

ANGÈLE. Good-morning, father.

*They hesitate for a moment as to whether they should
kiss one another, then make up their minds to do so. Dupont places a chill salute on either cheek of Angèle. Still
silent, Angèle goes up to Madame Dupont and kisses her
with the same frigidity.*

MME. DUPONT. Good-morning, Angèle.

ANGÈLE. Good-morning, mother. [*They look at one
another without a word*].

DUPONT [*overcoming a momentary emotion*] Let us
sit down. [*They sit. Then he addresses Angèle in the
tone he might have used if she had only gone away the
previous evening*] Thank you for coming.

ANGÈLE. I came for my sister's sake. For Caroline.
I was very fond of her. [*A pause*] Is she married?

DUPONT. No. She has never wished to marry.

ANGÈLE. Yet she is thirty-three.

DUPONT [*to his wife*] Thirty-three or thirty-four?

MME. DUPONT. Thirty-three.

ANGÈLE. I shall see her?

DUPONT. Yes. We will let her know you are here.

ANGÈLE. And my half-sister?

DUPONT. Julie?

ANGÈLE. Yes, Julie.

DUPONT. Your half-sister is married. She has made a good match. The son of a banker. The Mairauts. You remember M. Mairaut, the grandfather?

ANGÈLE. No.

DUPONT. Oh, yes; an old man with a long white beard.

ANGÈLE. No.

DUPONT. Anyhow, he was the grandfather of M. Antonin Mairaut, Julie's husband. [*He points to the door*] She is in there.

ANGÈLE. There?

DUPONT [*speaking rapidly to hide his mingled emotion and embarrassment*] Yes. She has come back with her husband to live with us for a time. Their house at St. Laurent is flooded. You remember the house at St. Laurent?

ANGÈLE. Yes.

DUPONT [*as before, his embarrassment growing*] I told them they ought to build a little wall along the river bank or their house would be flooded. They would n't listen to me and this is the consequence. Happily the water is going down, and they 'll be able to go home to-morrow. But they should have built a wall like their neighbors. Their neighbors built a wall and — and that 's how it was.

ANGÈLE [*after a pause*] How is the business doing? Well?

DUPONT. Oh, yes.

ANGÈLE. And you are all quite well?

DUPONT. All of us. I had a touch of bronchitis last year, but it passed off.

ANGÈLE. I am glad. [*A silence*].

DUPONT [*to Angèle, who is gazing at him*] You find me looking older, eh?

ANGÈLE. On the contrary. I was just thinking —

DUPONT. And you? You are well?

ANGÈLE. Quite, thank you. [*Another silence. Then Angèle rises and the Duponts rise too*].

DUPONT. You can't stay any longer?

ANGÈLE. No. I 'm afraid I must —   [*Another silence*].

DUPONT. You came straight from the station?

ANGÈLE. No. I had my things taken to the Lion d'Or.

DUPONT. You are staying at the Lion d'Or?

ANGÈLE. Yes.

DUPONT. Just so. Well, until to-morrow. Four o'clock at the lawyer's. His house is just opposite. [*He points through the window*] You can see his door from here. You can't miss it.

ANGÈLE. I understand. [*A pause*] Julie — she is there? [*She points to the door*].

DUPONT. Tut, tut, what am I thinking of? I had forgotten. Yes, she is there. They will take you to her. [*To Madame Dupont*] Go and see if — I 'll tell someone to go and find Caroline. [*He rings*].

MME. DUPONT [*opening a door and calling through it*] Julie: your sister Angèle is here.

JULIE [*from her room*] Angèle? Ask her to come in.

MME. DUPONT. You can go in to her.

Angèle goes. Dupont has rung and says a few words to the maid, who goes out at once.

DUPONT. Ouf! [*To Madame Dupont*] Ah, well, it

has all gone off excellently. I did n't say a word of what
I had got ready, but still it was all right. Don't you
think so?

MME. DUPONT. Quite. Poor girl! I felt sorry for her.

DUPONT. She is quite happy. She was very well
dressed; quite like a lady, in fact. Who would think to
see her — Eh? [*Madame Dupont nods*] And yet —
But when one has had a good education it always comes
out. It is curious. I thought I should be quite upset
when I saw her. Instead of which — Of course I don't
mean that I did n't feel it. Still it was n't so bad as I
expected. But now she 's no longer there I feel — I feel
my legs giving way under me! [*He sits down. A silence*] If I were not so sure it was my duty to do as I
did — for it was my duty? [*Pause*] You don't answer.
Was n't it my duty?

MME. DUPONT. I don't know.

Caroline comes in.

DUPONT. Angèle —

CAROLINE. Yes. Courthezon told me.

DUPONT [*with assumed carelessness, after a pause*]
You understand, Caroline, no reproaches. Don't make
any allusion to what you are doing for her sake.

CAROLINE. I understand.

DUPONT [*to his wife*] Tell her that Caroline is waiting for her.

The maid comes in.

MAID. M. and Madame Mairaut, monsieur. They
wish to speak to you.

DUPONT. Good. Where are they? In the office?

MAID. Yes, monsieur.

DUPONT [*to his wife*] I know what they want. [*To
the maid*] I will come down with you. [*He and the
maid go out*].

MME. DUPONT [*speaking at the door of Julie's room*]
Caroline is here.

Angèle comes in and makes a quick movement towards Caroline, but pulls herself up before the coldness of the other's demeanor.

ANGÈLE. Caroline!

CAROLINE. Angèle! [*They stand looking fixedly at one another for some moments*].

ANGÈLE [*sadly*] How changed you are!

CAROLINE. You are changed, too.

ANGÈLE. That is because life has not always gone smoothly with me. [*Caroline makes a gesture of incredulity*] You don't believe me?

CAROLINE. Yes, if you say so.

ANGÈLE. I have just seen Julie. She was kinder than you are. And she was only five when I left home; and she is only my half-sister. You and I have the same father and the same mother. We are almost of an age, and we used to love one another.

CAROLINE [*coldly*] That is true.

ANGÈLE. If you knew all about it you would forgive me.

CAROLINE. Are the things that were said about you untrue?

ANGÈLE. No. However bad they were they are true.

CAROLINE. Since that is so —

ANGÈLE [*without anger*] Since that is so, I still think your virtue very proud, and very hard. That is all. [*Changing her tone*] You understand what has brought me here?

CAROLINE. I understand that we are to meet at the lawyer's.

ANGÈLE. Very well. To-morrow at four.

CAROLINE. To-morrow at four at the lawyer's.

ANGÈLE [*turning at the door, greatly moved*] You have nothing else to say to me?

Caroline shakes her head. Angèle goes out. A moment after Dupont comes in.

DUPONT [*beaming*] She has gone?

CAROLINE. Yes.

DUPONT [*chuckling*] Where is your mother? Where is she? [*He calls Madame Dupont*].

MME. DUPONT. What is it?

DUPONT. I want you.

CAROLINE. I will go.

DUPONT. There's no need.

CAROLINE. I have some work to do.

DUPONT. Very well. Go, my child. Go. [*Calling after her*] To-morrow, remember. [*She goes out as M. Dupont rubs his hands, chuckling*] Guess what M. and Madame Mairaut came to ask me. You can't guess?

MME. DUPONT. No.

DUPONT. No wonder. They came to ask for the twenty-five thousand francs; the twenty-five thousand francs of Julie's dot, you remember, which I was to pay six months after her marriage.

MME. DUPONT. Well?

DUPONT. Well. It is six months to-day since Julie was married.

MME. DUPONT. Good heavens! What did you do?

DUPONT. Gave them nothing, of course.

MME. DUPONT. You could n't do otherwise.

DUPONT. As you say, I could n't.

MME. DUPONT. But they will make us bankrupt.

DUPONT [*still smiling broadly*] They can't. They have nothing but my word.

MME. DUPONT. Luckily.

DUPONT. However, I have n't refused the twenty-five thousand francs. Nor have I disputed the debt.

MME. DUPONT. What did you do then?

DUPONT. I wish you had been there. You would have laughed.

MME. DUPONT. Well?

DUPONT. I think I managed pretty well, though I say it who should n't. If you had seen the long faces they pulled. Especially Mother Mairaut. [*He bursts out laughing*] I should have liked a photograph of them. It would have cheered me in moments of depression. Ha! Ha! Ha!

MME. DUPONT [*smiling*] Tell me about it.

DUPONT. Well — I'd have given anything for a photograph. I said to them [*solemnly*]: "Dear monsieur and dear madame, I admit that I promised to pay you to-day twenty-five thousand francs. Only I am not in a position to pay them." Explosion! Rage! Dignified reproaches! Insults! Smiling, I let the storm pass by. Mother Mairaut sat there, her husband here, I here. All the time they were speaking I looked at them like this [*grins*]. As soon as they had finished I took up the tale again. "I do not deny the debt," said I, "only I ask to be allowed to postpone the payment. And this time I am ready to sign an undertaking, a binding undertaking, to pay." Complete change of front! Smiles. Apologies. Oh, they were devilish civil. Called me a man of honor, etc., etc. I let them run on, still smiling. Then, in the midst of an almost religious silence, I sat down at my desk, I took pen and paper, I wrote, I blotted, so, taking my time about it. Madame Mairaut positively slobbered with delight. I tell you she slobbered. I handed her the paper. On it was written simply: "Good for the sum of twenty-five thousand francs to be paid out of the money to be left by Uncle Maréchal." Ha! Ha! Ha!

MME. DUPONT [*laughing*] Splendid!

DUPONT. Funny, eh? Deuced funny!

MME. DUPONT. Yes.

DUPONT. You don't think so? You don't? Eh? Wasn't it funny?

MME. DUPONT. Yes. Yes.

DUPONT. When Mother Mairaut took it in I thought she was going to have a fit. "It's an insult!" she shrieked. I believe she actually even called me a cad! As for me, I was almost dying with laughter. They went away swearing they were going straight to the bank to tell Antonin. By Jove! I have n't enjoyed myself so much for ever so long.

MME. DUPONT [*becoming serious again*] I hope this won't make any difference to Julie.

DUPONT. Bah!

MME. DUPONT. Things are not going very well with her, I 'm afraid. Antonin is exacting and tyrannical, and she often locks herself into her room to cry.

DUPONT. That always happens in the early days of marriage. People's angles need rubbing off. That sort of marriage turns out best in the end. [*Julie comes in*] Here she is. Speak to her. Tell her these things are n't serious. Make her understand her duty. I must go back to my accounts. [*To Julie*] Well? What did your sister Angèle say to you?

JULIE. Hardly anything. She did n't know me, and I should n't have known her.

DUPONT. I told you so. Well, I must be off. Back soon. [*He goes out*].

MME. DUPONT. My dear — your husband may be rather put out when he comes in.

JULIE. I am getting used to that.

MME. DUPONT. More so than usual, I mean.

JULIE. Why?

MME. DUPONT. Your father has been unable to keep his promise.

JULIE. About the twenty-five thousand francs?

MME. DUPONT. Yes. Antonin will have just heard about it.

JULIE [*depressed*] No matter. [*Suddenly, alarmed*] I do believe I forgot to tell them to get out his grey suit. No: I remember. I did tell them. How angry he would have been if I had n't!

MME. DUPONT. Of course. He is your husband.

JULIE. You think it quite natural that he should fly into a rage as he did two days ago because something or other had been forgotten? And that it is only reasonable he should order me to go to Mass merely that Madame So-and-So may see me there? Well, he may order as much as he likes, I shall not go. I *will* not go!

MME. DUPONT. You make too much of it. My child, are n't you happy?

JULIE [*ironically*] Of course.

MME. DUPONT. Your husband is fond of you, is n't he?

JULIE. That depends on what you mean by fond.

MME. DUPONT. I mean he 's very much in love with you.

JULIE. I suppose so.

MME. DUPONT. You 're angry with him for that?

JULIE. No, I 'm angry with myself.

MME. DUPONT. My dear! What do you mean?

JULIE. I am ashamed of myself.

MME. DUPONT. I don't understand.

JULIE. Nor do I. Don't let us talk about it.

MME. DUPONT. Please, dear!

JULIE [*breaking out*] Well, I *detest* him. There!

MME. DUPONT. Tell me why.

JULIE. There is no why in that sort of dislike. It is born and grows with every moment we are together. Every moment there comes some little point on which we clash. We have n't the same ideas on a single subject. He and I are strangers. We are apart utterly, miserably. We are as far from one another as two human beings can be. [*With a deep sigh*] Oh, to realize that slowly, hopelessly. To feel that every fresh glimpse into each other's character only reveals a fresh source of offence. Till at last it has come to this, that I am certain the more we know each other the deeper will be our mutual loathing. Every day, every hour will add a fresh hatred to the accumulated hatreds of the others. Great heavens! And unless we are divorced this will go on all our lives. [*A pause*] Why, there are moments when he is sitting there in that chair, and I look at him fixedly, and it seems as if I had never seen him before. And why not? After all, it is only six months since I hardly recognized him when we passed in the street. And then I ask myself what am I doing here? I, in my dressing-gown, with my hair down, shut in with that man. And I long to run away screaming. And we are husband and wife. Oh, mother, I am *ashamed*.

MME. DUPONT. You must try to be reasonable. Antonin is a fine fellow. Many girls would have been glad to get him.

JULIE. Why did n't they then, in Heaven's name? Oh, if you knew how I long to have a child to console me for all this! If I should never have one! If I should never have one! [*Shudders*] But I must n't even think of that.

MME. DUPONT. My dear child, you must look at things more calmly. All this will gradually settle down until at last it passes away altogether.

JULIE. Yes. When I am an old woman.

MME. DUPONT. Exactly; when you are an old woman.

JULIE. Thank you.

MME. DUPONT. In any case, you should try to control yourself a little. If only for your father's sake and mine.

JULIE. I will try. [*Antonin comes in*] Hush! Here he is. Go away, mother. You will only make things worse. [*Madame Dupont goes out*].

ANTONIN [*furious*] Well! This is the last straw! Your father won't keep his word. You have heard?

JULIE [*sitting on the sofa*] Yes.

ANTONIN. It does n't disturb you apparently.

JULIE. He cannot do otherwise.

Antonin. It will be the ruin of me. But you seem to be all in league together, the whole lot of you. Oh, you 're a pretty family! Your father owes us twenty-five thousand francs. He won't pay them. The other day your sister promised us fifteen thousand francs. To-day she has changed her mind. As for you, you do everything in your power to compromise my position.

Julie. I?

Antonin. You! You disobey me!

Julie. In what?

Antonin. Were you at Mass this morning?

Julie. No.

Antonin. Why not?

Julie. It is not my fault if I no longer believe.

Antonin. I don't ask you to believe. I ask you to go to Mass. The two things are totally different. A woman ought to go to Mass. If she does n't believe she should appear to do so. It is usual among people of good position. I wish you to do as others do. Do you understand? I wish it. I have no desire to pass for a Freethinker when all my clients are Catholics, confound them!

Julie. I have not been and I do not intend to go.

Antonin. What do you say?

Julie. You heard what I said. If you were a believer, if you asked me to do this out of respect for your faith, I would do it. But it is a piece of commercial trickery that you want from me. I refuse.

Antonin. You wish to do as you like, you mean?

Julie [*breaking out*] Yes. You are quite right. I wish to do as I like. That is it. That is just it. For once in my life I wish to do as I like! All the time I was a girl I had to obey; to submit to authority that was often unreasonable. Now I am to go on obeying, obeying. I have had enough of this everlasting obedience.

Antonin. Then you should n't have married.

Julie. So that 's it, is it? The sole business of your

wife's life is to be your slave, to help the servant to make you comfortable, brush your clothes, taste your soup, and look up to you with admiring homage.

ANTONIN. That's all nonsense.

JULIE. What is nonsense?

ANTONIN. What you have been saying. You know quite well that you have other duties. You know quite well that it only rests with you to be a happy wife. You know that I love you.

JULIE. Yes, yes. I forgot. You *love* me! Which means that I am to submit to your caresses when the fancy takes you. They used to say of us women, " housekeeper or mistress." But we have moved with the times. Now you want the same woman to play both parts. Housekeeper and mistress. That is the only difference between us and the women you love before you marry us. A wife is a mistress who minds the house. That is not enough for me, thank you. No! No! No! I will not pass my whole life between cooking your dinner and accepting your kisses.

ANTONIN. That's right. Off we go on the old story of the wife who is not understood; the poor woman who is a slave and a martyr. If you really love me, if you thought a little more instead of cramming your head with ideas which you don't understand, you would be content with the part, modest no doubt but not dishonorable, with which plenty of women as good as you have contented themselves.

JULIE. Perhaps you are right. If I loved you, as you say, if we loved one another nothing would matter. But I say again I do not love you.

ANTONIN. Be silent.

JULIE. I do not love you.

ANTONIN. Julie, I shall end by losing my temper. You will force me to say things.

JULIE. To say things?

ANTONIN. Never mind.

JULIE. Oh, you may speak out. A little shame more or less does n't matter. We are alone. Let us speak out and clear up the matter once and for all. We *must*. It has been weighing on my mind for a long time. Say what you have to say.

ANTONIN. No.

JULIE. Then *I* will speak. I tell you that I do not love you, and you shrug your shoulders with a smile of self-complacency. But it 's no laughing matter, Heaven knows; and I don't imagine I am the only woman for whom this subject, amusing enough for you men, has meant a whole tragedy of sorrow and disgust.

ANTONIN. I don't understand you.

JULIE. Yes, you *do!* Your vanity makes you try to escape, but you shall understand. You think I dare n't speak, but I will. Do you suppose I will stay dumb and bear the kisses you give me, kisses which I end by returning. My lips when you kiss them draw back in repulsion and yet in the end they yield and go out to meet yours. Shall I go on? [*A pause. She looks him full in the face*] No! You understand now. You can never again imagine the tears I shed are tears of love. They are tears of remorse and misery. I hate you after your kisses. Our love is a duel in which I am worsted because what is best in me turns traitor. I blush at your victories because you could never have gained them without the help of what is base in me, without the baseness you know how to excite. It is not I who yield. It is the animal in me. It is all that is vile. I hate you for the crime of our loveless marriage, the crime you force me to share. I admit you are not the only guilty one, you are not the only one worthy of contempt. But I have had enough of it. Enough of it. I will no longer spend my days weeping over the shame of my nights. Every evening I have said I will regain my freedom. Till now I have not dared to say the words that would release me. Now I have done it. I am free.

ANTONIN [*shrugging his shoulders*] You are nothing of the sort.

JULIE. What do you mean?

ANTONIN. I mean that I have more common sense than you. I mean that it is my duty to guard you from these exaggerated fancies of yours. The bonds that join us are not to be broken by a whim. You are my wife and my wife you will remain. A divorce is impossible. I have given you no cause. You may leave me, of course, but you know the life of the woman who lives apart from her husband, a life without respect and without social position. No: you will stay with me.

JULIE. And it is this prison that we call marriage. [*A pause*] And when I think that I looked forward with longing to this: that I sighed for it: that all my girlhood I was hoping for it, dreaming of it. When I think that at this very moment there are girls kneeling by their bedsides, young girls whose hearts are yearning for this. [*She begins to cry*] Ah, poor girls! Poor girls! If they only knew! [*She wipes her eyes, after a moment*] Just Heaven, what a fool I am! Here am I, crying when I should be laughing. The thing is ludicrous. Why, if one dared, one would shake with laughter at it all. You may be tyrants, all of you, but you are so absurd that, when one thinks, one can scarcely hate you for it. What you have made of marriage! From start to finish: from the wedding morning, with its monkey tricks, its vanity, and its folly. When I think that there are still people who respect such mummery! [*She bursts out laughing*].

ANTONIN. Julie! Don't laugh like that!

JULIE. Oh, my dear sir, leave me alone. It's well for you I take it laughing. If I took it seriously, what sort of figure would you cut? Everything about a wedding is absurd, just because it is so detestable. Yes; everything. From the moment when you set it before us as a duty to hand ourselves over to our lords on such and such a day, at such and such an hour, at a date and a minute fixed beforehand. How is it that brides do not die of shame under the curious eyes of the wedding guests and the thoughts they hide? To think that they are passing the day among people who know. Pah! Oh, yes; I am quite aware how ridiculous the bride looks. [*She puts her hand familiarly on his shoulder*] But don't imagine the bridegroom cuts a very brilliant figure. [*She laughs*] You all wear a look of stupid complacency, like a contented animal sure of its prey. And there must be a dot, and you must be bought, and a price must be paid you in order that you may marry us. Oh, yes. You have arranged things finely among you, with your Deputies' scarves and your music and incense. And you need them. But do you think they impose on anyone nowadays? No.

ANTONIN. You make out too good a case for yourself. And it's not fair to make me responsible. All this is as much the result of your acts as of mine.

JULIE. Indeed! I am curious to hear what those acts are.

ANTONIN. I'll tell you.

JULIE. Have I ever failed in my duty? Haven't I been —

ANTONIN [*sternly*] Be silent. I'm going to have my say. It's no good your trying to play the injured victim. You did exactly the same as I did. When I proposed for you, I was not in love with you, I admit it. I didn't love you as you want to be loved. Yet you accepted me.

JULIE. Do you suppose I knew? What did I understand about life? How could I have guessed —

ANTONIN. You knew perfectly well the sort of love

I felt for you, — a sort of love every mother tries to rouse in any young man she wants to catch for her daughter. And the daughters take a hand in the game, too, bless their little hearts!

JULIE. Do you mean to say *I* did such a thing?

ANTONIN. Yes, I do. You began this plain speaking; I 'm going on with it. You wanted the cards on the table and you shall have them. Let us both own up. We know now what marriage is, our own and everybody else's. We know all the tricks, all the humbug of it. Let 's look it in the face. Your parents deceived mine.

JULIE. And yours?

ANTONIN. They did the same. I 'm not denying it. But did you help them? Yes or no?

JULIE. No.

ANTONIN. Yes, you did. I remember well enough how you helped them to cajole me, trap me, dupe me. Oh, I know it sounds ridiculous. I know each petty incident taken by itself amounts to nothing. But these deceptions of yours have their importance, for you only made use of them to catch me. You played on my weaknesses. You knew I was fond of money — we 're talking straight to each other, remember — you knew I was fond of money and you represented yourself as a model young woman who always made her own dresses. You remember that? And Wagner! Wagner, whose music you professed to admire so much, when you knew as little about him as I do. According to your own account lots of men had wanted to marry you. That was a lie. You had helped your father in keeping his books and were interested in my banking business. *That* was a lie, too.

JULIE. If that is all you have to reproach me with —

ANTONIN. It is not all. There was another lie to which you condescended. And that was a serious one, because you sacrificed your womanly dignity to your interest. You have forgotten it? I have not. Why it was here, here in this very room where we are at this moment, that you sat dressed for a ball. You were not going to a ball. I knew that later. But they told you to put on that dress, and you know why. Well, that trick came off all right. [*Julie, confused, hides her face in her hands*] I behaved as most men behave. I wanted to take your arm and kiss it. You objected as any decent woman would. But when you saw I was annoyed you said to yourself that a husband was well worth the sacrifice of a little modesty, and you came deliberately and let me kiss you as I wished. Is n't it true? Is n't it? I tried to deceive you, I admit it. But if I lied you lied, too. Marriages like ours may be shameful. I don't know. But don't try to thrust the whole responsibility on me when you 're equally guilty. [*Julie's head sinks lower. A pause*] The other things you say about me I dare say I deserve. I 'm ambitious. I want to succeed. Is it my fault that success is the only road to social consideration nowadays? In order to succeed I must truckle to people who can be useful to me and I ask you to help me. I 'm not a hero. I 'm like the rest of the world. I did n't make either myself or them. We are to be pitied, both of us. But I 'm more to be pitied than you are, for you don't love me and I can't help loving you. What shall I do if you leave me? My position will be compromised, my business ruined. And more than all that I shall have lost you. I don't speak as I ought; I am a fool, a dolt. I ought to have told you this at first instead of going over all that wretched business. But it 's true, it 's far worse for me than for you [*much moved*], for I love you in spite of all you can say, and the idea of losing you is like being told that I am going to die. [*He sobs*] And what have I done after all? I 've only done as other men do. Why should *I* be the only one to be punished? Ah, Julie, my little Julie, pity me. I'm very unhappy. [*He weeps, bowed over the table, his head in his hands*].

JULIE [*putting her hand upon his head and speaking in a low expressionless voice*]   Poor fellow!

ANTONIN [*still weeping*]   You *are* sorry for me, aren't you? Say you are.

JULIE. Yes, we are both of us victims.

ANTONIN. That's it. Ever since I was born my parents have taught me that the great thing in life was to be rich.

JULIE [*nodding sadly*]   Mine too.

ANTONIN. Unless one gets on nobody thinks anything of one.

JULIE. And marriage is one of the ways of getting on.

ANTONIN. That's what ruined us.

JULIE. Yes. It has ruined our lives as it has ruined so many others.

ANTONIN [*recovering his composure*]   You understand, then? You *do* understand, don't you?

JULIE [*dully*]   Yes.

ANTONIN [*taking her hand, which she does not draw away*]   You're not angry? [*Julie says nothing*]   It is all over, is n't it? [*patting her hand*]   All quite over and done with. [*She is still silent*]   You see that I mustn't do anything that might damage the business? You see that?

JULIE. Yes.

ANTONIN. And that it's better not to offend people who may be useful to us. Isn't it?

JULIE. Yes.

ANTONIN. After all, why shouldn't one go to Mass? Come, come. [*He smiles*]   We have been silly, haven't we, to say all that? It's forgotten now, isn't it? Say it's forgotten!

JULIE [*relucantly*]   Yes.

ANTONIN [*recovering his spirits*]   That's a good little

woman. There, there. One disputes, one flies into a passion, one runs on and on, one says terrible things [*laughing*]. What things you said to me. Oh, it was shocking. But there, we'll never speak of it again. Never. Never. Let's make it up. [*He takes her in his arms: hesitating, she lets him do so*] We're friends again, eh? And now go and wash your face, or people will see you've been crying. Are my eyes red, too? No, I expect not. Shall I tell you something? You won't believe it. You'll be shocked. Do you know, I almost think perhaps it's as well we've said all these things to each other. You see, now we know each other better. You understand about some of my worries. The business isn't going as I should wish. That makes my temper rather quick at times. No; things might be better. If you would say a word to Caroline, perhaps she would change her mind about that money.

JULIE [*still on her guard*] I will try.

ANTONIN. That's a good girl. And it's only for a little while that we shall have to be careful. We are only two and we shall pull through it. Luckily, we've only ourselves to think of. Imagine what it would be if we were expecting a baby!

JULIE. That would give me courage.

ANTONIN. Nonsense, my dear. We can do very well without that.

JULIE [*alarmed*] But we *are* going to have children, aren't we?

ANTONIN [*after a moment's hesitation, firmly*] No.

JULIE. Why not?

ANTONIN. How absurd you are. Because I don't choose, of course.

JULIE. But we've often talked of having children. You've made plans with me about what we should do with them.

ANTONIN [*laughing*] I know. You liked it, and it

was something to talk about. But for the future we 're
to be perfectly straight with one another.

JULIE. Do you mean that we are *never* to have any
children?

ANTONIN [*nods*] We can't afford them, my dear, at
present. And if we wait till we 're forty [*shrugs*],
people would laugh.

JULIE. Don't you know what it was that made me
willing to marry? Don't you know that it was this
thought of having children, this and this alone, that decided me? And you refuse me this? To be a wife, to be
a mother, is the natural end of life for me. And something will be wanting and my life will be incomplete, and
I shall not have *lived* if my arms have never clasped a
baby born of my flesh; if I have never suckled it, cried
over it, felt all the cares and all the joys that mothers
feel. And you would rob me of this? Merely because
you love money, because you are self-seeking and ambitious. Great Heavens, to think that you should have
such power over my life! People talk of tyranny; they
make revolts against Governments; there are women
who clamor for a vote; who demand that the marriage
law should be the same for women as for men; and they
don't understand that it is marriage itself they should
attack, that they should attack with fury, since it allows
such an infamy.

ANTONIN. For goodness' sake don't begin again. Remember, we made it up.

JULIE. Made it up! Just God! what name is there
vile enough for me to fling in your face? Are you so
utterly base that you think *now* there can be any thought
of reconciliation between us? After what you have just
told me, do you suppose that I would submit to — Think
what it means. Think what the thing you men call love
means to women if it has neither affection nor children
for its justification.

Antonin. I won't answer you. You don't know what you're saying. You're mad, and I shall treat you accordingly. To begin with, go to your room and try to calm yourself. Go! [*He tries to take her by the arm*].

Julie [*shrieking*] Don't touch me! Don't touch me! [*She pushes him violently away*].

Antonin [*furious*] Look here, Julie; I'm not going to stand this. I tell you to go to your room at once.

Julie. Don't touch me!

Antonin. I shall touch you if I please. Oh, you may scream if you like. You're my wife, and I've the right to do as I choose with you.

Julie. Take your hands off me! I hate you, I say! I hate you!

Antonin. You hate me? I dare say. But if you suppose that I'm a genteel husband out of a book, who lets his wife lock her door against him, you're vastly mistaken. I've married you, I love you, and I intend to keep you. Hate me, do you? Very well. Escape from me if you can. [*He takes her in his arms. There is a struggle. Furniture is overturned. No word is spoken, but you can hear their deep breathing. Suddenly Antonin cries out*] Curse you, you've bitten me!

Julie. Yes. And I will *kill* you if you don't let me go!

Antonin [*transported with rage*] We shall see which of us is master.

Julie. We shall see!

Antonin. We *shall!* [*Antonin goes out in a violent passion*].

Julie, left alone, straightens her hair and dress mechanically, muttering to herself inaudibly. Suddenly she falls upon a couch, and then upon the ground, where she lies sobbing in an agony of misery.

ACT IV

The same scene. M. and Madame Dupont are sitting together.

DUPONT. She's determined to leave him, then?

MME. DUPONT. Quite determined.

DUPONT. And he?

MME. DUPONT. After the scene I told you of he went straight out of the house and he has n't come back since.

DUPONT. He did n't sleep at home last night?

MME. DUPONT. No.

DUPONT [*scornfully*] He has gone back to "maman," no doubt. [*He goes to the window*].

MME. DUPONT [*after a pause*] Why do you keep looking out of that window?

DUPONT. I'm watching the lawyer's opposite. Caroline went in five minutes ago. I'm terribly afraid Angèle won't come. [*To himself*] Confound Caroline! Who the Dickens can have got hold of that other fifteen thousand francs? [*Joyfully*] There's Angèle. Look! She's going in now. What did you say? Bless my soul, my daughters give me worry enough. Yes; he has gone back to "maman." And you think this won't blow over, eh?

MME. DUPONT. I'm certain it won't. Julie will never forgive him.

DUPONT [*almost with triumph*] That means a divorce then, eh?

MME. DUPONT. Yes. A divorce.

DUPONT. Ah! And who was the clever one this time, too, eh? Who was it?

MME. DUPONT. I don't know.

DUPONT. Of course not. Well, *I* was.

MME. DUPONT. In what way?

DUPONT. You say she'll ask for a divorce?

MME. DUPONT. Unless he does.

DUPONT. Very well, then. Whichever way it is her money was settled on herself, and our good Antonin will have to give back the thirty thousand francs and my house. Thanks to me. Thanks to *me*. [*He rubs his hands*].

The maid comes in.

MAID. M. and Madame Mairaut.

DUPONT. Show them in. [*The maid goes out. To his wife*] Don't go.

M. and Madame Mairaut come in.

MME. MAIRAUT [*turning to the door and speaking to her husband, who hangs back*] Are you coming in or are you not?

MAIRAUT. I'm coming. [*He closes the door*].

Formal greetings are exchanged.

MME. MAIRAUT [*sitting down*] After what passed between us yesterday —

DUPONT [*with dangerous sweetness*] About Uncle Maréchal's money?

MME. MAIRAUT [*appearing not to have heard*] After what passed between us yesterday, I intended never to set foot in this house again.

DUPONT [*bowing*] It rested entirely with you, madame.

MME. MAIRAUT. Since then, however, grave differences have arisen between our children.

DUPONT. Very grave.

MME. MAIRAUT. You know, then?

DUPONT. Yes.

MME. MAIRAUT. We are come therefore, my husband and I, in the name of our son, formally to request your daughter, Madame Antonin Mairaut, to return to her husband's roof.

DUPONT. *His* roof?

MME. MAIRAUT. To St. Laurent. My son awaits her there.

DUPONT. He 'll have to wait some time. My daughter will not return to her husband. You are welcome to bring an officer of the Court to bear witness to the fact. It will provide your son with a ground for his divorce.

MME. MAIRAUT [*sweetly*] There is no question of a divorce.

DUPONT [*astonished*] What? No question of a divorce?

MME. MAIRAUT. None, monsieur.

DUPONT. In spite of my daughter's refusal —

MME. MAIRAUT. In spite of her refusal.

DUPONT. In spite of what she has said to her husband?

MME. MAIRAUT. In spite of that, too.

DUPONT. In spite of anything she may do in the future?

MME. MAIRAUT. In spite of anything she may do. There is no question of a divorce and there never will be.

DUPONT. On your part, you mean?

MME. MAIRAUT. On yours also. We shall give you no grounds. My son is waiting for his wife to return to him. He is ready to receive her whenever she sees fit to present herself.

DUPONT. Whatever she does?

MME. MAIRAUT. Whatever she does.

DUPONT. Even if —

MME. MAIRAUT. Even in that case. [*Movement of Mairaut*]. What is it, my dear?

MAIRAUT. Nothing.

DUPONT. The truth is you would rather risk your son's honor than give back the thirty thousand francs.

MME. MAIRAUT [*still very sweetly*] After all, thirty thousand francs is a considerable sum. [*Mairaut fidgets uneasily*].

DUPONT. Yesterday, when he went away, your son uttered certain threats.

MME. MAIRAUT [*still sweetly*] He has decided not to put them into execution.

MME. DUPONT. You know, of course, that Julie will never agree —

MME. MAIRAUT. I can't help that.

MME. DUPONT. All their lives they will be chained to one another. Young as they are, they must give up the idea of having a home.

MME. MAIRAUT. Your daughter has only to return to her duty. Antonin will receive her.

MAIRAUT [*breaking out*] No! I won't have it! I have a word to say on this.

MME. MAIRAUT. What's the matter now? Pray speak if you have anything to say.

MAIRAUT [*loudly*] What we are doing is an infamy.

MME. MAIRAUT. Hold your tongue!

MAIRAUT. I won't.

MME. MAIRAUT. Hold your tongue, I tell you!

MAIRAUT. No! And don't you try to shut me down. Do you hear?

MME. MAIRAUT. What's taken the man? I've never seen him like this before.

MAIRAUT. I tell you this is infamous! Infamous! I've thought so for a long time, ever since the day you would n't let me speak out about Uncle Maréchal. I said nothing because I was afraid of you. For thirty years I have said nothing. But now this is too much, and I say what I think. It's an infamy! Come what may, I will say it. Sit down! I tell you it's an infamy!

Rogues have been meddling with these children's lives
too long; it's time for honest men to take a hand in
them. I'm going to do it.

Mme. Mairaut.   Pay no attention to him. He's out
of his senses.

Mairaut.   Be silent, you! M. and Madame Dupont
this is what I have to say to you. An effort must be
made to reconcile Julie and Antonin. If this is impossible, *I* will pay you back the thirty thousand
francs.

Mme. Mairaut [*with a scream*]   Good Heavens, what
is he saying?

Mairaut.   I will return the thirty thousand francs,
and you'll see after that if my precious son won't be the
first to talk of a divorce.

Mme. Mairaut [*to her husband*]   You shall pay for
this when we get home.

Mairaut.   As you please. And now be off, and be
quick about it. [*Madame Mairaut goes out*]   Au revoir,
M. and Madame Dupont. Do what you can on your side,
and I will try and make Antonin come and beg his wife's
pardon.

Dupont.   Good-evening, M. Mairaut.

Mme. Dupont.   Count on me, M. Mairaut, and give
me your hand. You're a good man.

Mairaut [*as he goes*]   That's all right.   [*He goes*].

Dupont.   Are you really going to try?

Mme. Dupont.   Yes.

Dupont.   But since old Mairaut is willing to give
back the money?

Mme. Dupont.   I won't make up my mind to a divorce
until I'm absolutely convinced there's no other way.

Dupont.   But there is no other way. You said so
yourself.

Mme. Dupont.   Are you sure you aren't thinking
more of your money than of the happiness of your child?

DUPONT. I! Well, I declare! Are you taking a leaf out of old Mairaut's book?

MME. DUPONT [*gravely*] Perhaps so.
Madame Mairaut returns.

MME. MAIRAUT. I have come back for two things. First, to advise you not to count too much on my husband's promise. Next, to thank you for the fresh insult you have put upon us.

DUPONT. What insult?

MME. MAIRAUT. You don't know, I suppose, to whom Mlle. Caroline has given half her legacy?

DUPONT. No. But I shall be glad to learn.

MME. MAIRAUT. To your clerk, Courthezon.

DUPONT. Courthezon? It's a lie!

MME. DUPONT. Courthezon!

MME. MAIRAUT. She has just told me so herself.
Caroline comes in.

MME. DUPONT. Caroline, is it really to Courthezon that you've given the fifteen thousand francs?

DUPONT. You have given fifteen thousand francs to Courthezon?

MME. MAIRAUT. Isn't it to Courthezon that you have given the fifteen thousand francs?

CAROLINE. Yes.

DUPONT. You are crazy!

MME. DUPONT. What possessed you to do that?

MME. MAIRAUT. For his invention! An invention not worth twopence, Antonin says.

MME. DUPONT. You think more of strangers than your own flesh and blood.

DUPONT. Just at the very time when my plant needed renewing.

MME. MAIRAUT. And when her brother-in-law is on the verge of bankruptcy. Yes, mademoiselle, yes! And this money, which you give to a crack-brained inventor who is nothing to you, might perhaps have saved your sister from penury. That is all I have to say to you. Good-bye. [*She goes*].

DUPONT. Well! Perhaps now you 'll tell us why you have done this?

MME. DUPONT. What has taken you? How did such an idea come into your head?

DUPONT. Do you imagine his invention will make your fortune?

CAROLINE. No.

DUPONT. Do you know anything at all about it?

CAROLINE. No.

MME. DUPONT. Did he ask you to lend him money?

CAROLINE. No.

DUPONT. Then you ought to be put in an asylum. You 're out of your senses.

MME. DUPONT. I still can't make out how you came to have such an idea.

CAROLINE [*beginning to cry*] I was unhappy.

DUPONT. What! You give away fifteen thousand francs to the first comer because you are unhappy!

CAROLINE. I hope he will be grateful for what I have done for him, and that —

DUPONT. Well?

CAROLINE. I am no longer young, I know; but he is not young either.

DUPONT. You think he will *marry* you!

CAROLINE. Yes.

DUPONT. Then you don't know —

MME. DUPONT. Hush!

CAROLINE. I can't go on living alone. I am too wretched. For a long time I have thought — when I saw M. Courthezon, so steady and careful and quiet — I thought I could be happy with him. But I knew he would never marry me without money, and there was only enough for Julie. The time when I was most unhappy was when M. Antonin was here. He used to talk to Julie. They took no notice of me. They used to kiss one another. And though I don't think I'm jealous, it made me very wretched. So when this legacy came, and I knew M. Courthezon needed money for his invention, I thought I would give him some.

MME. DUPONT. You should at least have given him some idea of what you meant. It would have saved you from disappointment, my poor child.

DUPONT. You should have spoken to me. I could have told you why you had nothing to hope in that quarter.

CAROLINE. Nothing to hope? But why? Why?

DUPONT. Because for twenty years Courthezon has been living with a married woman. He does not speak of it, of course, but they have two children.

CAROLINE [*faintly*] God have pity on me! [*She almost falls*].

MME. DUPONT. Caroline! My child!

DUPONT. My child! Come, come! You must be reasonable.

MME. DUPONT. You must n't cry like that.

CAROLINE [*sobbing*] No.

DUPONT [*to his wife*] This is your fault. We should have told her that Courthezon — But you always said no.

MME. DUPONT. One can't tell things like that to a young girl. And afterwards, when she was grown up, it did n't seem worth while. [*To Caroline*] Don't cry any more, dear.

CAROLINE [*stifling her sobs by a great effort*] I am not crying any more.

DUPONT. There is only one thing to be done. We must try and get the money back from Courthezon.

CAROLINE. No! No!

DUPONT. We shall see. [*He hurries out*].

CAROLINE. Stop him! Stop him, mother! Go at once. Stop him, I beg of you!

MME. DUPONT. Very well, dear. [*She follows her husband*].

Caroline is left alone for a moment. Then Angèle comes in.

ANGÈLE [*very tenderly*] Caroline, are you in trouble?

CAROLINE [*in a low voice*] Yes.

ANGÈLE. What about? Tell me!

CAROLINE [*in an expressionless voice, but not angrily*] No. It is over now.

ANGÈLE. You won't tell me?

CAROLINE [*coldly*] It would be useless.

ANGÈLE. Who knows? Come! I can see you have been crying.

CAROLINE. Yes. We are very unfortunate, Julie and I.

ANGÈLE. Julie?

CAROLINE. She is leaving her husband.

ANGÈLE. Why?

CAROLINE. They cannot go on living together any longer.

ANGÈLE. And you?

CAROLINE. I? [*She makes a gesture of hopelessness*].
Julie comes in.

JULIE. I was looking for you, Caroline. I am going away sooner than I expected. They say my husband is coming here. I do not wish ever to see him again. So I am going.

CAROLINE. What will you do?

JULIE. I shall do as you do; hire a room somewhere and get work.

CAROLINE. What kind of work?

JULIE. I don't know. Anything I can get.

CAROLINE. Don't do that, Julie. Don't! [*Deeply distressed*] If you only knew!

JULIE. What?

CAROLINE. The wretchedness of living alone.

JULIE. I'm not afraid. I shall work so hard that I shall have no time for moping.

CAROLINE. You will work. [*She sighs*] It isn't easy for a woman who is alone to earn her living.

JULIE. Nonsense.

CAROLINE. I know what I'm talking about. Sometimes when I take my work to the shop they refuse it with an insolent contempt they would never dare to show to a man. It's true. For I am doubly unprotected since I am a woman and I need work.

JULIE. But in your own room, at least, you are free.

CAROLINE. Free! [*With a mirthless laugh*] If that is freedom, give me slavery.

JULIE. I shall have friends.

CAROLINE. Do you think so? The women will have nothing to do with you because you'll be a wife living apart from her husband, and because you will be dull. And the men? What will people say if they visit you?

JULIE. Little I care what people will say.

CAROLINE. Still for your own sake you will have to send them away.

JULIE. What do you advise, then? That I should remain with my husband?

CAROLINE. Ah, Julie dear, you complain of not being loved as you wish to be. What can *I* say to that, I whom no man will ever take in his arms? I who feel myself a thing apart, useless, absurd, incomplete. You don't know what a void that means for a woman: to have no one to forgive, no one to devote herself to. And the world sneers at women for remaining single. It makes their loneliness a reproach. Look at me, hardly allowed to dispose of my own property, black looks all round me because I have dared to use my own money in my own way.

JULIE. Poor Caroline!

CAROLINE. Yes. You may well pity me. And if I told you all. I turned to religion for consolation. For a while it cheated my craving for love; but it couldn't give me peace, and it has only left me more bitter and more disillusioned. For months I buoyed myself up on one last hope. I was a fool. [*Weeping*] Ah, no one need tell me how absurd it was. I know it well enough. I, at my age and in these clothes, much like everyone else's clothes, only everything looks ridiculous on me. *I* to fall in love! I must be crazy. Don't laugh at me. I have suffered so much. I knew he couldn't love me, but I hoped he would be grateful for what I — I only wanted his gratitude and his pity; no more, I swear to you. And now it seems there is some other woman. [*A pause*] Oh, what good was it to guard my good name as a miser guards his gold if this is all? No, Julie; don't spoil your life a second time. If you cannot resign yourself to living with your husband, at least don't follow my example. Don't try to live my life. One of us is enough. Don't try to earn your bread. It is too hard, and men have made it too humiliating.

JULIE. But, Caroline, if people see me accepting hardship with courage, living alone deliberately, because I choose, surely the dignity of my life will make them respect me?

CAROLINE. No one will believe in the dignity of your life.

JULIE. Then it is monstrous! That is all I can say. Monstrous! And since to pay for bread to eat and clothes to wear and a roof to cover me I must either give myself to a husband I hate or to a lover whom, perhaps, I may love, I choose the lover. If I must sell myself to someone, I prefer to choose the buyer.

ANGÈLE. You are mad! Mad! Be reconciled to
your husband. That is the best thing you can do.

JULIE. So everybody says. Well, I tell you I will
not! I will not!

ANGÈLE. You would soon be glad enough to have
your married life back again, bad as it may be; or
even Caroline's poverty.

JULIE [*scornfully*] You think so?

ANGÈLE [*passionately*] You don't know what you
are saying. You don't understand, Julie. You to talk
like that! You to wish — Oh, you don't understand.

JULIE. You did it, yourself.

ANGÈLE [*with great emotion*] Yes, I did it. But I
would strangle myself rather than begin it again.
Julie, I entreat you. What am I to say? How am I
to stop you? I can't tell you and Caroline all the
shame I have endured. Oh, don't make me do that.

JULIE. Well, you 're happy *now,* at least.

ANGÈLE. Happy! When I went off with Georges —
They told you, did n't they? Well, his people got him
away from me. His mother was dying of grief. Yes:
I know that is not what you wish to hear, but I must
tell you, that you may understand how I came to fall
as low as I did. I was left alone with the child. I
had to feed it, had n't I? You can understand that, at
least. But how? Work? I tried to get work. But
they told me to wait. How was I to wait? And then
— my God! that I should have to tell you all this —
then I let myself go. [*She sobs*] And afterwards —
No: I can't speak of it. But you understand, Julie.
You can guess. You can imagine what my life was
when you see that even now I can't bring myself to
tell you about it. [*Mastering herself*] You think
women — women like me — are happy because you
see us laugh. But to laugh is our trade. We are paid
for that. And I swear to you often we would ask

nothing better than just to sit and cry. And you talk of *choosing!* You poor child! Do you suppose we women *choose?* Oh, if you could but know how one comes to loathe the whole world, to be wicked, *wicked!* They despise us so. We have no friends, no pity, no justice. We are robbed, exploited. I tell you all this, anyhow, just as it comes, but you understand, don't you? And once you start downhill you can't stop. That is our life, the life of women like me. That is the slough in which I have struggled ten years. No, no, Julie! No, little sister! I implore you don't do as I did. It is too horrible, too abject, too degraded.

JULIE. Poor Angèle.

ANGÈLE. You understand, don't you?

JULIE. Yes.

ANGÈLE [*rising*] I must go. Good-bye. I dare not look either of you in the face again now that you know everything, now that I remember what I once was. I knew you could never have anything more to do with me. But I felt such a craving to be loved that I half fancied you, at least, Caroline — I see I was wrong. Well, good-bye, I am going away. Forgive me, both of you, for what I have done. Good-bye. [*She turns to the door*].

CAROLINE. Angèle! [*A pause. Angèle turns at the door*] I pity you with all my heart. [*Another pause*] May I kiss you? [*Angèle throws herself into her arms*].

ANGÈLE. Caroline! My kind, good Caroline!

The three sisters embrace with tears.

Dupont, Antonin, and Mairaut come in.

ANTONIN [*pushed forward by his father. To Julie*] My dear wife, I have come to ask you to forgive me.

JULIE. It is I who ask *you* to forgive *me*. I was full of romantic ideas. I thought marriage something quite different from what it is. Now that I understand

I will be reasonable. One must make allowances. I will make some — to myself.

DUPONT. That's right.

ANTONIN. That's right. You can't imagine how glad I am that you understand me at last. It seems to me it's only from to-day that our marriage really begins.

JULIE. Perhaps.

ANTONIN. To celebrate our reconciliation I will give a grand dinner. I will invite the Pouchelets, the Rambourgs, Lignol —

JULIE [sadly and with meaning] Exactly — Lignol.

DUPONT. Ah, my children, everything comes right when once you make up your mind to be like the rest of the world.

JULIE [slowly] Yes: like the rest of the world. I dreamed of something better. But it seems it was impossible.

DAMAGED GOODS

[Les Avariés]

Translated by

JOHN POLLOCK

Before the play begins the manager appears upon the stage and says: —

Ladies and Gentlemen,

I beg leave to inform you, on behalf of the author and of the management, that the object of this play is a study of the disease of syphilis in its bearing on marriage.

It contains no scene to provoke scandal or arouse disgust, nor is there in it any obscene word; and it may be witnessed by everyone, unless we must believe that folly and ignorance are necessary conditions of female virtue.

ACT I

The doctor's consulting room. To the right a large stained-glass window representing a religious subject. In front of this, on pedestals, bronzes and statues. Parallel to it a large Louis XIV writing-table littered with papers and statuettes. Between the desk and the window the doctor's chair. On the other side an arm-chair nearly facing the footlights and a stool. To the left the entrance door, which, when opened, reveals a corridor lined with tapestries, statues, and paintings. Beyond the door a large glass bookcase, above which hang portraits of Wallace, Dupuytren, and Ricord. Busts of celebrated physicians. A small table and two chairs. At the back a small door. The room is sumptuously furnished and literally encumbered with works of art.

George Dupont, in great distress and ill at ease, enters by the door at the back, takes his stick, gloves, and hat from the stool, and sits down on the sofa before the writing-table. He is a big fellow of twenty-six, with large, round eyes, and simple, but not ludicrous appearance. A heavy sigh escapes him. The doctor, a man of forty, with the ribbon of the Legion of Honor in the buttonhole of his frock-coat, follows and takes his seat. He gives the impression of a man of strength and intellect.

GEORGE. Well, doctor?

DOCTOR. Well! There is no doubt about your case.

GEORGE [*wiping his forehead*] No doubt — How do you mean no doubt?

187

DOCTOR. I mean it in the bad sense. [*He writes.
George turns pale, and stays silent for a moment in
terror. He sighs again*] Come, come! You must have
thought as much.

GEORGE. No, no.

DOCTOR. All the same!

GEORGE [*utterly prostrated*] Good God!

DOCTOR [*stops writing and observes him*] Don't be
frightened. Out of every seven men you meet in the
street, or in society, or at the theatre, there is at least
one who is or has been in your condition. One in seven,
fifteen per cent.

GEORGE [*quietly, as if to himself*] Anyhow, I know
what to do.

DOCTOR. Certainly. Here is your prescription. You
will take it to the chemist's and have it made up.

GEORGE [*taking the prescription*] No.

DOCTOR. Yes: you will do just what everyone else
does.

GEORGE. Everyone else is not in my position. I
know what to do. [*He raises his hand to his temple*].

DOCTOR. Five times out of ten the men who sit in
that chair before me do that, perfectly sincerely. Everyone thinks himself more unfortunate than the rest. On
second thoughts, and after I have talked to them, they
realize that this disease is a companion with which one
can live; only, as in all households, domestic peace is to
be had at the price of mutual concessions. Come now,
I repeat, there is nothing in all this beyond the ordinary.
It is simply an accident that might happen to anybody.
I assure you it is far too common to merit the name
" French disease." There is, in fact, none that is more
universal. If you wanted to find a motto for the creatures who make a trade of selling their love, you could
almost take the famous lines, " There is your master.
. . . It is, it was, or it must be."

GEORGE [*putting the prescription in the outer pocket of his coat*] But I at least ought to have been spared.

DOCTOR. Why? Because you are a man of good position? Because you are rich? Look round you. Look at these works of art; five are copies of John of Bologna's Mercury, six of Pigallo's, three are reproductions — in wax, to be sure — of the lost Wounded Love by Paccini; do you think that all these have been presented to me by beggars?

GEORGE [*groaning*] I 'm not a rake, doctor. My life might be held up as an example to all young men. I assure you, no one could possibly have been more prudent, no one. See here; supposing I told you that in all my life I have only had two mistresses, what would you say to that?

DOCTOR. That one would have been enough to bring you here.

GEORGE. No, doctor, not one of those two. No one in the world has dreaded this so much as I have; no one has ever taken such infinite precautions to avoid it. My first mistress was the wife of my best friend. I chose her on account of him; and him, not because I cared most for him, but because I knew he was a man of the most rigid morals, who watched his wife jealously and did n't let her go about forming imprudent connections. As for her, I kept her in absolute terror of this disease. I told her that almost all men were taken with it, so that she might n't dream of being false to me. My friend died in my arms: that was the only thing that could have separated me from her. Then I took up with a young seamstress.

DOCTOR. None of your other friends had sufficiently reassuring morals?

GEORGE. No. You know what morals are nowadays.

DOCTOR. Better than anyone.

GEORGE. Well, this was a decent girl with a family in needy circumstances to support. Her grandmother was an invalid, and there was an ailing father and three little brothers. It was by my means that they all lived. They used to call me Uncle Raoul — I was not so green as to give my real name, you see.

DOCTOR. Oh! Your Christian name, well — besides, it is always safer.

GEORGE. Why, of course. I told her and I let the others know that if she played me false I should leave her at once. So then they all watched her for me. It became a regular thing that I should spend Sunday with them, and in that sort of way I was able to give her a lift up. Church-going was a respectable kind of outing for her. I rented a pew for them and her mother used to go with her to church; they liked seeing their name engraved on the card. She never left the house alone. Three months ago, when the question of my marriage came up, I had to leave her. They all cried over my going. I 'm not inventing or exaggerating: they all cried. You see, I 'm not a bad sort. People do regret me.

DOCTOR. You were very happy. Why did you want to change?

GEORGE [*surprised at the question*] I wanted to settle down. My father was a notary, and before his death he expressed the wish that I should marry my cousin. It was a good match; her dowry will help to get me a practice. Besides, I simply adore her. She 's fond of me, too. I had everything one could want to make life happy. My acquaintances all envied me. [*Miserably*] And then a lot of idiots must give me a farewell dinner and make me gad about with them. See what has come of it! I have n't any luck, I 've never had any luck! I know fellows who lead the most racketty lives: nothing happens to them, the beasts! But I — for a wretched

lark — What is there left for a leper like me? My
future is ruined, my whole life poisoned. Well then,
is n't it better for me to clear out of it? Anyway, I shan't
suffer any more. You see now, no one could be more
wretched than I am. [*Crying*] No one, doctor, I tell
you, no one! [*He buries his face in his handkerchief*]
Oh, oh, oh!

DOCTOR [*rising and going to him with a smile*] You
must be a man, and not cry like a child.

GEORGE [*still in tears*] If I had led a wild life and
spent my time in bars and going about with women, I
should understand: I should say I deserved it.

DOCTOR. No.

GEORGE. No?

DOCTOR. No. You would not say so: but it does n't
matter. Go on.

GEORGE. Yes, I know I should. I should say I deserved it. But for nothing! nothing! I have cut myself
off from all pleasures. I have resisted attractions as you
would the devil. I would n't go with my friends to
places of amusement: ladies I knew actually pointed me
out to their boys as an example. I stuck to my work: I
forced myself to be more regular in my habits. Why, my
two friends helped me to prepare for my law exams.
I taught them to make me cram, and it 's thanks to them
that I got through. Oh, I should have liked to come
home at four o'clock in the morning with my coat-collar
turned up, smoking a cigar lit in some ballet-girl's rooms!
I 've longed as much as anyone for the taste of rouged
lips and the glitter of blacked eyes and pale faces! I
should have liked larks and jolly suppers and champagne and the rustle of lace and all the rest of it! I 've
sacrificed all that to my health, and see what I 've got
for it. Ah, if I had known! If I had only known!
Then I should have let myself go; yes, altogether!
That would have been something to the good, anyway!

When I think of it! When I think of the beastliness, the frightful horrors in store for me!

DOCTOR. What's all that nonsense?

GEORGE. Yes, yes, I know — hair falling out, camomile for a cocktail, and a bath chair for a motor car, with a little handle for the steering wheel and a fellow shoving behind instead of the engine; and I shall go, Gug, gug, gug, gug! [*Crying*] That's what will be left of handsome Raoul — that's what they called me, handsome Raoul!

DOCTOR. My dear sir, kindly dry your eyes for the last time, blow your nose, put your handkerchief in your pocket, and listen to me without blubbering.

GEORGE [*doing so*] Yes, doctor; but I warn you, you are wasting your time.

DOCTOR. I assure you —

GEORGE. I know what you are going to tell me.

DOCTOR. In that case you have no business here. Be off with you!

GEORGE. As I am here, I'll listen, doctor. It's awfully good of you.

DOCTOR. If you have the will and the perseverance, none of the things you are dreading will happen to you.

GEORGE. Of course. You are bound to tell me that.

DOCTOR. I tell you that there are a hundred thousand men in Paris like you, sound and in good health, I give you my word. Come, now! Bath chairs! You don't see quite so many as that.

GEORGE [*struck*] Nor do you.

DOCTOR. Besides, those who are in them are not all there for the reason you think. Come, come! You will not be the victim of a catastrophe any more than the other hundred thousand. The thing is serious: nothing more.

GEORGE. There, you see. It is a serious disease.

DOCTOR. Yes.

GEORGE.   One of the most serious.

DOCTOR.   Yes; but you have the good luck —

GEORGE.   Good luck?

DOCTOR.   Relatively, if you like; but you have the good luck to have contracted just that one among serious diseases which we have the most effective means of combating.

GEORGE.   I know: remedies worse than the disease.

DOCTOR.   You are mistaken.

GEORGE.   You 're not going to tell me that it can be cured?

DOCTOR.   It can.

GEORGE.   And that I am not condemned to —

DOCTOR.   I give you my word on it.

GEORGE.   You 're not — you 're not making some mistake?   I have been told —

DOCTOR [*shrugging his shoulders*]   You have been told! You have been told! No doubt you know all the ins and outs of the law of property.

GEORGE.   Yes, certainly; but I don't see what connection —

DOCTOR.   Instead of being taught that, it would have been much better if you had been told the nature of the disease from which you are suffering. Then, perhaps, you would have been sufficiently afraid to avoid contracting it.

GEORGE.   But this woman was so — well, who could have thought such a thing of her? I did n't take a woman off the streets, you know. She lives in the Rue de Berne — not exactly a low part of the town, is it?

DOCTOR.   The part of the town has nothing to do with it. This disease differs from many others; it has no preference for the unfortunate.

GEORGE.   But this woman lives almost straight. One of my chums has a mistress who 's a married woman. Well, it was a friend of hers. Her mother — she lives

with her mother — was abroad at the time. At first she
would n't listen to me: then, finally, after I had spent
a whole half-hour persuading her I had to promise her a
ring like one of her friend's before she would give way.
She even made me take off my boots before going upstairs so that the porter might n't hear.

Doctor. Well, if you had been taught, you would
have known that these circumstances are no guarantee.

George. That 's true; we ought to be taught.

Doctor. Yes.

George. At the same time it 's not a subject that can
be broached in the papers.

Doctor. Why not?

George. I can speak of my own knowledge, for my
father used to own a small provincial paper. If we had
ever printed that word, the circulation would have
dropped like a stone.

Doctor. Yet you would publish novels about adultery.

George. Of course. That 's what the public wants.

Doctor. You are right. It is the public that needs
to be educated. A respectable man will take his wife
and daughters to a music-hall, where they hear things
to make a doctor blush. His modesty is only alarmed
by serious words.

George. And then, after all, what would one gain
by being posted up about this disease?

Doctor. If it were better understood it would be
more often avoided.

George. What one wants is some means of avoiding
it altogether.

Doctor. Oh! That is quite simple.

George. Tell me.

Doctor. It is no longer any concern of yours; but
when you have a son you will be able to tell him what
to do.

George. What 's that?

DOCTOR. To love only one woman, to be her first lover, and to love her so well that she will never be false to you.

GEORGE. That's easy, is n't it? And if my son does not marry till he is twenty-eight, what then?

DOCTOR. Then, that he may run the least risk, you will tell him to go to the licensed dealers —

GEORGE. With a guarantee from the government.

DOCTOR. And to choose them a little stale.

GEORGE. Why so?

DOCTOR. Because at a certain age they have all paid their toll. The prettiest girl in the world can give all she has, not what she has no longer. That is what you will tell your sons.

GEORGE.. But do you mean that I can have children?

DOCTOR. Certainly.

GEORGE. Healthy ones?

DOCTOR. Perfectly healthy. I repeat: if you take proper and reasonable care of yourself for the necessary length of time, you have little to fear.

GEORGE. Is that certain?

DOCTOR. Ninety-nine times out of a hundred.

GEORGE. Then I shall be able to marry?

DOCTOR. You will be able to marry.

GEORGE. You're not deceiving me, are you? You would n't give me false hopes? You would n't — How soon shall I be able to marry?

DOCTOR. In three or four years.

GEORGE. What! three or four years? Not before?

DOCTOR. Not before.

GEORGE. Why? Am I going to be ill all that time? You said just now —

DOCTOR. The disease will no longer be dangerous to you yourself, but you will be dangerous to others.

GEORGE. But, doctor, I am going to be married in a month!

DOCTOR. Impossible.

GEORGE. I can't help it. The contract is all ready: the banns have been published. I have given my word.

DOCTOR. Here's a pretty patient! A moment ago you were feeling for your pistol; now you want to be married in a month!

GEORGE. But I must!

DOCTOR. I forbid you.

GEORGE. You can't mean that seriously. If this disease is not what I imagined, and if I can be cured, I shan't commit suicide. If I don't kill myself, I must take up the ordinary course of my life. I must fulfill my engagements: I must be married.

DOCTOR. No.

GEORGE. If my engagement were broken off it would be absolutely disastrous. You talk of it like that because you don't know. I didn't want to get married. I have told you — I had almost a second family; the children adored me. It is my old aunt, who owns all the property, who has pushed on the match. Then my mother wants to see me " settled " as she says. The only thing in the world she wants is to see her baby grand-children, and she wonders twenty times a day whether she will live long enough. Since the question first came up she simply hasn't thought of anything else; it's the dream of her life. And then I tell you I have begun to adore Henriette. If I draw back now my mother would die of grief, and I should be disinherited by my aunt. Even that isn't all. You don't know my father-in-law's character. He is a man of regular high old principles; and he has a temper like the devil. What's more, he simply worships his daughter. It would cost me dear, I can assure you. He would call me to account — I don't know what would happen. So there are my mother's health, my aunt's fortune, my future, my honor, perhaps my life, all at stake. Besides, I tell you I have given my word.

DOCTOR. You must take it back.

GEORGE. Well, since you stick to it, even if that were possible, I could not take back my signature to the contract for the purchase of a notary's practice in two months' time.

DOCTOR. All these —

GEORGE. You won't tell me that I have been imprudent because I have not disposed of my wife's dowry till after the honeymoon —

DOCTOR. All these considerations are foreign to me. I am a physician, nothing but a physician. I can only tell you this: if you marry before three or four years have elapsed you will be a criminal.

GEORGE. No, no! You are more than a physician: you are a confessor as well. You are not only a man of science. You can't observe me as you would something in your laboratory and then simply say: " You have this, science says that. Now be off with you!" My whole life depends upon you. You must listen to me; because when you know everything you will understand the situation and will find the means to cure me in a month.

DOCTOR. I can only tell you over and over again that no such means exist. It is impossible to be certain of your cure — as far as one can be certain — under three or four years.

GEORGE. I tell you that you must find one. Listen to me: if I am not married, I shall not get the dowry. Will you kindly tell me how I am to carry out the contract I have signed?

DOCTOR. Oh, if that is the question, it is very simple. I can easily show you the way out of the difficulty. Get into touch with some rich man, do everything you can to gain his confidence, and when you have succeeded, rook him of all he has.

GEORGE. I'm not in the mood for joking.

DOCTOR. I am not joking. To rob that man, or even

to murder him, would not be a greater crime than you would commit in marrying a young girl in good health to get hold of her dowry, if to do so you exposed her to the terrible consequences of the disease you would give her.

GEORGE.   Terrible?

DOCTOR.   Terrible; and death is not the worst of them.

GEORGE.   But you told me just now —

DOCTOR.   Just now I did not tell you everything. This disease, even when it is all but suppressed, still lies below the surface ready to break out again. Taken all round, it is serious enough to make it an infamy to expose a woman to it in order to avoid even the greatest inconvenience.

GEORGE.   But is it certain that she would catch it?

DOCTOR.   Even with the best intentions, I won't tell you lies. No; it is not absolutely certain. It is probable. And there is something else I will tell you. Our remedies are not infallible. In a certain number of cases — a very small number, scarcely five per cent. — they have no effect. You may be one of these exceptions or your wife may be. In that case — I will use an expression you used just now — in that case the result would be the most frightful horrors.

GEORGE.   Give me your advice.

DOCTOR.   The only advice I can give you is not to marry. To put it in this way, you owe a debt. Perhaps its repayment will not be exacted; but at the same time your creditor may come down on you suddenly, after a long interval, with the most pitiless brutality. Come, come! You are a man of business. Marriage is a contract. If you marry without saying anything, you will be giving an implied warranty for goods which you know to be bad. That is the term, is n't it? It would be a fraud which ought to be punishable by law.

George. But what can I do?

Doctor. Go to your father-in-law and tell him the un-varnished truth.

George. If I do that, it will not be a delay of three or four years that he will impose on me. He will refuse his consent for good.

Doctor. In that case, tell him nothing.

George. If I don't give him a reason, I don't know what he won't do. He is a man of the most violent tem-per. Besides, it will be still worse for Henriette than for me. Look here, doctor; from what I have said to you, no doubt you think I simply care for the money. Well, I do think it is one's primary duty to make certain of a reasonable amount of comfort. From my youth upwards I have always been taught that. Nowadays one must think of it, and I should never have engaged myself to a girl without money. It's perfectly natural. [*With emotion*] But she is so splendid, she is so much better than I am that I love her — as people love one another in books. Of course it would be a frightful dis-appointment not to have the practice that I have bought, but that would not be the worst for me. The worst would be losing her. If you could see her, if you knew her, you would understand. [*Taking out his pocket-book*] Look here; here's her photograph. Just look at it. [*The doctor gently refuses it*] Oh, my darling, to think that I must lose you or else — Ah! [*He kisses the photograph, then puts it back in his pocket*] I beg your pardon. I am being ridiculous. I know I am some-times. Only put yourself in my place. I love her so.

Doctor. It is on that account that you must not marry her.

George. But how can I get out of it? If I draw back without saying anything the truth will leak out and I shall be dishonored.

Doctor. There is nothing dishonorable about being ill.

George. Ah, yes! But people are such idiots. Even yesterday I myself should have laughed at anyone I knew who was in the position that I am in now. Why, I should have avoided him as if he had the plague. Oh, if I were the only one to suffer! But she — she loves me, I swear she does, she is so good. It will be dreadful for her.

Doctor. Less so than it would be later.

George. There 'll be a scandal.

Doctor. You will avoid a bigger one.

George quietly puts two twenty-franc pieces on the desk, takes his gloves, hat, and stick, and gets up.

George. I will think it over. Thank you, doctor. I shall come back next week as you told me to — probably. [*He goes toward the door*].

Doctor [*rising*] No: I shall not see you next week, and what is more you will not think it over. You came here knowing what you had, with the express intention of not acting by my advice unless it agreed with your wishes. A flimsy honesty made you take this chance of pacifying your conscience. You wanted to have someone on whom you could afterwards throw the responsibility of an act you knew to be culpable. Don't protest. Many who come here think as you think and do what you want to do. But when they have married in opposition to my advice the results have been for the most part so calamitous that now I am almost afraid of not having been persuasive enough. I feel as though in spite of everything I were in some sort the cause of their misery. I ought to be able to prevent such misery. If only the people who are the cause of it knew what I know and had seen what I have seen, it would be impossible. Give me your word that you will break off your engagement.

George. I can't give you my word. I can only repeat: I will think it over.

DOCTOR.   Think over what?

GEORGE.   What you have told me.

DOCTOR.   But what I have told you is true.   You cannot make any fresh objections.   I have answered those
you have made.   You must be convinced.

GEORGE.   Well, of course you are right in thinking that
I posted myself up a bit before coming to see you.   In
the first place, is it certain that I have the disease you
think?   You say so, and perhaps it is true.   But even the
greatest doctors are sometimes deceived.   Have n't I
heard that Ricord, your master, used to maintain that this
disease was not always contagious?   He produced cases
to prove his point.   Now you produce fresh cases to
disprove it.   Very well.   But I have the right to think it
over.   And when I think it over, I realize the results you
threaten me with are only probable.   In spite of your
desire to frighten me, you have been compelled to admit
that my marriage will quite possibly produce no ill results
for my wife.

DOCTOR [restraining himself with difficulty]   Go on.
I will answer you.

GEORGE.   You tell me that your drugs are powerful,
and that for the catastrophes you speak of to happen I
must be one of the five exceptions per cent. you allow,
and that my wife must be an exception too.   Now, if a
mathematician calculated the probabilities of the case,
the chance of a catastrophe would prove so small that,
when the slight probability of a disaster was set against
the certainty of all the disappointments and the unhappiness and perhaps the tragedies which my breaking off the match would cause, he would undoubtedly
come to the conclusion that I was right and you were
wrong.   After all, mathematics is more scientific than
medicine.

DOCTOR.   Ah, you think so!   Well, you are wrong.
Twenty cases identical with yours have been carefully

observed — from the beginning to the end. Nineteen
times — you hear, nineteen times in twenty — the woman
was contaminated by her husband. You think that the
danger is negligible: you think you have the right to
make your wife take her chance, as you said, of being
one of the exceptions for which we can do nothing!
Very well: then you shall know what you are doing.
You shall know what sort of disease it is that your wife
will have five chances per cent. of contracting without
so much as having her leave asked. Take this book —
it is my master's work — here, read for yourself, I
have marked the passage. You won't read it? Then I
will. [*He reads passionately*] " I have seen an unfortunate young woman changed by this disease into the
likeness of a beast. The face, or I should rather say,
what remained of it, was nothing but a flat surface
seamed with scars."

GEORGE. Stop, for pity's sake, stop!

DOCTOR. I shall not stop. I shall read to the end.
I shall not refrain from doing right merely for fear
of upsetting your nerves. [*He goes on*] " Of the
upper lip, which had been completely eaten away, not
a trace remained." There, that will do. And you are
willing to run the risk of inflicting that disease on a
woman whom you say you love, though you cannot support even the description of it yourself? And pray, from
whom did that woman catch syphilis? It is not I who
say all this: it is this book. " From a man whose criminal folly was such that he was not afraid to enter into
marriage in an eruption, as was afterwards established,
of marked secondary symptoms, and who had further
thought fit not to have his wife treated for fear of
arousing suspicion." What that man did is what you
want to do.

GEORGE. I should deserve all those names and worse
still, if I were to be married with the knowledge that

my marriage would bring about such horrors. But I do not believe that it would. You and your masters are specialists. Consequently you fix the whole of your attention on the subject of your studies, and you think that these dreadful, exceptional cases never have enough light thrown on them. They exercise a sort of fascination over you.

DOCTOR. I know that argument.

GEORGE. Let me go on, I beg. You have told me that one man in every seven is a syphilitic, and further that there are a hundred thousand such men going about the streets of Paris in perfect health.

DOCTOR. It is the fact that there are a hundred thousand who are not for the moment visibly affected by their complaint. But thousands have passed through our hospitals, victims to the most frightful ravages that our poor bodies can endure. You do not see them: they do not exist for you. Again, if it were only yourself who was in question, you might take that line well enough. But what I affirm, and repeat with all the strength of my conviction, is that you have no right to expose a human being to this appalling chance. The chance is rare, I know: I know still better how terrible it is. What have you to say now?

GEORGE. Nothing. I suppose you are right. I don't know what to think.

DOCTOR. Is it as if I were forbidding you ever to marry when I forbid you to marry now? Is it as if I were telling you that you will never be cured? On the contrary, I give you every hope. Only I ask a delay of three or four years, because in that time I shall be able to ascertain whether you are one of those unhappy wretches for whom there is no hope, and because during that time you will be a source of danger to your wife and children. The children: I have not spoken to you about them. [*Very gently and persuasively*] Come, my dear sir, you are too young and too generous to be insensible to pity. There are things that cannot fail to move you: it is incredible that I should not be able to touch or to convince you. Indeed, I feel most deeply for you; but on that account I implore you all the more earnestly to consider what I say. You have admitted you have no right to expose your wife to such torture: but there is not only your wife — there are her children, your children, whom you may contaminate, too. For the moment I will not think of you or of her: it is in the name of those innocent little ones that I appeal to you; it is the future of the race that I am defending. Listen to me. Of the twenty marriages I spoke of only fifteen produced children. They produced twenty-eight. Do you know how many of them survived? Three: three out of twenty-eight. Above all else syphilis is a child-murderer. Ah, yes! Every year produces a fresh massacre of the innocents. Herod still reigns in France and all the world over. And though it is my business to preserve life, I tell you that those who die are the lucky ones. If you want to see the children of syphilitic parents, go round the children's hospitals. We know the type: it has become classical. Any doctor can pick them out from the rest; little creatures old from their birth, stamped with the marks of every human infirmity and decay. You will find children with every kind of affliction: hump-backed, deformed, club-footed, hare-lipped, ricketty, with heads too big and bodies too small, with congenital hip-disease. A large proportion of all these are the victims of parents who were married in ignorance of what you now know. If I could, I would cry it aloud from the house-tops. [*A slight pause*] I have told you all this without the slightest exaggeration. Think it over. Weigh the pro and the con: tot up the sum of possible suffering and certain misery. But remember that on the one side is your own suffering — and on the other the suffering of other people. Remember that. Distrust yourself.

GEORGE. Very well. I give in. I will not be married. I will invent some excuse. I will get it put off for six months. More than that is impossible.

DOCTOR. I must have three years at least, if not four.

GEORGE. No, no! For pity's sake! You can cure me before that.

DOCTOR. No, no, no!

GEORGE. Yes, you can. I implore you. Science can do everything.

DOCTOR. Science is not God Almighty. The day of miracles is past.

GEORGE. Oh, you could if you wanted to. I know you could. Invent something, discover something! Try some new treatment on me. Double the doses! Give me ten times the ordinary ones, if you like! I'll stand anything, absolutely! Only there must be some way of curing me in six months. Look here, I can't be responsible for myself after that. For the sake of my wife and her children, do something.

DOCTOR. Nonsense!

GEORGE. If only you'll cure me, I don't know what I won't do for you. I'll be grateful to you all my life. I'll give you half my fortune. For God's sake, do something for me!

DOCTOR. You want me to do more for you than for all the rest?

GEORGE. Yes.

DOCTOR. Let me tell you, sir, that everyone of our patients, whether he is the richest man in the land or the poorest, has everything done for him that we can do. We have no secrets in reserve for the rich or for people who are in a hurry to be cured.

GEORGE. Good-bye, doctor.

DOCTOR. Good-day.

ACT II

George's study. To the left a window. In front of the window a desk of moderate size, facing away from the audience, and a writing-chair. On the desk a telephone. To the right of the desk an arm-chair, a small table with a work-box and embroidery, and between the window and the footlights a deep easy-chair. At the back a dainty bookcase, and in front of it a pretty table with flowers. At the back, to the right, a door, and, nearer, a piano and a music-stool. To the left another door. Two small chairs.

Henriette is sitting by the small table and working at a baby's cap. After a moment she holds it up on her hand.

HENRIETTE. Another little cap to send to nurse. How sweet my little Germaine will look in it! Come, sweetheart, laugh at mother! Oh, my love! [*She kisses the cap and goes on working*].

George enters at the back.

GEORGE [*opening the door and taking off his coat in the hall*] Hullo! Are you there? Are you there? Ha, ha, ha!

HENRIETTE [*rising gaily*] Oh, you know I recognized your voice.

GEORGE. What a story! [*Kissing her*] Poor little darling! — was she taken in? — poor little woman! Ha, ha, ha!

HENRIETTE [*laughing too*] Don't laugh like that!

GEORGE. "Hullo! Hullo! Madame George Du-

206

pont?" [*Imitating a woman's timid voice*] "Yes, yes; I am here!" I could feel you blushing at the end of the wire.

HENRIETTE [*laughing*] I did n't say " I am here " in that voice. I simply answered " Yes."

GEORGE. "Hullo! Madame George Dupont. Is George there? [*Laughing*] You were taken in! You can't say you were n't! [*In the woman's voice*] "George is out. Who is it speaking to me?" I could hardly keep it up. "Me — Gustave." You thought it was, too.

HENRIETTE. What is there astonishing in your friend Gustave telephoning?

GEORGE. And when I added [*imitating Gustave's voice*] "How are you this morning, dearest?" you gave a "What?" all flustered, like that: "What?"

HENRIETTE. Yes; but then I guessed it was you.

GEORGE. I went into fits. What a lark! [*He sits down in front of her on the arm of the chair close to the fireplace and watches her happily*].

HENRIETTE [*sitting down and returning his glance*] What a funny little fellow you are!

GEORGE. Me?

HENRIETTE [*gaily*] Do you think I don't understand you, after knowing you for fifteen years and being married to you a twelvemonth?

GEORGE [*curious*] Ah, well! go on. Say what you think of me.

HENRIETTE. To begin with, you 're anxious. Then you 're jealous. And suspicious. You spend all your time in making a tangle of things and then inventing ingenious ways of getting out of it.

GEORGE [*happy to hear himself talked about*] So that 's what you think of me? Go on, let us have some more.

HENRIETTE. Is n't it true?

GEORGE [*admitting it with a laugh*] Well?

HENRIETTE. Was n't it a trap that you set for me this morning?

GEORGE [*in the same tone*] No.

HENRIETTE. Yes; you wanted to be sure that I had not gone out. You asked me not to go to the Louvre to-day.

GEORGE [*innocently*] So I did.

HENRIETTE. See how suspicious you are, even of me.

GEORGE. No; not of you.

HENRIETTE. Yes, you are. But you have always been, so I don't mind. And then I know at the bottom you feel things so keenly that it makes you rather afraid.

GEORGE [*seriously*] I was laughed at so much when I was a boy.

HENRIETTE [*gaily*] Besides, perhaps you have reasons for not having too much confidence in men's friendships with their friends' wives. Gay deceiver!

GEORGE [*laughing*] I should like to know what you mean by that.

HENRIETTE. Suppose I had thought it was Gustave and answered: "Very well, thanks. How are you, darling?"

GEORGE [*laughing*] Well, it is a trick that I should n't like to try on everyone. [*Changing the conversation*] By the way, as I came in, Justin spoke to me.

HENRIETTE. Well?

GEORGE. He says he wants a rise.

HENRIETTE. He has chosen a likely moment.

GEORGE. Has n't he? I asked him if the sale of my cigars was not enough for him.

HENRIETTE. How did he take that?

GEORGE. He lost his temper and gave warning. This time I took him at his word. He's simply furious.

HENRIETTE. Good.

GEORGE. He'll go at the end of the month, and we shall be well rid of him. Mother will be delighted. I say, she hasn't wired, has she?

HENRIETTE. No.

GEORGE. Then she's not coming back till to-morrow.

HENRIETTE. If she had her way, she would never leave our little girl.

GEORGE. You're not going to be jealous, are you?

HENRIETTE. I'm a little anxious. Still, if there had been anything the matter, I know your mother would have telegraphed to us.

GEORGE. We agreed that she should, if there was anything since yesterday.

HENRIETTE. Perhaps after all we should have done better to keep baby with us.

GEORGE. Oh, are you going to begin again?

HENRIETTE. No, no. Don't scold. I know the air of Paris didn't suit her.

GEORGE. You still think that the dust of my papers was better for her than the air of the country?

HENRIETTE [*laughing*] No; I don't.

GEORGE. Of course, there is the square, with the smell of fried fish and all the soldiers.

HENRIETTE. Don't tease. I know you are right.

GEORGE. Aha! I'm glad you admit that for once at least.

HENRIETTE. Besides, nurse takes good care of her. She is a good girl.

GEORGE. And how proud she is to nurse the granddaughter of her deputy.

HENRIETTE. Father is not deputy for that district. All the same —

GEORGE. All the same he is deputy for the department.

HENRIETTE. Yes; he is.

GEORGE. Can't you hear her talking to her friends?

[*Imitating the nurse's voice*] " Have n't I had a bit of luck, neither? Yes, ma'am; she 's our deputy's daughter's daughter, she is. She 's as fat as a calf, the little duck; and that clever with it, she understands everything. That 's not a bit of luck, neither, is n't it? "

HENRIETTE [*laughing*] You great silly! She does n't talk like that at all.

GEORGE. Why not say at once that I can't do imitations?

HENRIETTE. Now I did n't say that.

GEORGE. As if mother would have engaged nurse for us if she had not been absolutely certain that baby would be well looked after. Besides, she goes down to see her every week, and she would have brought her back already —

HENRIETTE. Twice a week, sometimes.

GEORGE. Yes.

HENRIETTE. Ah, our little Germaine knows what it is to have a granny who dotes on her.

GEORGE. Does n't she, though?

HENRIETTE. Your mother is so good. You know I adore her, too.

GEORGE. Runs in the family!

HENRIETTE. Do you know, the last time we went down there with her — you had gone out somewhere or other —

GEORGE. To see that old sixteenth century chest.

HENRIETTE [*laughing*] Of course, your wonderful chest.

GEORGE. Well, what were you going to say?

HENRIETTE. You were out, and nurse had gone to mass, I think.

GEORGE. Or to have a drink. Go on.

HENRIETTE. I was in the little room, and your mother thought she was alone with Germaine. But I could hear her: she was telling baby all sorts of sweet little things

— silly little things, but so sweet that I felt like laughing and crying at the same moment.

GEORGE.   Did n't she call her "my own little Saviour"?

HENRIETTE.   Why, were you listening?

GEORGE.   No; but that's what she used to call me once on a time.

HENRIETTE.   It was that day she said she was sure baby had recognized her and laughed at her.

GEORGE.   One day, too, I went into mother's room here.   The door was ajar, so that she did n't hear me come in; and I found her looking at one of the little christening slippers she wanted baby to have.   You know.

HENRIETTE.   Oh, yes.

GEORGE.   And then she took it up and kissed it.

HENRIETTE.   What did you say to her?

GEORGE.   Nothing.   I went out as softly as I could and blew a kiss to her from the other side of the door.

HENRIETTE.   When nurse's letter came the other day, it did n't take her long to get ready and catch the 8.59.

GEORGE.   However, there was n't anything the matter.

HENRIETTE.   No; but still perhaps she was right. Perhaps I should have gone with her.

GEORGE.   Poor innocent little Henriette!   You believe everything you are told.   Now I saw at once what was up.   The nurse simply wanted to humbug us into raising her screw.   I bet she did.   Look here.   Will you bet me she did n't?   Come, what will you have?   Look here. I bet you that lovely necklace — you know, the one with the big pearl.

HENRIETTE.   No;   I should be too much afraid of winning.

GEORGE [laughing]   Silly!   I believe you think I don't care for baby as much as you do.   Why, you don't even know how old she is!   No, no, — exactly!   Let's see.

Aha! Ninety-one days and eight hours, there! [*He laughs*]. Ah, when she can get on by herself, then we 'll have her back with us. Six months more to wait.

HENRIETTE. Six months is a long time to wait. When I think that if you had not put off our marriage for six months, we should have her back now!

GEORGE. I have told you over and over again that I only did what was right. Just consider, how could I marry when the doctor told me I had traces of consumption?

HENRIETTE. Your doctor is a donkey. As if you looked like a consumptive!

GEORGE. Generally speaking, doctors are a bit that way, I grant.

HENRIETTE. And you actually wanted to wait three or four years.

GEORGE. Yes; to be quite certain I had nothing wrong with my lungs.

HENRIETTE. You call me innocent, me! And here were you, just because a doctor —

GEORGE. But you know it seems that I really had the beginning of some bronchial trouble. I used to feel something when I breathed rather hard — like that, only a little harder. There, that 's it. There was a sort of heaviness each side of my chest.

HENRIETTE. It was n't anything to put off our marriage for.

GEORGE [*getting up*] Yes, yes; I assure you I was right. I should have been wrong to expose you to the chance of having a consumptive husband. No; I 'm not at all sorry we waited. Still, those specialists — I can afford to laugh at them now. If I knew someone now who was ill, I should tell him: " My dear chap, those bigwigs at forty francs a consultation — well, just don't you consult them, you know! "

HENRIETTE. That one wanted four years to cure you!

GEORGE. Hang it, doctors are only men. After all, they must live; and when their consultations are forty francs apiece, why, the more the merrier.

HENRIETTE. And some quite unknown little doctor cured you in three months!

GEORGE. Yes; he was quite unknown. The odd thing is I have absolutely forgotten his address. I found it in the paper, I remember. I know vaguely that it was somewhere near the Halles; but if I was to have my head chopped off for it, I could n't find it again. Idiotic, is n't it?

HENRIETTE. Consequently, Germaine is six months less old than she ought to be.

GEORGE. What of that? We shall keep her so much the longer. She will be married six months later, that 's all.

HENRIETTE. Oh, don't speak of it. It 's odious to think even now that we shall lose her some day.

GEORGE. Ah! I can see myself going up the steps of the Madeleine with her on my arm.

HENRIETTE. ˙Why the Madeleine?

GEORGE. I don't know. She 'll have on a great white veil and I shall have an order in my buttonhole.

HENRIETTE. Indeed! Pray what will you have done to get an order?

GEORGE. I don't know, but I shall have one. Say what you like, I shall. What a glorious crowd there 'll be!

HENRIETTE. That 's all in the dim, distant future.

GEORGE. Ah, yes.

HENRIETTE. Yes, happily. [*Getting up*] Well, do you mind if I go and pay my visits now?

GEORGE. Run along, run along. I shall work hard while you are out. Look at all these papers! I shall be up to my eyes in them before you 're downstairs. Goodbye.

HENRIETTE. Good-bye. [*She kisses him and goes out at the back by the right*].

George lights a cigarette, looks at himself in the glass, and throws himself into the easy-chair to the left, humming a tune. By way of being more comfortable, he moves away the writing-chair and puts his feet on the desk, smoking and humming in perfect contentment. Madame Dupont comes in by the door on the left.

GEORGE [*getting up*] Hullo! Why, mother! We had no wire, so we did n't expect you till to-morrow. Henriette has just gone out. I can call her back.

MME. DUPONT. No; I did not want Henriette to be here when I came.

GEORGE. What 's the matter?

The conversation that follows is broken by long silences.

MME. DUPONT. I have brought back the child and the nurse.

GEORGE. Is baby ill?

MME. DUPONT. Yes.

GEORGE. What 's wrong with her?

MME. DUPONT. Nothing serious; at least for the moment.

GEORGE. We must send for the doctor.

MME. DUPONT. I have just come from the doctor's.

GEORGE. Good. I 'm not going out. I 'll wait for him.

MME. DUPONT. I have seen him.

GEORGE. Ah, you found him in?

MME. DUPONT. I telegraphed to him from the country. I took the child to see him.

GEORGE. It was so urgent as that?

MME. DUPONT. After what the nurse's doctor had told me, I wished to be reassured immediately.

GEORGE. And after all there is nothing serious?

MME. DUPONT. For the moment.

GEORGE. When you got down there, how did you find baby?

MME. DUPONT. Fairly well, but I sent for the doctor at once.

GEORGE. What did he say?

MME. DUPONT. That you must make a change; that the child must be brought up on the bottle.

GEORGE. What an extraordinary idea.

MME. DUPONT. He told me that what she was suffering from might become very serious. So without saying anything to nurse, I made her come with me and we took the train back.

GEORGE. Well, what is the matter with the child?

MME. DUPONT [*after a thoughtful pause*] I do not know.

GEORGE. Did n't you ask him?

MME. DUPONT. Yes.

GEORGE [*beginning to be anxious*] Well?

A silence.

MME. DUPONT. He replied evasively.

GEORGE [*tonelessly*] He probably did not know himself.

MME. DUPONT [*after a silence*] Probably.

During what follows they avoid looking at one another.

GEORGE. But our own doctor, did n't he say —?

MME. DUPONT. It was not to him that I went.

GEORGE. Ah! [*A very long silence. Then lower*] Why?

MME. DUPONT. The nurse's doctor had so terrified me.

GEORGE. Seriously?

MME. DUPONT. Yes; it is a disease — [*Silence*]

GEORGE [*in anguish*] Well?

MME. DUPONT. I asked him if the matter was too serious for our own doctor to deal with.

GEORGE.   What did he answer?

MME. DUPONT.   That if we had the means it would be preferable to see a specialist.

GEORGE [*trying to pull himself together*]   And — where did he send you?

MME. DUPONT [*handing him a visiting card*]   There.

GEORGE.   He sent you to that doctor?

MME. DUPONT.   Yes.   Do you know him?

GEORGE.   No — yes — I think I have met him — I don't know.   [*Very low*]   My God!

MME. DUPONT [*after a silence*]   He is coming to speak to you.

GEORGE [*scarcely daring to pronounce the words*] Then is he anxious?

MME. DUPONT.   No.   He wants to speak to you.

GEORGE.   He wants to speak to me?

MME. DUPONT.   Yes.

GEORGE [*resigning himself*]   Very well.

MME. DUPONT.   When he saw the nurse, whom I had left in the waiting room, he called me back and said: " It is impossible for me to continue attending on this child unless I can see its father and speak to him at once."   I answered " Very well," and gave him your address.   He will not be long.

GEORGE [*to himself in a low voice*]   My poor little child!

MME. DUPONT [*looking at him*]   Yes; she is a poor little child.

GEORGE [*after a long silence*]   Mother —

MME. DUPONT [*hearing the door opened*]   Hush! [*A maid comes in and speaks to her. To George*]   It is he!   [*To the maid*]   Show him in.   [*To George*]   I shall be there if you want me.

She goes out by the left.   The doctor enters by the right.

DOCTOR [*to the maid*]   You will let me know here when the child wakes up, will you not?

MAID. Yes, sir.

She goes out.

GEORGE [*with the greatest emotion*] Good-day, doctor: you don't recognize me?

DOCTOR [*simply: more discouraged than angry*] You! — it is you! You married and had a child after all I said to you? [*Almost to himself*] Scoundrel!

GEORGE. Let me explain.

DOCTOR. I can listen to no explanation of what you have done.

A silence.

GEORGE [*imploring him*] You will look after my little girl all the same, won't you?

DOCTOR [*shrugging his shoulders. Low*] Fool!

GEORGE [*not hearing*] I could only get my marriage put off six months.

DOCTOR. Enough, enough! That is not my business. I was wrong even to show you my indignation. I should have left you to judge yourself. I am here only concerned with the present and the future, with the child and with the nurse.

GEORGE. She is not in danger?

DOCTOR. The nurse is in danger of being contaminated.

GEORGE. No; but — my child?

DOCTOR. For the moment the symptoms are not disquieting.

GEORGE. Thank you. [*More easily*] About the nurse — you were saying — Do you mind if I call my mother? She knows more about these things than I do.

DOCTOR. As you please.

GEORGE [*going to the door and coming back much moved*] There is one thing I should like to ask you. Could you contrive that no one — my wife — should know what has happened? If my poor wife knew that it was I who was the cause — It is for her sake that I beg you. She is not to blame.

DOCTOR. I promise you that I will do everything in my power to save her from learning the real nature of the child's illness.

GEORGE. Oh, thank you! Thank you!

DOCTOR. You need not. If I tell lies, it will be for her sake and not for yours.

GEORGE. And my mother?

DOCTOR. Your mother knows the truth.

GEORGE. But —

DOCTOR. Please, please. We have many very serious matters to discuss.

George goes to the door and brings in his mother. She bows to the doctor, makes a sign to him to be seated in the arm-chair near the fireplace, and sits down herself on the chair near the little table. George takes a seat to the left in front of the desk.

DOCTOR. I have written a prescription for the child which will, I hope, improve its condition and prevent any fresh disorders. But my duty, and yours, does not stop there. If it is not too late, the health of the nurse must be protected.

MME. DUPONT. Tell us what we must do.

DOCTOR. She must stop giving milk to the child.

MME. DUPONT. You mean that we must change the nurse?

DOCTOR. No. I mean that the child cannot continue to be fed at the breast either by this nurse or by any healthy nurse.

MME. DUPONT. Why?

DOCTOR. Because the child would communicate its complaint to the person who gave it milk.

MME. DUPONT. But, doctor, if the baby is brought up on the bottle it will die.

GEORGE [*breaking into sobs*] Oh, my poor little girl! Oh, my God! it's me! Oh! oh!

DOCTOR. Careful treatment, with sterilized milk —

MME. DUPONT. That may succeed with healthy children, but at the age of three months a sickly child such as ours cannot be fed by hand. Such a child has all the more need of being fed at the breast. That is true?

DOCTOR. Yes; but —

MME. DUPONT. In that case you will realize that between the life of the child and the health of a nurse I have no choice.

GEORGE [*sobbing*] Oh! oh! oh!

DOCTOR. Your affection leads you to express an incredible sentiment. But it is not for you to choose. I shall forbid the child to be brought up at the breast. The health of this woman does not belong to you.

MME. DUPONT. Nor the life of our child to you. If there is one way to save its life, it is to give it every possible attention, and you want me to treat it in a way that you doctors condemn even for healthy children. My little one! You think I will let her die like that! Oh, I shall take good care she does not! Neglect the one single thing that can save her! It would be criminal! As for the nurse, we will indemnify her. We will do everything in our power, everything but that. No, no, no! Whatever can be done for our baby shall be done, cost what it may. But that — You don't consider what you are asking. It would be as if I killed my child. [*Bursting into tears*] Oh, my little angel, my own little Saviour!

George has not stopped sobbing since he first began. At his mother's last words his sobs become almost cries. His anguish is pitiable to see.

GEORGE. Oh, oh, oh! My little child! My little child! Oh, oh! [*In an undertone*] Oh, what a scoundrel I am! What a criminal!

DOCTOR. Calm yourself, madam, I beg. You will not improve matters in this way. Try to consider them coolly.

MME. DUPONT. You are right. I beg your pardon.

But if you knew how much this child is to me. I lost one at the same age. I am old and widowed — I did not expect to live to see my grandchildren. You are right. George, be calm — we will show our love by being calm. Now then, we will talk seriously and coldly. But I warn you that you will not succeed in making me consent to any but the very best conditions for the child. I shall not let her be killed by being taken from the breast.

DOCTOR. This is not the first time I have found myself in this situation, and I must begin by telling you that parents who have refused to be guided by my advice have invariably repented of it most bitterly.

MME. DUPONT. The only thing of which I shall repent —

DOCTOR. You are evidently unaware of what the rapacity and malice of peasants such as this nurse are capable, especially against those of superior station. In this case, moreover, her enmity would be legitimate.

MME. DUPONT. Oh! What can she do?

DOCTOR. She can bring an action against you.

MME. DUPONT. She is far too stupid to think of such a thing.

DOCTOR. Others will put it into her head.

MME. DUPONT. She is too poor to pay the expenses of going to law.

DOCTOR. Then you propose to profit by her ignorance and her poverty? Besides, she could obtain the assistance of the court.

MME. DUPONT. Never! Surely, never!

DOCTOR. Indeed? For my part I know at least ten such cases. In every case where the fact was proved, judgment was given against the parents.

MME. DUPONT. Not in a case like this! Not where the life of a poor innocent little child was at stake! You must be mistaken!

DOCTOR. Many of the facts have been identical. I can give you the dates.

GEORGE [*rising*] I have the law reports here. [*He takes a volume and hands it to the doctor*].

MME. DUPONT. It is needless.

DOCTOR [*to George*] You can convince yourself. In one or two cases the parents have been ordered to pay a yearly pension to the nurse; in the others sums of money varying from three to eight thousand francs.

MME. DUPONT. If we had to fight an action, we should retain the very best lawyer on our side. Thank heaven we are rich enough. No doubt he would make it appear doubtful whether the child had not caught this disease from the nurse, rather than the nurse from the child.

DOCTOR. Allow me to point out that such conduct would be atrocious.

MME. DUPONT. Oh, it is a lawyer's business to do such things. I should not have to say anything. In any case you may be sure that he would win our suit.

DOCTOR. And have you considered the scandal that would ensue.

GEORGE [*turning to a page in the reports*] Here is the judgment you were speaking of — six thousand francs.

DOCTOR. You can make Madame Dupont read it afterwards. Since you have the reports there, kindly give me the volume before this. [*George goes again to the bookcase. To Madame Dupont*] Have you thought of the scandal?

GEORGE [*coming back*] But, doctor, allow me to point out, in reports of this kind the names are suppressed.

DOCTOR. They are not suppressed in court.

GEORGE. True.

DOCTOR. Are you sure that no paper would publish a full account of the case?

Mme. Dupont. Oh, how infamous!

Doctor. You see what a horrible scandal it would be for you. [*George nods*] A catastrophe, absolutely.

George. Particularly for a notary like me. [*He goes to get the other volume*].

Mme. Dupont. We will prevent her from bringing an action. We will give her what she wants.

Doctor. Then you will expose yourself to be indefinitely blackmailed. I know one family which has paid hush-money of this kind for twelve years.

George. We could make her sign a receipt.

Doctor. In full settlement of all claims?

George. Exactly so. Here is the volume.

Mme. Dupont. She would be only too glad to go back to her people with enough money to buy a little house and a plot of land. To a woman of her position it would be wealth.

The nurse comes in.

Nurse. Baby's waked up, sir.

Doctor. I will come and see her. [*To Madame Dupont*] We will finish what we were saying presently.

Mme. Dupont. Very well. Do you want the nurse?

Doctor. No, thank you.

The doctor goes out.

Mme. Dupont. Nurse, just wait a minute. I want to speak to you. [*In an undertone to her son*] I know how we can manage. If we warn her and she agrees to stay, the doctor will have nothing more to say; will he?

George. I suppose not.

Mme. Dupont. I will promise her two thousand francs when she goes if she consents to stay on as wet-nurse.

George. Is that enough, do you think?

Mme. Dupont. At any rate I will try. If she hesitates I will make it more.

George. All right.

MME. DUPONT [*turning to the nurse*] Nurse, you know that baby is a little ill?

NURSE. Oh, no, ma'am.

MME. DUPONT. Indeed she is.

NURSE. I've looked after her as well as possible; I know I have, ma'am.

MME. DUPONT. I do not say you have not. But she is ill: the doctors say so.

NURSE. That's a fine story! As if doctors were n't always finding something, so that you may n't think they don't know their business!

MME. DUPONT. But our doctor is a great doctor; and you have seen yourself that baby has little pimples.

NURSE. Oh, ma'am, that's nothing but the heat of her blood. Don't you worry about it, I tell you it's only the strength of her blood. It is n't my fault. I've always done everything for her and kept her that clean and proper.

MME. DUPONT. No one says that it is your fault.

NURSE. Then what are you finding fault with me about? Ah, there is n't anything the matter with her. The pretty little darling, she's a regular town baby she is, just a bit poorly; but she's all right, I promise you.

MME. DUPONT. I tell you she is ill: she has a cold in her head and there are sores at the back of her throat.

NURSE. Then that's because the doctor scratched her with the spoon he put into her mouth by the wrong end. And if she has a little cold, I don't know when she caught it, I'm sure I don't: I always keep her that well wrapped up, she has three thicknesses of things on. It must have been when you came the time before last and opened all the windows in the house.

MME. DUPONT. But I tell you that nobody is finding fault with you at all.

NURSE. Oh, yes, I know. That's all very well. I'm only a poor country girl.

MME. DUPONT. What do you mean?

NURSE. Oh, that's all very well, it is!

MME. DUPONT. But I have told you over and over again that we have no fault to find.

NURSE [*sticking to her idea*] I never expected any unpleasantness when I came here. [*She begins to whimper*].

MME. DUPONT. We have no fault to find with you. Only we want to warn you, you may catch the baby's illness —

NURSE [*sulkily*] Well, if I do catch a cold, it won't be the first time I've had to blow my nose, I suppose.

MME. DUPONT. Perhaps you may get her pimples.

NURSE [*sneering*] Oh, ma'am, we country folks haven't got nice, delicate, white skins like Paris ladies have. When you have to work in the fields all day, rain or shine, you don't need to plaster your face all over with cream, I can tell you. No offence meant, but if you want to find an excuse, that isn't much of a one.

MME. DUPONT. What do you mean? What excuse?

NURSE. Oh, yes, I know.

MME. DUPONT. What do you know?

NURSE. I'm only a poor country girl, I am.

MME. DUPONT. I have not the slightest idea what you mean.

NURSE. Oh, I know what I mean.

MME. DUPONT. Then tell me what you mean.

NURSE. Oh, what's the good?

MME. DUPONT. Tell me, please. I insist!

NURSE. Oh, very well —

MME. DUPONT. Go on.

NURSE. Oh, all right. I may be only a poor country girl, but I'm not quite so stupid as that. I know what it is you want. Just because master's cross at your having promised me thirty francs a month more

if I came to Paris. [*Turning to George*] Well, and
what do you expect? Mustn't I have my own little
boy looked after? And hasn't his father got to eat
and drink? We're only poor country folks, we are.

GEORGE. You're making a mistake, nurse. There's
nothing at all the matter. My mother was quite right
to promise you the thirty francs extra, and the only
thing in my mind is that she did not promise you
enough. Now I have decided when baby is old enough
to have a dry nurse and you leave us, just to show how
grateful we are, to give you, er —

MME. DUPONT. We shall make you a present, you
understand, over and above your wages. We shall give
you five hundred francs, or perhaps a thousand. That
is, of course, if baby is in perfectly good health.

NURSE [*stupefied*] You'll give me five hundred
francs — for myself —   [*Struggling to understand*]
But you haven't got to. We didn't agree to that.

MME. DUPONT. No.

NURSE [*to herself*] What's up, then?

MME. DUPONT. It is simply because baby will require more attention. You will have rather more
trouble with her. You will have to give her her medicine and so on. It may be a little difficult for you.

NURSE. Ah, I see. So that you may be sure I shall
look after her well. You say to yourself: " Nurse has
an interest in her." I see.

MME. DUPONT. That is understood, then?

NURSE. Yes, ma'am.

MME. DUPONT. Very good. You will not come
afterwards and complain of the way we have treated
you. We have warned you that the child is ill and
that you may catch her illness. To make up for that,
and because you will have more trouble with her, we
will give you five hundred francs when your time here
is over. That is understood?

Nurse. But you said a thousand francs, ma'am.

Mme. Dupont. Very well; a thousand francs, then.

George [*passing to the right behind the other two and drawing his mother aside*] It's a pity that we can't get her to sign that.

Mme. Dupont [*to the nurse*] So that there may be no misunderstanding about the sum — you see I forgot just now that I said a thousand francs — we will draw up a little paper which we shall sign on our side and you will sign on your side.

Nurse. Very good, ma'am; I understand.

The doctor comes back.

Mme. Dupont. Here is the doctor. You may go, nurse; that is all right.

Nurse. Yes, ma'am. [*To herself*] What's up, then? A thousand francs? What's the matter with the baby? Has she got something bad, I wonder? [*She passes to the left, between the desk and window, and goes out*].

Doctor. The condition is unchanged. There is no need for anxiety. [*He sits down at the desk to write a prescription*].

Mme. Dupont. I am glad to tell you, doctor, that you can now devote yourself to the baby and the nurse without misgiving. While you have been away we have informed the nurse of the circumstances, and agreed with her that she shall stay with us in return for a certain sum of money.

Doctor. The disease which the nurse will almost infallibly contract in giving her milk to the child is, I fear, too serious to be made the subject of a bargain, however large the sum of money. She might be completely crippled, even if she did not die of it.

Mme. Dupont. But she accepts!

Doctor. It is not only that she would be rendered incapable of serving in future as wet nurse without danger to the infants she suckled. The results of the disease to herself might be inconsiderable; but at the same time, I repeat, they might, in spite of everything we could do, cast a terrible blight upon her life.

MME. DUPONT. But I tell you she accepts! She has the right to do what she pleases.

DOCTOR. I am not sure that she has the right to sell her own health, but I am sure that she has not the right to sell the health of her husband and of her children. If she contracts this disease, she will almost certainly communicate it to both of them; and, further, the life and health of any children she might afterwards have would be gravely endangered. You understand now that it is impossible for her to make a bargain of this kind. If the mischief is not already done, every effort must be made to prevent it.

MME. DUPONT. You say: "If the mischief is not done." Can you not be certain?

DOCTOR. Not as yet. There is a period of five or six weeks between the moment of contracting the disease and the appearance of its first symptoms.

MME. DUPONT. You think of nothing but the nurse. You do not think of our poor little baby. What can we do? We cannot let her die!

GEORGE. We can't, we can't!

DOCTOR. Neither can you endanger the life of this woman.

MME. DUPONT. You are not defending our interests!

DOCTOR. I am defending those of the weakest.

MME. DUPONT. If we had called in our own doctor, he would have taken our side.

DOCTOR. I doubt it. [*Rising*] But there is still time to send for him.

GEORGE. Mother! I beg you not to go, doctor.

MME. DUPONT [*supplicating him*] Oh, don't abandon us! You can make allowances — If you only knew what this child was to me! I feel as if I had staved off death to wait for it. Have pity on us! Our poor little girl! — she is the weakest, surely. Have pity on her! When you saw her tiny, suffering body, did you not feel any pity for her? Oh, I beseech you!

GEORGE. Doctor, we implore you!

DOCTOR. Indeed I pity her and I will do everything in my power to save her. But you must not ask me to sacrifice the health of a young and strong woman to that of a sickly infant. I will be no party to giving this woman a disease that would embitter the lives of her whole family, and almost certainly render her sterile.

MME. DUPONT [in a stifled voice] Oh, are there not enough of these peasants in the world!

DOCTOR. I beg your pardon?

MME. DUPONT [in the same tone] I said that if she had no more children, there would only be the fewer to be unhappy.

DOCTOR. It is useless for us to continue this discussion.

MME. DUPONT [rousing herself] I shall not take your advice! I shall not listen to you!

DOCTOR. There is one here already who regrets not having done so.

GEORGE. Yes; O, God, yes!

MME. DUPONT [more and more exalted] I do not care! I do not care if I am punished for it in this world and the next! If it is a crime, if it is a sin, I accept all the responsibility, however heavy it may be! Yes, yes! If it must be, I will lose my soul to save our child's life, our little one's! I know that hell exists for the wicked: that is one of my profoundest convictions. Then let God judge me — if I am damned, so much the worse for me!

DOCTOR. I shall not allow you to take that responsibility. To enable you to do so, my consent would be necessary, and I refuse it.

MME. DUPONT.   What do you mean?

DOCTOR.   I shall speak to the nurse and give her the fullest particulars, which I am convinced you have not done.

MME. DUPONT.   What! you, a doctor, would betray family secrets entrusted to you in the strictest confidence! Secrets of this kind!

DOCTOR.   The betrayal, if it is one, is forced on me by the law.

MME. DUPONT.   The law! I thought you were bound to secrecy?

DOCTOR [*turning the pages of the volume of reports*] Not in this case.   Here is a judgment given by the court at Dijon: I thought that I might have to read it to you. [*Reading*] " A doctor who knowingly omits to inform a nurse of the dangers incurred by her in giving milk to a syphilitic child may be held responsible in damages for the results caused by her ignorance." You see that the law is against you, as well as your conscience; and I may add that, even were it not so, I should not allow you to be led by your feelings into committing such a crime.   If you do not consent to have the child fed by hand, I shall either speak to the nurse or give up the case.

MME. DUPONT.   You dare to threaten us!   Oh, you know the power that your knowledge gives you!   You know what need we are in of your services, and that if you abandon us perhaps our child will die!   And if we give way to you, she will die all the same!   [*Wildly*]   O, my God, my God, why cannot I sacrifice myself?   Oh, if only my aged body could take the place of this woman's young flesh, and my poor dry breasts give to our child the milk that would save her life!   With what joy I would give myself up to this disease!   With what rapture I would suffer the most horrible ravages that it could inflict on me!   Oh, if I could but offer myself, without fear and without regret!

GEORGE [*flings himself into her arms with sobs and cries of*] Mother! Mother! Mother!

They weep.

DOCTOR [*to himself, moved*] Poor people! Poor people!

MME. DUPONT [*sitting down with an air of resignation*] Tell us what we must do.

DOCTOR. Keep the nurse here as dry-nurse so that she may not carry the infection elsewhere. We will feed the child by hand, and I beg you in all sincerity not to exaggerate the danger that will result from the change. I have every hope of restoring the baby to health in a short space of time; and I assure you that I will use every possible effort to bring about a happy conclusion. I will call again to-morrow. Good-day.

MME. DUPONT [*without moving*] Thank you, doctor.

GEORGE [*going to the door and shaking hands*] Thank you, thank you! [*The doctor goes out. George comes back and goes to his mother with outstretched arms*] Mother!

MME. DUPONT [*repulsing him*] Let me be.

GEORGE [*checking himself*] Are we not unhappy enough, without hating one another?

MME. DUPONT. It is God who visits upon your child the sins of its father.

GEORGE [*raising his shoulders gloomily*] You believe that, when there is not a man alive so wicked and unjust as to commit such an act!

MME. DUPONT. Oh, I know you believe in nothing.

GEORGE. Not in that kind of God.

The nurse, who comes in by the left soon after the doctor has gone out, appears.

NURSE. If you please, ma'am, I've been thinking I would rather go away at once, and only have the five hundred francs.

MME. DUPONT. What do you say? You want to leave us?

NURSE. Yes, ma'am.

GEORGE. But ten minutes ago you did n't want to.

MME. DUPONT. What has happened?

NURSE. I 've been thinking.

MME. DUPONT. Thinking! About what?

NURSE. Well, I want to go back to my baby and my husband.

GEORGE. But ten minutes ago — There must be something else.

MME. DUPONT. Evidently there is something else.

NURSE. No, ma'am.

MME. DUPONT. But there must be!

NURSE. Well, then, I 'm afraid that Paris does n't suit me.

MME. DUPONT. How can you tell without waiting to try?

NURSE. I 'd rather go back home at once.

MME. DUPONT. At least tell us why.

NURSE. I have told you. I 've been thinking.

MME. DUPONT. What about?

NURSE. I 've been thinking.

MME. DUPONT. Oh, don't say that over and over again! "I 've been thinking, I 've been thinking." What have you been thinking about?

NURSE. About everything.

MME. DUPONT. Can't you tell us about what?

NURSE. I tell you, about everything.

MME. DUPONT. Idiot!

GEORGE [*stepping in front of his mother*] Let me speak to her.

NURSE. I know we 're only poor country folk.

GEORGE. Listen to me, nurse. Just now you were not only satisfied with your wages, but you were afraid we were going to send you away. In addition to your wages we have promised to give you a large sum of money at the end of your time here — and now you want to leave us, at once! Come now, you must have some sort of reason. Has anyone been doing anything to you?

NURSE. No, sir.

GEORGE. Well, then?

NURSE. I've been thinking.

GEORGE [*exasperated*] Don't go on repeating that silly thing! What do you mean by it? [*Gently*] Come, come! Tell me why you want to go away. [*Silence*] Eh?

NURSE. I have told you.

GEORGE. One might as well talk to a block of wood.

MME. DUPONT [*coming forward*] But you have no right to leave us.

NURSE. Yes; I want to go away.

MME. DUPONT. I shall not allow you to go!

GEORGE. Oh, well, let her go; after all we can't keep her by force. [*To the nurse*] Since you want to go, you shall go; but I can only say that you're as stupid as a cow.

NURSE. I don't mind if I am.

GEORGE. I shall not pay you for the month that has just begun, and you will pay for your own railway ticket.

NURSE. We'll see about that.

GEORGE. Yes; you will see. You'll see this moment, too! Be off with you! I don't want you any longer. Now, then!

MME. DUPONT. Don't fly into a rage, George. [*To the nurse*] You don't mean it seriously, nurse, surely?

NURSE. I would rather go back home at once and only have my five hundred francs.

GEORGE. What's that?

MME. DUPONT. What are you talking about?

GEORGE. Five hundred francs?

MME. DUPONT. What five hundred francs?

NURSE. The five hundred francs you promised me, to be sure!

GEORGE. We never promised you anything of the sort!

NURSE. Yes, you did.

MME. DUPONT. Yes; when you had finished nursing the baby, and if we were satisfied with you.

NURSE. No; you said you would give me five hundred francs when I left. Now I 'm going away, so I want them.

MME. DUPONT. You will please not address me in that tone; you understand?

NURSE. You 've only got to give me my money and I shan't say a word more.

GEORGE. Oh, that 's it, is it? Very well, I discharge you on the spot. Now, then, be off with you!

MME. DUPONT. I should think so, indeed.

GEORGE. Off you go!

NURSE. Give me my five hundred francs.

GEORGE [pointing furiously at the door] Take your blasted carcase out of this! Do you hear?

NURSE. Hullo, hullo! You speak to me a bit more politely; can't you?

GEORGE. Will you get out of this, or have I got to send for the police?

NURSE. The police! What for, eh, what for?

GEORGE. To chuck you out, you —

NURSE. Well, and what am I? I 'm only a country girl, I am. I may be a bit stupid —

MME. DUPONT. Stupid! I should think you were. You have no more brains than a mule.

NURSE. I may be stupid, but I 'm not —

MME. DUPONT [interrupting] You have no more heart than a stone. You are a wicked woman.

GEORGE. You 're no better than a thief.

NURSE. Oh, a thief am I? I should like to know why.

GEORGE. Because you 're trying to get money that is n't yours.

MME. DUPONT. Because you are deserting our baby. You are a wicked woman.

GEORGE. Do you want me to put you out? [*He takes her by the arm*].

NURSE. Oh, that's it, is it? So you want me to tell you why I'm going?

GEORGE. Now, then, out with it.

MME. DUPONT. Well, why is it?

Henriette enters at the back. In the noise of the quarrel no one perceives her.

NURSE. Very well, then. I'm going away because I don't want to catch your beastly diseases here.

MME. DUPONT. Be quiet, will you?

GEORGE. Shut up, can't you?

NURSE. Oh, you need n't be afraid; everyone knows about it. Justin listened at the door to what your doctor was saying and told me what was up. Oh, I may be stupid, but I'm not so stupid as that. I'm going to have my money and get out of this.

GEORGE. Shut up!

MME. DUPONT. [*taking her by the arm*] Hold your tongue, I tell you!

NURSE. Let me go! Let me go! I know your brat's not going to live. I know it's rotten through and through because its father's got a beastly disease that he caught from some woman of the streets.

Henriette, with two hoarse cries, falls to the ground in a fit of nervous sobbing.

GEORGE [*rushing towards her*] My God!

Henriette eludes him and pulls herself up with disgust, hatred, and horror depicted all over her.

HENRIETTE [*shrieking like a mad woman*] Don't touch me! Don't touch me!

ACT III

The doctor's room in the hospital where he is chief physician. The doctor enters with a medical student, both in their hospital clothes, and takes off his apron while talking.

DOCTOR. By the way, my dear fellow, is the gentleman we passed in the passage waiting for you?

STUDENT. No, not for me.

DOCTOR. Then it's my deputy. Do you know this name? Where did I put his card? [*He looks on his desk*] Ah, here. "Loches, deputy for Sarthes."

STUDENT. That's the famous Loches.

DOCTOR. Ah, yes, deputy for Sarthes. A regular orator, is n't he?

STUDENT. Tremendous, I believe.

DOCTOR. That's the man we want then. He busies himself a great deal with social questions?

STUDENT. Just so.

DOCTOR. I suppose he wants to start an agitation in the Chamber in favor of the laws for which we have been clamoring so long. No doubt he means to post himself up first. This is what he writes: "Loches, deputy for Sarthes, presents his compliments," etc. . . . would be much obliged if I would see him to-morrow, Sunday, not for a consultation.

STUDENT. It's very likely he has some idea of the sort.

DOCTOR. Now that I have a deputy I will post him up, I can assure you. That's why I have had the case from St. Charles' ward and number 28 brought here.

STUDENT. Shall you want me?

DOCTOR. Not at all, my dear fellow. Good-bye.

STUDENT. Good-bye, sir.

DOCTOR [*calling to the other as he goes out*] Would you mind telling them to show in M. Loches? Thanks very much. Good-bye.

The student goes out.

Loches enters and bows. The doctor motions him to be seated.

LOCHES. I must thank you for being so kind as to receive me out of your regular hours. The business that brings me here is peculiarly distressing. I am the father-in-law of M. George Dupont. After the terrible revelation of yesterday, my daughter has returned to me with her child, and I have come to ask you to be so good as to continue attending on the infant, but at my house.

DOCTOR. Very good.

LOCHES. Thank you. Now, as to the scoundrel who is the cause of all these misfortunes.

DOCTOR [*very gently*] You must excuse me, but that is a subject on which I cannot enter. My functions are only those of a physician.

LOCHES [*in a thick voice*] I ask your pardon, but I think when you have heard me for a moment, you will agree with me. I shall not trouble you with the plans of vengeance I formed yesterday, when my poor daughter fled to me with her child in her arms after the revelation that you know. You will excuse me if I speak to you in this state — oh, I can scarce contain my indignation! I had intended to talk of this calmly: but when I think of that man and of his infamous conduct — the brutal, cowardly blow he has struck at me and mine — I cannot control myself — I — I — It is abominable! My daughter! A girl of twenty-two! Twenty-two!

A silence.

Doctor. I understand and respect your feelings; but, believe me, you are not in a fit state to form any decision at this moment.

Loches [*with an effort*] Yes, yes: I will command myself. All last night I spent in profound reflection; and after rejecting the ideas I mentioned, this is the conclusion to which I have come in conjunction with my daughter: we desire to obtain a divorce as soon as possible. Consequently I have come to ask you for the certificate which will be the basis of our action.

Doctor. What certificate?

Loches. A certificate attesting the nature of the disease which this man has contracted.

Doctor. I regret that I am unable to furnish you with such a certificate.

Loches. How is that?

Doctor. The rule of professional secrecy is absolute.

Loches. It is impossible that it should be your duty to take sides with a criminal against his innocent victims.

Doctor. To avoid all discussion, I may add that even were I free, I should refuse your request.

Loches. May I ask why?

Doctor. I should regret having helped you to obtain a divorce.

Loches. Then just because you hold this or that theory, because your profession has rendered you sceptical or insensible to the sight of misery like ours, my daughter must bear this man's name to the end of her life!

Doctor. It would be in your daughter's own interest that I should refuse.

Loches. Indeed! You have a strange conception of her interest.

Doctor [*very gently*] In your present state of excitement you will probably begin to abuse me before five minutes are over. That will not disturb a man of my experience, but you see why I refused to discuss these subjects. However, since I have let myself in for it, I may as well explain my position. You ask me for a certificate in order to prove to the court that your son-in-law has contracted syphilis?

LOCHES. Yes.

DOCTOR. You do not consider that in doing so you will publicly acknowledge that your daughter has been exposed to the infection. The statement will be officially registered in the papers of the case. Do you suppose that after that your daughter is likely to find a second husband?

LOCHES. She will never marry again.

DOCTOR. She says so now. Can you be sure that she will say so in five or in ten years time? Besides, you will not obtain a divorce, because I shall not furnish you with the necessary proof.

LOCHES. I shall find other ways to establish it. I shall have the child examined by another doctor.

DOCTOR. Indeed! You think that this poor little thing has not been unlucky enough in her start in life? She has been blighted physically: you wish besides to stamp her indelibly with the legal proof of congenital syphilis?

LOCHES. So when the victims seek to defend themselves they are struck still lower! So the law provides no arms against the man who takes an innocent, confiding young girl in sound health, knowingly befouls her with the heritage of his debauchery, and makes her mother of a wretched mite whose future is such that those who love it most do not know whether they had better pray for its life or for its immediate deliverance! This man has inflicted on his wife the supreme insult, the most odious degradation. He has, as it were, thrust her into contact with the streetwalker with whose vice he is stained, and created between her and that common thing a bond of blood to poison herself and her child. Thanks to him, this abject creature, this prostitute, lives our life, makes one of our family, sits down with us at table. He has smirched my daughter's imagination as he has tarnished her body, and bound up for ever in her mind the ideal of love that she placed so high with heaven knows what horrors of the hospital. He has struck her physically and morally, in her dignity and her modesty, in her love and in her child. He has hurled her into the depths of shame. And the state of law and opinion is such that this woman cannot be separated from this man save at the cost of a scandal which will overwhelm herself and her child. Very well, then, I shall not ask the aid of the law. Last night I wondered if it was not my duty to go and shoot down that brute like a mad dog. It was cowardice that prevented me. Weakly I proposed to invoke the law. Well, since the law will not do justice, I will take it into my own hands. Perhaps his death will serve as a warning to others.

DOCTOR [*putting aside his hat*]   You will be tried for your life.

LOCHES.   And I shall be acquitted.

DOCTOR.   Yes; but after the public narration of all your troubles. The scandal and the misfortune will be so much the greater, that is all. And how do you know that the day after your acquittal you will not find yourself before another and less lenient judge? When your daughter, realizing that you have rendered her unhappiness irreparable, and seized with pity for your victim, demands by what right you have killed the father of her child, what will you say? What will you say when that child one day asks the same question?

LOCHES [*speaking before the other has done*]   Then what can I do?

DOCTOR [*immediately*]   Forgive.
A silence.

LOCHES [*without energy*]   Never.

DOCTOR. Are you quite sure that you have the right to be so inflexible? Was it not within your power at a certain moment to spare your daughter the possibility of this misery?

LOCHES. Within my power! Do you imply that I am responsible?

DOCTOR. Yes; I do. When the marriage was proposed you doubtless made inquiries concerning your future son-in-law's income; you investigated his securities; you satisfied yourself as to his character. You only omitted one point, but it was the most important of all: you made no inquiries concerning his health.

LOCHES. No.

DOCTOR. And why?

LOCHES. Because it is not the custom.

DOCTOR. Well, it ought to be made the custom. Before giving his daughter in marriage a father ought to take as much care with regard to her husband as a house of business takes in engaging an employee.

LOCHES. You are right; a law should be passed.

DOCTOR. No, no! We want no new laws: there are too many already. All that is needed is for people to understand the nature of this disease rather better. It would soon become the custom for a man who proposed for a girl's hand to add to the other things for which he is asked a medical statement of bodily fitness, which would make it certain that he did not bring this plague into the family with him. It would be perfectly simple. Once it was the custom, the man would go to his doctor for a certificate of health before he could sign the register, just as now, before he can be married in church, he goes to his priest for a certificate that he has confessed. As things are, before a marriage is concluded the family lawyers meet to discuss matters: a meeting between the two doctors would be at least as useful and would pre-

vent many misfortunes. Your inquiry, you see, was incomplete. Your daughter might well ask you, who are
a man and a father, and ought to know these things, why
you did not take as much trouble about her health as
about her fortune. I tell you that you must forgive.

LOCHES. Never!

DOCTOR. Well, there is one last argument which,
since I must, I will put to you. Are you yourself without sin, that you are so relentless to others?

LOCHES. I have never had any shameful disease, sir!

DOCTOR. I was not asking you that. I was asking
you if you had never exposed yourself to catching one.
[*He pauses. Loches does not reply*] Ah, you see!
Then it is not virtue that has saved you; it is luck. Few
things exasperate me more than that term " shameful
disease," which you used just now. This disease is like
all other diseases: it is one of our afflictions. There is
no shame in being wretched — even if one deserves to
be so. [*Hotly*] Come, come, let us have a little plain
speaking! I should like to know how many of these
rigid moralists, who are so choked with their middle-
class prudery that they dare not mention the name
syphilis, or when they bring themselves to speak of it
do so with expressions of every sort of disgust, and treat
its victims as criminals, have never run the risk of contracting it themselves? It is those alone who have the
right to talk. How many do you think there are? Four
out of a thousand? Well, leave those four aside: between all the rest and those who catch the disease there
is no difference but chance. [*Bursting out*] And by
heavens, those who escape won't get much sympathy
from me: the others at least have paid their fine of
suffering and remorse, while they have gone scot-free!
[*Recovering himself*] Let's have done, if you please,
once for all with this sort of hypocrisy. Your son-in-
law, like yourself and like the immense majority of men,

has had mistresses before he married. He has had the ill-luck to catch syphilis, and married supposing that the disease was no longer dangerous when in fact it still was. It is a misfortune that we must do our best to remedy, and not to aggravate. Perhaps in your youth you deserved what he has got even more than he; at any rate your position towards him is as that of the culprit who has escaped punishment towards his less fortunate comrade. That is a reflection that should, I think, touch you.

LOCHES. You put it in such a way —

DOCTOR. Am I not right?

LOCHES. Perhaps; but I can't tell my daughter all this to persuade her to return to her husband.

DOCTOR. There are other arguments that you can use.

LOCHES. What, then, good heavens?

DOCTOR. Any number. You can tell her that a separation will be a calamity for all parties and that her husband is the only person interested in helping her at any price to save her child. You can tell her that out of the ruins of her first happiness she can construct a life of solid affection that will have every chance of being lasting and most sincerely enviable. There is much truth in the saying that reformed rakes make the best husbands. Take your son-in-law. If your daughter consents to forgive and forget, he will not only respect her, he will be eternally grateful. You can tell her all this and you will find much else to say besides. As for the future, we will make sure that when they are reunited their next child shall be healthy and vigorous.

LOCHES. Is that possible?

DOCTOR. Yes, yes! A thousand times yes! I have one thing that I always tell my patients: if I could I would paste it up at every street corner. "Syphilis is like a woman whose temper is roused by the feeling that her power is disdained. It is terrible only to those who

think it insignificant, not to those who know its dangers."
Repeat that to your daughter. Give her back to her husband, — she has nothing more to fear from him, — and
in two years' time I guarantee that you will be a happy
grandfather.

LOCHES. Thank you, doctor. I do not know if I can
ever forget. But you have made me so uneasy on the
score of these responsibilities that I have ignored and
given me back so much hope, that I will promise you to
do nothing rash. If my poor child can, after a time,
bring herself to forgive her husband, I shall not stand in
the way.

DOCTOR. Good! But if you have another daughter,
take care not to make the same mistake that you made
over the marriage of your first.

LOCHES. How was I to know?

DOCTOR. Ah, there it is. You did n't know! You are
a father and you did n't know! You are a deputy and
have the honor and the burden of making laws for us,
and you did n't know! You did n't know about syphilis,
just as you probably do not know about alcoholism and
tuberculosis.

LOCHES. Really, I —

DOCTOR. Well, if you like I will except you. But
there are five hundred others, are there not, who sit in
the Chamber and style themselves Representatives of the
people? Here are the three unspeakable gods to whom
every day thousands of human sacrifices are offered up.
What single hour do your colleagues find for the organization of our forces against these insatiable monsters?
Take alcoholism. The manufacture of poisonous liquors
should be prohibited and the number of licences cut
down. But we are afraid of the power of the great distillers and of the voting strength of the trade: consequently we deplore the immorality of the working classes
and quiet our conscience by writing pamphlets and

preaching sermons. Pah! Then take tuberculosis: everyone knows that the real remedy is to pay sufficient wages and have insanitary workmen's dwellings knocked down. But no one will do it, although the working class is the most useful we have as well as the worst rewarded. Instead, workmen are recommended not to spit. Admirable, is n't it? Finally, syphilis. Why do you not concern yourselves with that? You create offices of state for all sorts of things: why do you not one day set about creating an office of public health?

LOCHES. My dear doctor, you are falling into the common French mistake of attributing all the ills in the world to the government. In this case it is for you to show us the way. These are matters for scientific experts. You must begin by pointing out the necessary measures, and then —

DOCTOR. And then — what? Ha! It is fifteen years since a scheme of this kind, worked out and approved *unanimously* by the Academy of Medicine, was submitted to the proper authorities. Since that day it has never been heard of again.

LOCHES. Then you think that there really are measures to be taken?

DOCTOR. You shall answer that question yourself. I must tell you that when I received your card yesterday I imagined that it was in your public capacity that you were about to interest yourself in these matters. Consequently, after naming the hour of your visit, I told off two of my hospital patients to show to you. You need not be alarmed. I shall not shock your nerves. To outward appearance they have nothing the matter with them. They are not bad cases; they are simply the damaged goods of our great human cargo. I merely wished to give you food for reflection, not a lesson in pathology. You came on another matter. So much the worse for you. I have you and I shall not let you go.

[*A slight pause*].   I will ask you, therefore, to raise
your mind above your personal sorrow and to conceive
in the mass the thousands of beings who suffer from
similar causes.   Thousands, mark you, from every rank
of society.   The disease jumps from the hovel into the
home, frequently with few intermediate steps; so that
to cleanse the gutter, where preventive measures can be
taken, means practically to safeguard the family life.
Our greatest enemy of all, as you shall see for yourself,
is ignorance.   Ignorance, I repeat.   The refrain is
always the same: " I did n't know."   Patients, whom
we might have saved had they come in time, come too
late, in a desperate condition, and after having spread
the evil far and wide.   And why?   " I did n't know."
[*Going towards the door*]   What can we do?   We can't
hunt them out from the highways and hedges.   [*To a
woman in the passage*]   Come in, please.   [*The woman
enters.   She is of the working class.   The doctor turns
again to Loches*]   Here is a case.   This woman is very
seriously ill.   I have told her so, and I told her to come
here once a week.   [*To the woman*]   Is that so?

WOMAN.   Yes, sir.

DOCTOR [*angrily*]   And how long is it since you came
last?

WOMAN.   Three months.

DOCTOR.   Three months!   How do you suppose I can
cure you like that?   It is hopeless, do you hear, hopeless!
Well, why did n't you come?   Don't you know that you
have a very serious disease?

WOMAN.   Oh, yes, sir.   I know it is.   My husband
died of it.

DOCTOR [*more gently*]   Your husband died of it?

WOMAN.   Yes, sir.

DOCTOR.   Did he not go to the doctor?

WOMAN.   No, sir.

DOCTOR.   And is n't that a warning to you?

WOMAN. Oh, sir, I 'd come as often as you told me to, only I can't afford it.

DOCTOR. How do you mean, you can't afford it?

LOCHES. The consultations are gratis, are they not?

WOMAN. Yes, sir. But they 're during working hours, and then, it 's a long way to come. One has to wait one's turn with all the others, and sometimes it takes the best part of the day, and I 'm afraid of losing my place if I stop away so much. So I wait till I can't help coming again. And then —

DOCTOR. Well?

WOMAN. Oh, it 's nothing, sir. You 're too kind to me.

DOCTOR. Go on, go on.

WOMAN. I know I ought n't to mind, but I have n't always been so poor. We were well off before my husband fell ill, and I 've always lived by my own work. It 's not as it is for a woman who has n't any self-respect. I know it 's wrong, but having to wait like that with everyone else and to tell all about myself before everyone — I know I 'm wrong, but it 's hard all the same, it 's very hard.

DOCTOR. Poor woman! [*A pause. Then very gently*] So it was from your husband that you caught this disease?

WOMAN. Yes, sir. We used to live in the country and then my husband caught it and went half mad. He did n't know what he was doing, and used to order all kinds of things we could n't pay for.

DOCTOR. Why did he not get himself looked after?

WOMAN. He did n't know. We were sold up and came to Paris; we had n't any more money. Then he went to the hospital.

DOCTOR. Well?

WOMAN. He got looked after there, but they would n't give him any medicines.

DOCTOR. How was that?

WOMAN. Because we had only been three months in Paris. They only give you the medicines free if you have lived here six months.

LOCHES. Is that so?

DOCTOR. Yes, that is the rule.

WOMAN. You see it is n't our fault.

DOCTOR. You have no children, have you?

WOMAN. I could n't ever bring one to birth, sir. My husband was taken at the very beginning of our marriage, while he was doing his time as a reservist. There are women that hang about the barracks.

A silence.

DOCTOR. Ah! Well, this is my private address; you come to see me there every Sunday morning. [*At the door he slips a piece of money into her hand. Roughly*] There, just take that and run along. What 's that? Tut, tut! Nonsense! Nonsense! I have n't time to listen to you. Run along, now. [*He pushes her out. To someone who is invisible to the audience*] What can I do for you?

MAN [*outside*] I am the father of the young man you saw this morning. I asked leave to speak to you after the consultation was over.

DOCTOR. Ah, yes, just so, I recognize you. Your son is at college, is n't he?

MAN [*in the doorway*] Yes, sir.

DOCTOR. Come in, come in. You can talk before this gentleman.

MAN [*entering*] You know, sir, the disaster that has befallen us. My son is eighteen; as the result of this disease he is half paralyzed. We are small tradespeople; we have regularly bled ourselves in order to send him to college, and now — I only wish the same thing may n't happen to others. It was at the very college gates that my poor boy was got hold of by one of these women. Is it right, sir, that that should be allowed? Aren't there enough police to prevent children of fifteen from being seduced like that? I ask, is it right?

DOCTOR. No.

MAN. Why don't they stop it, then?

DOCTOR. I don't know.

MAN. Look at my son. He'd be better in his grave. He was such a good-looking chap. We were that proud of him.

DOCTOR. Never despair. We'll do our best to cure him. [*Sadly*] But why did you wait so long before bringing him to me?

MAN. How was I to know what he had? He was afraid to tell me; so he let the thing go on. Then when he felt he was really bad with it, he went, without letting me know, to quacks, who robbed him without curing him. Ah, that too; is that right? What's the government about that it allows that? Isn't that more important than what they spend their time over?

DOCTOR. You are right. Their only excuse is that they do not know. You must take courage. We have cured worse cases than your son's. As for the others, perhaps some day they will have a little attention paid them. [*He goes with the man to the door. Turning to Loches*] You see, the true remedy lies in a change of our ways. Syphilis must cease to be treated like a mysterious evil the very name of which cannot be pronounced. The ignorance in which the public is kept of the real nature and of the consequences of this disease helps to aggravate and to spread it. Generally it is contracted because "I didn't know"; it becomes dangerous for want of proper care because "I didn't know"; it is passed on from person to person because "I didn't know." People ought to know. Young men ought to be taught the responsibilities they assume and the misfortunes they may bring on themselves.

LOCHES. At the same time these things cannot be taught to children at school.

DOCTOR. Why not, pray?

LOCHES. There are curiosities which it would be imprudent to arouse.

DOCTOR [*hotly*] So you think that by ignoring those curiosities you stifle them? Why, every boy and girl who has been to a boarding school or through college knows you do not! So far from stifling them, you drive them to satisfy themselves in secret by any vile means they can. There is nothing immoral in the act that reproduces life by the means of love. But for the benefit of our children we organize round about it a gigantic conspiracy of silence. A respectable man will take his son and daughter to one of these grand music halls, where they will hear things of the most loathsome description; but he won't let them hear a word spoken seriously on the subject of the great act of love. No, no! Not a word about that without blushing: only, as many barrack room jokes, as many of the foulest music hall suggestions as you like! Pornography, as much as you please: science, never! That is what we ought to change. The mystery and humbug in which physical facts are enveloped ought to be swept away and young men be given some pride in the creative power with which each one of us is endowed. They ought to be made to understand that the future of the race is in their hands and to be taught to transmit the great heritage they have received from their ancestors intact with all its possibilities to their descendants.

LOCHES. Ah, but we should go beyond that! I realize now that what is needed is to attack this evil at its source and to suppress prostitution. We ought to hound out these vile women who poison the very life of society.

DOCTOR. You forget that they themselves have first been poisoned. I am going to show you one of them. I warn you, not that it matters much, that she won't

express herself like a duchess. I can make her talk by
playing on her vanity: she wants to be a ballet-dancer.

*He opens the door and admits a pretty girl of some
twenty years: she is very gay and cheerful.*

DOCTOR. Getting on all right? [*Without waiting for
an answer*] You still want to go on the stage, don't you?

GIRL. Rather.

DOCTOR. Well, this gentleman's a friend of the manager of the opera. He can give you a line to him; will
that do?

GIRL. Why, of course. But if they want character,
I'm done, you know.

DOCTOR. They won't. You just tell the gentleman
about yourself; what you want to do and what you've
done. Talk to him a bit.

GIRL. My parents were people of good position.
They sent me to a boarding school —

DOCTOR [*interrupting*] You needn't tell him all that;
he won't believe a word of it.

GIRL. Eh? Well, but if I tell him the truth, it's
all up with me.

DOCTOR. No, no; he won't mind. Now then, you
came to Paris —

GIRL. Yes.

DOCTOR. You got a place as maid-servant?

GIRL. Well, yes.

DOCTOR. How old were you then?

GIRL. Why, I was turned seventeen.

DOCTOR. And then you had a baby?

GIRL [*astonished at the question*] Of course I did;
next year.

DOCTOR. Well, who was its father?

GIRL [*treating it as a matter of course*] Why, it was
my master, of course.

DOCTOR. Go on, go on. Tell us about it. Your mistress found out. What happened then?

GIRL [*in the same tone*] She sent me packing. I 'd have done the same, if I 'd been her.

DOCTOR. Go on; what are you stopping for? Talk away. The gentleman 's from the country; he does n't understand about these things.

GIRL [*gaily*] Right oh! I 'll tell you all about it. One night the boss comes up to my room in his socks and says: " If you shriek out, off you go! " Then —

DOCTOR. No, no. Begin after you lost your place.

GIRL. All right, if you think he 'll think it funny.

DOCTOR. Never mind that. Say what you 're doing now.

GIRL. Why, I come here every day.

DOCTOR. But before you come here?

GIRL. Oh, I do my five hours on the streets.

DOCTOR. Well, how 's that? The gentleman 's from the country, I tell you. He wants to know. Go on.

GIRL. There now, I would n't have thought there was anyone did n't know that. Why, I rig myself out as a work-girl, with a little bag on my arm — they make togs special for that, y' know — and then I trot along by the shop windows. Pretty hard work, too, 'cause to do it real well you have to walk fast. Then I stops in front of some shop or other. Nine times out of ten that does the trick. It just makes me laugh, I tell you, but you 'd think all the men had learnt what to say out of a book. There 's only two things they say, that 's all. It 's either: " You walk very fast " or else: " Are n't you afraid, all alone? " One knows what that means, eh? Or else I do the " young widow " fake. You 've got to go a bit fast like that, too. I don't know why, but it makes 'em catch on. They find out precious soon I 'm not a young widow, but that does n't make any odds. [*Seriously*] There 're things like that I don't understand.

DOCTOR. What sort are they, then? Shopwalkers, commercial travellers?

GIRL. I like that! Why, I only take real gentlemen.

DOCTOR. They say that's what they are.

GIRL. Oh, I can see well enough. Besides, a whole lot of 'em have orders on. That makes me laugh, too. When they meet you, they've got their little bits of ribbon stuck in their buttonhole. Then they follow you and they haven't anything. I wanted to find out, so I looked over my shoulder in a glass and saw my man snap the ribbon out with his finger and thumb just as you do when you're shelling peas. You know?

DOCTOR. Yes; I know. Tell us about your child. What became of it?

GIRL. Oh, I left it at that place in the Rue Denfer.

DOCTOR [to Loches] The foundlings' hospital.

LOCHES. Did you not mind doing that?

GIRL. It was better than dragging it about with me to starve.

LOCHES. Still, it was your child.

GIRL. Well, what about its father? It was his child, too, wasn't it? See here, I'm not going to talk about that again. Anyway, just tell me what I could have done, you two there. Put it out to nurse? Well, of course, I would have, if I'd been sure of having the money for it. But then I wanted to get another place; and how was I to pay for nursing it with the twenty-five or thirty francs a month I should have got, eh? If I wanted to keep straight, I couldn't keep the kid. See?

LOCHES. It's too horrible.

The doctor stops him with a gesture.

GIRL [angrily] It's just as I tell you. What else could I have done, eh? If you'd been in my place you'd have done just the same. [Quieting down] See here, what's the good of making a fuss about it? You'll say: "But you haven't been living straight." No more I have, but how could I help it? I couldn't stay in my places; and then, when you're hungry and a jolly young

chap offers you a dinner, my word, I 'd like to see the
girl who 'd say no. I never learnt any trade, you see.
So that the end of it all is that I found myself in St.
Lazare because I was ill. That 's pretty low down, too.
These beastly men give you their foul diseases and it 's
me they stick in prison. It 's a bit thick, that is.

DOCTOR. You gave them as good as you got, did n't
you, though?

GIRL [*gaily*] Oh, I had my tit for tat! [*To Loches*]
I suppose you 'd like to have that, too? Before they
carted me off there, the day I found out I was in for it,
I was going home in a pretty temper when who do you
think I met in the street but my old boss! I was that
glad to see him! Now, thinks I to myself, you 're going
to pay me what you owe me — with interest, too! I just
winked at him: oh, it did n't take long, I can tell you.
[*Tragically*] Then when I left him, I don't know what
came over me — I felt half mad. I took on everyone I
could, for anything or for nothing! As many as I could,
all the youngest and the best looking — well, I only gave
'em back what they gave me! Now somehow I don't
care any more: where 's the use in pulling long faces
about things? It only makes me laugh. Other women,
they do just the same; but then they do it for their
bread and butter, d' ye see. A girl must live even if
she is ill, eh? [*A pause*] Well, you 'll give my name
to the chap at the theatre, won't you? The doc here 'll
tell you my address.

LOCHES. I promise you I will.

GIRL. Thank ye, sir.

She goes out.

DOCTOR. Was I not right to keep that confession for
the end? This poor girl is typical. The whole problem
is summed up in her: she is at once the product and the
cause. We set the ball rolling, others keep it up, and it
runs back to bruise our own shins. I have nothing more

to say. [*He shakes hands with Loches as he conducts him to the door, and adds in a lighter tone*] But if you give a thought or two to what you have just seen when you are sitting in the Chamber, we shall not have wasted our time.

MATERNITY

[New Version]

Translated by

JOHN POLLOCK

A second version of Maternity was lately undertaken by M. Brieux. It differs in so many respects from the original one performed in England by the Stage Society, that it has been decided to include both versions in this volume. That which follows is the later one, and is presented by its author as the final form of the play.

ACT I

Brignac's drawing-room. An octagonal room, five sides of which are visible. Right, the door of Brignac's study, and beyond it the mantelpiece, in front of which are arm-chairs and a marquetry table with seats round it. At the back the door of the bedroom, which, being opened, shows the bed. Left, the door into the hall, then that of Annette's room, and beyond, a large window with a piano and music-stool in front of it. In the corners, at the back, on both sides, flowers in stands. The room is pretty and comfortable, without being luxurious. At the rise of the curtain the stage is empty. The door, left, opens, and Josephine, the maid, shows in Madeleine, a woman of twenty-eight.

JOSEPHINE. Madame Brignac must be there. I 'll tell her.

She goes across to the door at the back and disappears. After a moment Lucie enters. She is twenty-five years old, and her simple, but becoming, dress contrasts with her elder sister's exquisite and fashionable appearance.

LUCIE [*going gaily to Madeleine and kissing her*] My dear, how are you?

MADELEINE. Lucie, sweet!

LUCIE. How ravishing you look!

MADELEINE. One must, to please one's husband. Tell me — but first, how are the children?

LUCIE. About as usual.

257

MADELEINE. I 've a piece of good news. You know
Dr. Hourtin?

LUCIE. No, no; I don't think so.

MADELEINE. Yes; you do. The famous Hourtin,
you know. The man they call Providence for nervous
diseases.

LUCIE. Oh, yes, yes.

MADELEINE. Dr. Bar wanted to have a consultation
with him about your children, did n't he?

LUCIE. Of course; I know.

MADELEINE. I 've just met him at the Parmillets'.

LUCIE. What, he 's at Chartres!

MADELEINE. He 's going to see his brother somewhere
or other not far off, and so he came through Chartres to
visit the wonderful cave. In the one week since they
found it he must be at least the twentieth man of science
to come and pore over these old prehistoric bones.

LUCIE. But I thought he was a specialist for —

MADELEINE. Yes; the skeletons are just a relaxation.

LUCIE. Oh! Well —

MADELEINE. He 's a great friend of the Parmillets.
So, as I had the chance, I asked him to come here, and he
said he would.

LUCIE. But the children are with their granny in the
country.

MADELEINE. Oh, dear! Could n't you send for
them?

LUCIE. Yes, certainly. But when is Dr. Hourtin
going?

MADELEINE. At five o'clock. He wanted to go to his
brother first.

LUCIE. There 'd hardly be time.

MADELEINE. No. Suppose we were to ask him to
come this evening on his way back?

LUCIE. Do you think he would?

MADELEINE. Oh, yes; he 's a charming man.

LUCIE. What a piece of luck! If he could only cure my poor babies!

MADELEINE. They say he works wonders. And where is our little Annette?

LUCIE. Annette is with the Bernins. Tuesday is her day for going there.

MADELEINE. And your husband?

LUCIE. My husband? Why, he's at his meeting, of course.

MADELEINE. What, is it this afternoon?

LUCIE. You naughty woman! Not even to know the date of your brother-in-law's meeting!

MADELEINE [*making a face*] No. To me, you know, all these questions — birth-rate, repopulation — ugh!

LUCIE. France has need of it.

MADELEINE. I suppose so. [*A pause*] How is it you're not at the meeting?

LUCIE. It's only for working-men.

MADELEINE. M. de Forgeau's constituents?

LUCIE. Yes; but some day they may be Julien's constituents.

MADELEINE. How do you mean?

LUCIE. Listen! It's a secret, but I can't help telling you. M. de Forgeau has promised Julien to get him adopted by his committee at the election to the Chamber two months from now.

MADELEINE. Do you find the idea of being wife of a deputy fascinating?

LUCIE [*laughing*] He didn't ask my opinion. [*Seriously*] It seems that if he were in the Chamber, Julien might look forward to going very far.

MADELEINE. It was he who said that?

LUCIE. He, and M. de Forgeau. You know we're not rich. My husband's professional income would hardly be enough to secure the future of our two little girls, even if one were not, alas, an invalid.

Madeleine.   Are n't you afraid that Julien may be once again letting his imagination run away with him?

Lucie [*melancholy*]   What would be the good of my trying to dissuade him?   I must make myself try to share his illusions — for instance, in the success of his meeting this afternoon.

Madeleine.   But what can he find to say to working-men about all that?   That they ought to have large families?

Lucie.   That 's it.

Madeleine.   Of course, I know nothing about it, but I should think the best way to encourage them was not to let the children they have already perish of want.

Lucie.   Just what I tell Julien.   It 's the rich who ought to have children.

Madeleine.   So I think.

Lucie.   You 're rich — why have you only got one, then?

Madeleine.   That 's another question.   Don't let 's talk about that.   Talk of something cheery.

Josephine [*entering*]   If you please, ma'am, Catherine is here.

Lucie.   Ask her to come in.   [*To Madeleine*]   It 's ever so long since I 've seen nursie.

Josephine shows in Catherine, a working-woman of forty, dressed simply and very neatly in a black cloak and bonnet.

Catherine [*to Lucie and Madeleine*]   Good-day, ma'am.   Good-day.

Lucie and Madeleine [*shaking hands*]   How do you do, Catherine?

Catherine.   And your sister, ma'am, how 's she?

Lucie.   Annette?   Your darling 's very well.

Catherine.   That 's good to hear.   I thought I 'd just look in to say good-day.

Lucie.   I 'm glad you came.

CATHERINE. And to ask if you have n't any errands for me in Paris.

MADELEINE [*teasing her good humouredly*] Ah! So Catherine 's off to Paris — quite the lady!

LUCIE. Shall you stay there long?

CATHERINE. Oh, no. I expect to be back to-morrow. My big boy there is n't very well. So I 'm going to see him, too.

MADELEINE [*in order to say something*] This early heat, no doubt.

CATHERINE. May be. Then you have n't any errands for me?

LUCIE and MADELEINE. No, no. No, thank you.

CATHERINE. You don't know what I 'm going for?

LUCIE. I have no idea.

CATHERINE. I 'm going to see my eldest girl.

MADELEINE. You know where she 's living, then?

CATHERINE. Yes, I 've seen someone who met her.

LUCIE. And why did n't she write to you?

CATHERINE. We 'd got angry with one another.

MADELEINE. Ah!

CATHERINE. After she was turned off from the sewing-place she could n't get any work. And what must she do but want money from me? As if we had so much to spare!

LUCIE. What 's she doing now?

CATHERINE. She 's in work again. It seems she 's got a good place.

LUCIE. Come and tell us about her, won't you?

CATHERINE. Yes, indeed I will.

MADELEINE. And when you 're my way come in to see me, too. I 'll have a little packet of things for your youngsters.

CATHERINE. Ah, there it is! My husband won't let me take anything more from you or Mme. Brignac.

LUCIE. Why?

CATHERINE. Because of his politics. He says he's not going to vote for M. Brignac, so he does n't want to owe him anything.

MADELEINE. But why not from me? I don't ask him to vote for me!

CATHERINE. That's all one. You see, when you're in want, it turns a body sulky.

LUCIE. In want? He's still at the electric works, is n't he? He makes a good living.

CATHERINE. So he does. If there were just the two of us, we'd live like lords. But it's the little ones, that's what it is: there are too many of us.

MADELEINE. Oh, come, come, Catherine!

CATHERINE. Well, ma'am, I ask you. We don't go spending our money at the theatre —

Brignac enters. He is a dark, good-looking fellow of five-and-thirty, rather stout, with a strong, vibrating voice, and a southern accent.

BRIGNAC [*to Josephine*] And bring me the biscuits and the bottle I told you to bring up this morning. The one with the green seal.

JOSEPHINE. Yes, sir.

BRIGNAC. Aha, Lucie! A kiss, quick! Congratulate me!

LUCIE. It went well?

BRIGNAC. Splendidly. How are you, Madeleine? Immensely! Ah, Catherine, it's you? How are you?

CATHERINE. I was just going, sir.

BRIGNAC. I did n't see your husband at the meeting.

CATHERINE. He was n't there, sir.

BRIGNAC. Ah, yes, yes. A regular fire-eater now, is n't he? Well, I hope his Socialism is profitable.

CATHERINE. Well, we might —

BRIGNAC. Get along better? I thought so. [*In a changed tone*] Ah, Catherine, I used to know you and your family when your husband went more to church than to his club. You had faith then to help you bear up against your troubles! You put your trust in Providence! Yes, you brought up your children according to the Scriptures: " Consider the lilies of the field, how they grow. They toil not, neither do they spin, and yet I say unto you, that even Solomon in all his glory was not arrayed like one of these."

MADELEINE [*shrugging her shoulders. Low*] Don't, Julien.

CATHERINE. Good-bye, ma'am. Good-bye, sir. [*She goes out*].

BRIGNAC [*to Madeleine*] What is it?

MADELEINE. You should have more tact.

LUCIE [*interposing*] Come now, don't quarrel, you two. [*To Madeleine*] You're not to get cross again. Tell us about your meeting.

BRIGNAC. First, just to get back my strength! [*He drinks a glass of the wine that Josephine has brought*]. My meeting? Well, it was a huge success. On the battlefield Napoleon used to say: " One night of Paris will make up for all this." If he lived now, he'd say: " One night of Paris — after an address from Brignac!" I tell you, I did magnificently. And the audience was by no means only my friends. I know that, because when I said — when I was inspired to say — " God blesses large families — "

MADELEINE. Someone answered: " But he doesn't support them."

BRIGNAC. Were you there?

MADELEINE. No, but the retort is so well known that nowadays people don't allude to blessings from above. There's too much suffering here below. It looks like a bad joke.

BRIGNAC. Ah, that spirit of Voltaire! [*He pours out another glass of wine*].

LUCIE. Don't you think you've had enough, dear?

BRIGÑAC [*holding up the glass*] What, of this wine? From a vineyard that my father planted?

LUCIE. That makes no difference.

BRIGNAC. Have you ever seen me drunk?

LUCIE. No.

BRIGNAC. Well, then! [*He drinks*] Ah! Pure sunshine! It brightens my heart to drink it! M. de Forgeau was enchanted. Have you told Madeleine that I'm going to stand?

LUCIE. Everyone knows about it.

BRIGNAC. So much the better. After to-day, I have reason to think that there's every chance of my being elected. At last, we'll have done with this narrow life of a provincial lawyer! You'll see! And who knows — between ourselves, of course — who knows that some day I shan't have men on the bench coming to beg favors of the Minister that they used to refuse to the simple lawyer! Aha, and why not? Stranger things have happened. [*Walking about and rubbing his hands*] Ah, there'll be some who'll cut a queer figure then. [*He pulls himself up*] Well, well. In the meantime the essential thing is the deputation.

LUCIE. Yes.

BRIGNAC. We're working at it. And what could be finer than to advance one's own interests in the very act of defending one's country? That is the best defence of it, to help in the production of the human race itself, for it means true morality within and the respect of other countries from without.

MADELEINE. You didn't forget that in your speech, I hope?

BRIGNAC [*simply*] No, no; that was part of my peroration. All Frenchmen ought to do like old Féchain.

LUCIE. Who's he?

BRIGNAC. Old Féchain — he was one of the audience. You'll see him presently. He came to shake hands with me after the meeting. He has twelve children — magnificent! Magnificent! I repeat. I told him to come round here.

MADELEINE. What for?

BRIGNAC. I don't know, he was so worked up, I wanted to show him a mark of my sympathy. He'll tell you how it went off; you don't believe me, Madeleine?

MADELEINE. Indeed I do.

BRIGNAC. I saw you smiling. Yes, he'll tell you. [*Josephine brings a card in*] Dr. Hourtin? I know that name.

LUCIE. Oh, yes, I forgot. It's Dr. Hourtin, the professor at Paris.

MADELEINE. I'll see him, and explain.

LUCIE. Yes, do. [*Madeleine goes out*] It's the doctor we wanted to consult about the children, you know. He happens to be at Chartres, and Madeleine met him at some friends.

Madeleine returns with Dr. Hourtin. He is a man of thirty-five, with short hair and a pointed beard.

HOURTIN [*to Madeleine, as they come in*] No apology is needed.

MADELEINE [*introducing him*] My sister, Madame Brignac; Monsieur Brignac. Professor Hourtin. [*Greetings*].

HOURTIN. I hear that your babies are in the country. If you like, I could come in to see them to-morrow on my way back. But only after dinner, I fear — my train gets in late.

LUCIE. Of course! We shall be extremely grateful.

MADELEINE [*to Lucie*] I shall arrange to come as soon as possible to hear what the doctor says.

BRIGNAC. Sit down, won't you? I'm really delighted. [*Ringing*] Let me offer you a biscuit and a glass of Alicante.

HOURTIN. No, thank you.

BRIGNAC [*speaking first in an undertone to Josephine, who answers the bell*] Just for the sake of company! And so, here you are at Chartres — a stroke of luck for the town and for us.

HOURTIN. I was going to see my brother at Château-dun and thought that I would visit the town on the way.

BRIGNAC. And see our famous cave — these pre-historic remains?

HOURTIN. Anthropology interests me.

BRIGNAC. A thoroughly genuine discovery, too.

HOURTIN. Oh, yes, there is no doubt.

LUCIE. I saw a photograph of some of the remains. It was horrible.

HOURTIN. Don't say that!

LUCIE. I dreamed of it all night. Were they really human beings?

HOURTIN. The remains are undoubtedly those of a household of the stone age. The man's skeleton is intact, the woman's skull is fractured.

LUCIE. Poor woman! By a falling rock?

HOURTIN. Oh, no. The human, fist of that date was well able to give such a blow.

BRIGNAC. In fact, a little domestic difference?

HOURTIN [*laughing*] I can't diagnose at such an interval. But it is easy to imagine the man trying to drag the woman into his den. She refuses. He raises his fist — a blow to stun her, only he hits rather too hard.

LUCIE. How terrible!

HOURTIN. Those were the manners of our ancestor, the cave man.

BRIGNAC. The world has changed.

MADELEINE. Yes. Since the cave man hypocrisy has been invented.

HOURTIN. And we can imagine further. A rival springs on the ravisher, strangles him, and leaves the two corpses in the midst of the flint weapons and the kitchen utensils of polished stone.

LUCIE. It's enough to give one a nightmare.

HOURTIN [*rising, to Lucie*] Forgive me. [*To Brignac*] I should have begun instead of ended by congratulating you on the success of your meeting.

Josephine enters with a bottle and glasses on a tray.

BRIGNAC. You must not go without drinking to it, then. Aha, I'm not from Chartres! Montpellier is my native town; close by Montpellier, at least. Palavas — Palavas-les-Flots. In my part of the country an honest man isn't afraid of a glass of wine. Alicante, you know!

HOURTIN. No, thank you, really.

BRIGNAC [*filling his glass*] I see. You're afraid that my Alicante comes from the grocer's? No, no! My dear sir, I am the son of a wine grower and I can answer for my cellar, I assure you.

HOURTIN. I only drink water.

BRIGNAC. Ah! You belong to that school of doctors to whom wine is anathema. Let me tell you you're ruining at one stroke the stomach of the north and the purse of the south. Pessimists, that's what you are. It's nothing short of treason to slander the good wine of France. Here's to your health, and to mine, and to France! [*He drinks*].

HOURTIN [*laughing*] Allow me to point out that it's Spanish wine you are drinking.

BRIGNAC [*laughing too*] Yes; but I only drink this in a small glass. Look here, I'll prove to you that you're wrong. My father — you see, I don't need to go far — died at seventy-five, as strong as an oak. He kept his vines and his vines kept him. I can promise you he didn't only drink water. I don't say that now and then — market day and so on — he didn't get a bit lively, a bit too lively, perhaps. Well, did he suffer for it? On the contrary, it gave him strength to support life and made him charitable to other people's little failings. A good glass of wine never hurt anybody — there's my witness you see — and my dear father did n't drink by the thimbleful, I can tell you. But nowadays you think you see drunkards everywhere.

HOURTIN. With good reason.

BRIGNAC. Well, take me! Do I look healthy? Fit?

HOURTIN. I don't judge people by their looks.

BRIGNAC. Well, then, I am fit. Ask my wife if I 've ever been ill? That 's the result of following my father's example. Never once ill at thirty-five. Only, only — mark my words — I drink nothing but good wine. You must admit I 'm right, for I 've never been — I won't say drunk, but even ordinarily elevated. No, never! Is n't that so, Lucie? I 'll hold my own with anyone. I 've often won bets about it.

LUCIE. But you know you sometimes have fits of passion.

BRIGNAC. That has nothing to do with it. That 's my temperament. I 'm built nervously.

HOURTIN. Never having been drunk proves nothing.

BRIGNAC. Oh, come!

HOURTIN. No. There are a large number of men who drink, perhaps, a glass of vermouth before lunch, a bottle of wine at lunch, and two or three glasses of liqueur after. The same at dinner, after an absinthe and a glass or two of beer in the afternoon. They would be much astonished to learn that they are thoroughly alcoholized.

BRIGNAC. Well, I do all that, and I 'm as well as can be. What is more, as a baby I was very delicate. I could n't walk till I was eighteen months old or talk before two years. And I 'm from the South. Ha, ha! You 'll say I 'm making up for lost time?

HOURTIN [laughing] I shan't try to convince you. Time will do that.

BRIGNAC [glass in hand] In one way I 'm of your mind. I firmly believe that drink is a social evil, and I fight against it. For poor people, who are underfed and drink adulterated stuff. That's different. There you're right. But alcohol is only bad on an empty stomach.

HOURTIN. Poor empty stomachs. But why don't you preach sobriety to them, instead of inciting them to have children?

BRIGNAC. Don't you approve of that?

HOURTIN. My own opinion is that the poor and the sick have too many children and the rich not enough.

BRIGNAC. But — [*To Josephine, who enters*] What is it?

HOURTIN. Then I'll be going. [*To Lucie*] Till to-morrow.

BRIGNAC [*to Josephine*] Show him in. [*To Hourtin*] Wait a moment — five minutes — two minutes only. I'll show you a workman who has twelve children. Let's see what you say to that. [*To Féchain*] Come in, my friend, come in.

Enter Féchain, a man of fifty, dressed in a workman's Sunday clothes. Where he stands on coming in he is unable to see Hourtin.

FÉCHAIN. Good-day, ladies and gentlemen.

LUCIE [*to Madeleine*] What a gay old thing!

MADELEINE. Ha, ha!

BRIGNAC. I am glad to see you here in my house and in the midst of my family, and I congratulate you as a living example of the fulfilment of duty. Give me your hand.

FÉCHAIN. Here you are, sir. [*They shake hands*].

BRIGNAC. What's your name?

FÉCHAIN. Féchain.

BRIGNAC. Do you live at Chartres?

FÉCHAIN. Yes, sir, close by, in the valley.

BRIGNAC. What are you by trade?

FÉCHAIN. I do a job here and a job there.

BRIGNAC. And you have twelve children?

FÉCHAIN. The thirteenth coming, too.

BRIGNAC. What! My best congratulations.

MADELEINE. Your wife might have some of the congratulations as well.

FÉCHAIN. Thank you, ma'am. I 'll tell her what you say.

MADELEINE. Is she in good health?

FÉCHAIN. Perfect.

BRIGNAC. That 's fine. You 're a grand fellow, a real example of public virtue.

FÉCHAIN. It 's just the way I 'm made, so I can't help it. [*Laughing with stupid vanity*] Aha, if only everyone were like you or me! The way you talked, you know! Why number thirteen had to be on the way after that. How many have you?

BRIGNAC. Two.

FÉCHAIN [*making a face*] What! what! Oh, you must make up for lost time.

MADELEINE [*to Lucie, low*] Nasty old beast!

BRIGNAC [*a little awkwardly*] There, splendid! You 're the right sort. Come and see me again some day. If you want a recommendation — [*He takes him to the door*].

FÉCHAIN. Thank you kindly.

BRIGNAC. Good-bye.

FÉCHAIN. If I might make so bold, sir, could you lend me twenty-eight francs? I 'm a bit behind with my rent.

BRIGNAC. I 'll lay your request before the town authority and second it warmly, I promise you.

MADELEINE. But perhaps he 's in need of it at once. [*To Féchain*] Give me your address and I 'll bring you the money. I shall be glad to pay my respects to that fine wife of yours.

FÉCHAIN. Oh, ma'am; but you 'd be likely to miss her. She 's often out of the house.

MADELEINE. That does n't matter. I shall see the children, anyway. Where do you live?

FÉCHAIN.   You're very kind, but I should n't like a lady like you to come to our sort of place.   My landlord 'll wait so long as he knows that M. Brignac is going to help me.   Thank you all the same.

HOURTIN [*to Brignac*]   Let me say a word to this fellow.   I feel sure I 've seen him somewhere.   [*Brignac nods. To Féchain*]   Pardon me —

FÉCHAIN [*starting*]   Oh! Good-day, doctor.

HOURTIN.   Ah, I thought so! I was sure I knew you. You were working at the hospital once?

FÉCHAIN.   Yes, sir.

HOURTIN.   Quite so.   No; you do *not* live at Chartres.

FÉCHAIN [*after a silence*]   No, sir.   I live at Paris. Only when I see there 's to be a meeting like this not far away, I go to it.   I 'm a poor man, and then —

HOURTIN.   Then you get a loan from the chairman?

FÉCHAIN.   If I can.   Sometimes I 'm asked to dinner.

HOURTIN.   Is it true you have twelve children?

FÉCHAIN [*smiling*]   That? Oh, yes; I 've got the proofs.   [*He takes some papers from his pocket*]   Here are their birth certificates, all twelve.   I always have them about me — never go without them — so as I can show them.   You can count them.

HOURTIN [*taking the papers*]   Do all your children live with you?

FÉCHAIN.   Oh, no.   Why there are n't more than seven left.

HOURTIN.   The others are dead?

FÉCHAIN.   Poor folks can't hope to keep all they have.

HOURTIN.   When you had had five, you must have seen that you could n't support them?

FÉCHAIN.   Of course.

HOURTIN.   And you had more all the same?

FÉCHAIN.   We could n't have been worse off than we were.   One more or less makes no odds; and then, after seven, things are easier.

HOURTIN. How's that?

FÉCHAIN. This way. If you have three or four children, no one bothers about you, you're like everyone else; but with seven or eight, then they have to help you. Relief charities, or the authorities, or just people, that's all one. They daren't say no. If you have ten, then it's first class. Only you mustn't mind moving. But there, there's nothing to be had for nothing, is there?

HOURTIN. How many of your children are living with you?

FÉCHAIN. Two.

HOURTIN. And the other five?

FÉCHAIN. The two girls are big enough to do for themselves. The other three are in hospital. [*A silence*].

HOURTIN [*looking at the papers*] All your children are not of the same mother, I see.

FÉCHAIN. No; I've been a widower twice. Oh, yes; I've had my troubles. This is my third. It's her fourth she's expecting.

MADELEINE [*after a pause, to Lucie*] A man like that ought to be shut up.

HOURTIN [*giving him back the papers*] Thank you.

FÉCHAIN. Good-day, sir. Good-day, ladies. [*To Brignac*] You couldn't just let me have the money for the railway and my ticket to the meeting? It's only just a trifle.

HOURTIN [*giving him some money*] There!

FÉCHAIN. Thank you kindly, sir. [*He goes out*].

HOURTIN [*taking leave*] You see! Children who cannot be kept ought not to be born. And I would add that those who are born ought to be properly kept.

BRIGNAC. A pretext that would justify the shirking of all duty. It's impossible to see ahead like that.

HOURTIN. You don't ask more people to dinner than

you have room for, nor before dinner is ready. It will be time to think of increasing our population when our housing and means of livelihood are up to the mark of our existing needs.

BRIGNAC. But each new generation is itself a means of production.

HOURTIN. Certainly. I only ask that the poor should have few children and the degenerate none. No child ought to be brought into the world handicapped by illness or want.

BRIGNAC. And as the result of your precautions our country would fall in point of population to a fifth or a tenth rate power.

HOURTIN [at the door] History teaches us that not even military supremacy belongs to the largest nations. M. de Marigny's reflection, not mine. [Bowing to the ladies] Till to-morrow. [Shaking Brignac's hand] And when you have a moment, just consider how society behaves to the mothers of whom it demands children. You'll find that an entertaining subject — unless it makes you cry. Good-bye.

LUCIE [showing him out] Then you will really come to see my babies?

HOURTIN. Most certainly. [Lucie goes out with him].

MADELEINE. Well, my dear brother-in-law, what do you say to that?

BRIGNAC [shrugging his shoulders] Oh, if I had wanted to answer him —

MADELEINE. Why did n't you?

BRIGNAC. Surely you can see that I was not going to annoy a man whom we want to consult professionally. [A pause. He looks at his watch. Lucie returns] Well, five o'clock. I'm off to the club for my game of dominoes. Ta, ta! You dine here, Madeleine, of course?

MADELEINE. No; I can't. We've some official people

to go to in the evening. But I 'll look in for news of the chicks.

BRIGNAC. Very well. I 'll upset all Dr. Hourtin's theories for you in five seconds. You wait and see.

MADELEINE. All right.

BRIGNAC. Good-bye. [*He goes out*].

MADELEINE. Annette not back yet?

LUCIE. She won't be long now.

MADELEINE. Lucie, don't you think perhaps she goes rather too often to the Bernins?

LUCIE. Gabrielle 's her best friend.

MADELEINE. Hm! yes.

LUCIE. They 're both so keen on music. Besides, the poor little dear does n't get too much fun. It 's dull for her here. I can see she feels it, particularly lately. She only brightens up when she goes to see Gabrielle.

MADELEINE. Yes; but that girl has a brother.

LUCIE. Jacques.

MADELEINE. Just so; Jacques.

LUCIE. Have you heard people talking about Annette in connection with him?

MADELEINE. No. Well, then, yes; I have. Listen, dear. We 're rather peculiarly placed, are n't we? Three orphan girls. I 'm married twice, though I 'm only twenty-eight, and you 're married for the first time.

LUCIE. And for the last, I should hope.

MADELEINE [*laughing*] Tut, tut!

LUCIE [*laughing too*] Monster!

MADELEINE. Then you took our youngest sister to live with you. A perfect arrangement, so long as you look after her as you would after your own girl, or as mother would have done.

LUCIE. She 's eighteen.

MADELEINE. That 's just it.

LUCIE. I don't see what danger there is for Annette.

MADELEINE. Nor do I. But we're not alone in the world. As it is, people look astonished — of course it's a silly little provincial place — at her going out alone.

LUCIE. Oh, to see Gabrielle, five minutes off!

MADELEINE. I know, I know! Tell me, do you think that the Bernin boy would be a possible match for Annette?

LUCIE. I never thought about it. Well, why not?

MADELEINE. Hm! hm!

LUCIE. He's about the right age. He seems to be a good fellow.

MADELEINE. Oh, yes.

LUCIE. His family is well enough.

MADELEINE. And — the money?

LUCIE. Yes; that's true. The Bernins are rich and Annette has nothing. Yes; you're right. She was going to spend a week with them in the country. I'll find an excuse for her not going. Perhaps I had better say something to her about it.

MADELEINE. There's no hurry; but we must see that no harm happens to our little pet.

LUCIE. Good heavens! I should never forgive myself.

Annette, fair, eighteen years old, runs in, overflowing with joy.

ANNETTE. What luck! Madeleine, too! Here, Josephine! [*She throws her hat to Josephine, who drops it on the floor*] Oh, stupid! [*Recovering herself*] All right, there! Don't be cross, Fifine. [*She kisses Josephine and shoves her out*].

LUCIE. What's the matter?

MADELEINE. Why so radiant?

ANNETTE. Yes, I am! I am! Oh, I'm so happy!

LUCIE. Is that why you kissed Josephine?

ANNETTE. Josephine! Why, I could have kissed the passers-by in the street!

MADELEINE [*laughing*] Our little girl's gone cracked.

ANNETTE. No, no; only — oh, I 'm so happy! [*She bursts into a fit of sobbing*].

LUCIE. Annette, what 's the matter?

MADELEINE. Annette!

ANNETTE [*through her tears*] Oh, I am happy, happy!

LUCIE. She 'll make herself ill. Madeleine, call someone.

ANNETTE. No, no; don't worry. Don't say anything. It 's only my nerves. [*Laughing and crying at the same time*] Oh, I am happy, only — how silly to cry like that! But I can't help it. [*She puts her arm round Lucie's neck, who is kneeling beside her, and draws Madeleine's head towards her*] Lucie, darling! Madeleine, dearest! [*She kisses them, then sobs again*] How silly! It 's no good; I must. There [*she dries her eyes*], there! Now I can tell you. [*With a pure look of deeply felt happiness*] I 'm going to be married. M. and Madame Bernin are coming.

LUCIE. Why?

ANNETTE. Because they 're going to the country tomorrow.

MADELEINE. They 're going away?

ANNETTE. Yes; Jacques has told them.

LUCIE. Jacques?

ANNETTE [*in a sudden rush*] Yes. It all happened like that, with our music — Gabrielle and me. That was how, and he guessed everything. He sings tenor — oh, not very well. Once [*with a laugh*] — but I 'll tell you later. That was how it came about; and we 're to be married soon. [*Crying again, then gravely pressing Lucie to her*] I love him so! Oh, if you only knew! If he had n't married me, it would have been so dreadful! You don't understand?

MADELEINE [*smiling*] Perhaps we can guess.

ANNETTE. Shall I tell you everything, everything from the beginning?

LUCIE. Yes.

ANNETTE. I should love to tell you. You won't mind?

MADELEINE. Go on.

ANNETTE. It was like that, when Gabrielle and I were playing duets. At first I hated him because he always laughs at everything, but at bottom he 's good. Do you know what he once —

LUCIE. Never mind that. Go on about the music.

ANNETTE. Well, as I was saying, Gabrielle and I used to play duets. He used to come and listen to us. He stood behind and turned over the pages. Then once he put his hand on my shoulder —

MADELEINE. And you did n't say anything?

ANNETTE. He had his other hand on Gabrielle's. I should have looked so idiotic.

LUCIE. Gabrielle 's not the same thing.

ANNETTE. Just what I was going to say. My heart beat so hard and I felt my face all scarlet, that I hardly knew what I was playing. Then another time, when he could n't follow, he bent right over. Oh, but I can't tell you everything, little by little. We love one another, that 's all.

MADELEINE. And he has told you that he loves you?

ANNETTE [*gravely*] Yes.

LUCIE. And you kept all that from me! That was n't right, Annette.

ANNETTE. Oh, forgive me; but it came about so gradually, I could hardly say when it began. I said to myself that it could n't be true, and when — when we did tell one another what we had n't ever said, though we knew it ourselves, then I knew I 'd done wrong, only I was so ashamed that I could n't tell you about it.

LUCIE [*gently*] But it was wrong, my little pet.

ANNETTE. Oh, don't scold me! Please, please, don't! If you knew how I 've been feeling — oh, how dreadfully badly! You did n't notice.

LUCIE. Yes, I did.

MADELEINE. Has he spoken to his parents?

ANNETTE. Oh, a long time ago.

LUCIE. They consent?

ANNETTE. They 're coming here this afternoon.

MADELEINE. Why did n't they come sooner?

ANNETTE. Because — Jacques told them you see; but they did n't want it talked about. They wanted Gabrielle to get married first. So we agreed that I should seem not to think they knew anything about it. Then to-day I met Jacques in the street —

LUCIE. In the street!

ANNETTE. Yes. He 's given up coming to the music, so I meet him —

LUCIE. In the street!

ANNETTE. As a rule, we only bow to each other; but to-day, as he passed me he said: " My parents are going to your sister's to-day." He was quite pale. Don't scold me, please! I 'm so happy! Do forgive me!

MADELEINE [*to Lucie, who looks silently at Annette*] Come, forgive her.

LUCIE [*kissing her*] Oh, yes, I forgive her. So you want to leave us, bad girl?

ANNETTE. Yes. I am bad and ungrateful, I know.

LUCIE. Hush, hush! Nonsense!

MADELEINE. Marriage is a serious thing, Annette. Are you sure that your characters agree together?

ANNETTE. Oh, yes, yes! Why, we 've quarrelled already!

LUCIE. What about?

ANNETTE. About a book he lent me.

MADELEINE. What book?

ANNETTE. Anna Karenina. He liked Vronsky better than Levine. He said such silly things. And he could n't understand Anna Karenina killing herself — you know — when she throws herself underneath the train that he 's in. You remember, don't you?

Lucie. And then?

Annette. Then — there's the bell. Perhaps it's them.

A pause. Josephine enters with a card.

Lucie. Yes.

Annette. Oh, heavens!

Lucie. Madeleine, take Annette. Go through her room.

Madeleine. All right.

Lucie [*to Josephine*] Show Madame Bernin in.

Annette [*to Lucie*] Don't be long.

Annette goes out with Madeleine. Lucie arranges herself before a glass. Josephine shows in Madame Bernin.

Lucie. How do you do?

Mme. Bernin. How are you?

Lucie. Very well, thank you. And you?

Mme. Bernin. I need not ask news of M. Brignac. I know he is busy fighting the good fight.

Lucie. And M. Bernin?

Mme. Bernin. He's very well, thanks. I hope your children —

Lucie. About the same. But won't you sit down?

Mme. Bernin. Thank you. What lovely weather!

Lucie. Yes; is n't it?

Mme. Bernin. I hear there was a large audience at M. Brignac's meeting.

Lucie. Yes, indeed.

Mme. Bernin. In spite of the heat.

Lucie. You are happy to be able to go to the country. Annette was so delighted to get your kind invitation.

Mme. Bernin. That was precisely my object in calling here to-day — apart from the pleasure of seeing you — to talk about that plan of ours.

Lucie. And about another one, I think?

Mme. Bernin. Another?

Lucie. No?

MME. BERNIN. No; I don't know what you are referring to.

LUCIE. Oh, I beg your pardon, then. Please go on. About Annette?

MME. BERNIN. My daughter has had an invitation to join our cousins, the Guibals, for some time, and we absolutely cannot refuse to send Gabrielle to them. So I came to ask you to excuse us, as Gabrielle will not be there.

LUCIE. Will you forgive me for being indiscreet?

MME. BERNIN. I am sure you could n't be.

LUCIE. I wanted to ask you, is it long since Gabrielle received this invitation?

MME. BERNIN. About a week.

LUCIE. Indeed!

MME. BERNIN. Why should that surprise you?

LUCIE. She said nothing about it to Annette.

MME. BERNIN. She was probably afraid of disappointing her.

LUCIE. Only yesterday Annette was telling me of all the excursions that your daughter had planned to make with her. Please, please, tell me the truth! This invitation is merely an excuse; I feel convinced it is. Please tell me! Annette is only my sister, but I love her as though she were my child. Think it 's her mother who is speaking to you. I won't try to be clever. I 'm not going to stand on my dignity. This is what has happened. Annette believes that your son loves her, and when your card was brought in she imagined that you had come to ask her for him. Now you know everything that I know, and I beg you to talk as candidly to me, so that we may avoid as much unhappiness as possible.

MME. BERNIN. You have spoken to me so simply and feelingly that I can't help answering openly — from the bottom of my heart. Yes, then, this invitation to Ga-

brielle is only an excuse. We have invented it to prevent
Jacques and Annette from meeting again.

LUCIE. You don't want them to meet again?

MME. BERNIN. No; because I don't want them to
marry.

LUCIE. Because Annette is poor?

MME. BERNIN [*hesitates, then*] Well, since we have
agreed to be perfectly candid, that is the reason.

LUCIE. You would not consent to the idea of their
marrying?

MME. BERNIN. No.

LUCIE. Is that absolutely final?

MME. BERNIN. Absolutely final.

LUCIE. Because Annette has no dowry?

MME. BERNIN. Yes.

LUCIE. But your son knew that she was poor. It's
monstrous of him to have made her love him.

MME. BERNIN. If he had acted as you describe, I
admit it would be monstrous. But he had no intention
of engaging her affections. Annette was a friend of his
sister's. I am sure he had no idea in meeting her beyond
that of simple good comradeship. Very likely he went
on to pay her some attention; indeed he might well have
been attracted by her. Your sweet little Annette, who is
the most innocent of creatures, has fallen more easily
and more deeply, perhaps, in love. Innocence like hers
is closely akin to ignorance. But that my son has more
to reproach himself with! You can easily see that he
has not, because it was he who told me about it himself.

LUCIE. How long ago?

MME. BERNIN. Just now. He told me that he was in
love with Annette, as she, no doubt, thinks herself with
him; and, in fact, he begged me to come and ask for her
hand.

LUCIE. Only to-day?

MME. BERNIN. A couple of hours since.

Lucie. Annette implored him to tell you. He said he had already done so and that you had given your consent.

Mme. Bernin. Never!

Lucie. A month ago.

Mme. Bernin. Until to-day he never said anything to me.

Lucie. Annette told me so herself!

Mme. Bernin. He never said anything to me.

Lucie. Do you mean that she lied?

Mme. Bernin. He never said anything to me.

Lucie. Do you think her truthful?

Mme. Bernin. Yes.

Lucie. Candid, honest?

Mme. Bernin. Yes.

Lucie. Well, then?

Mme. Bernin. Well, it is possible that he did not tell her the truth. After all, he 's a man.

Lucie. And in love, men have the right to lie?

Mme. Bernin. They think so.

Lucie. And when you told him to give up Annette, he agreed?

Mme. Bernin. Yes, he did. He is a sensible, practical fellow, and he could not help seeing the force of what I said. He realizes that however hard it may be for him to break with Annette, it is necessary. I need hardly say he feels it keenly, but at these children's age feelings change.

Lucie. I see. A week hence your son won't think of her. But she?

Mme. Bernin. She will forget him, too.

Lucie. I don't know about that. Oh, my poor darling! If you could have seen her here just now when she came to tell us! She cried with joy! It 's not for joy that she 'll cry now. Oh, my God! [*She breaks into tears*].

Mme. Bernin [*moved*] Oh, don't! Please, please!

I understand your grief; indeed I do. Ah, if it were possible, how happy it would make me for Annette to marry my boy. I tell you I have had to stop myself from loving her. What a contrast to the girl he will have to marry — tiresome, affected creature!

LUCIE. If what you say is true, are n't you rich enough to let your son marry a poor girl?

MME. BERNIN. No; we are not so well off as people suppose. And then we must give Gabrielle a dowry.

LUCIE. You 'll find her a husband who will want her for herself.

MME. BERNIN. Even if we did, which I doubt, I would not desire a man like that for her, because he would be blind to the realities of the situation. Gabrielle has not been brought up to poverty, but to a life of luxurious surroundings.

LUCIE. Give your children an equal amount, then.

MME. BERNIN. All that we can give Gabrielle will not be too much. Life is hard, and becomes a harder struggle every day. Young men tend to ask more with their wives, because they know the power of money in the keen competition of modern existence.

LUCIE. Oh, yes; they know it! Their creed is to have enjoyment as soon as possible, without making the least sacrifice for it, and a fig for gentleness or emotion!

MME. BERNIN. You may be right. I want Gabrielle to be rich because riches will attract more bidders for her hand, so that she will have more choice.

LUCIE. You have to speak of it even like a business transaction.

MME. BERNIN. Consequently there will be little or nothing for Jacques.

LUCIE. People who have no money work.

MME. BERNIN. He has not been brought up to work.

LUCIE. Then he ought to have been.

MME. BERNIN. The professions are already overstocked. Do you propose that he should become a clerk at two hundred francs a month? He and his wife wouldn't be able to keep a servant.

LUCIE. There are clerks who get more than that.

MME. BERNIN. Even if he got five hundred, would that enable him to keep up his social position? Of course it would not. He would owe his inferiority to his wife, and would soon begin to reproach her with it. And have you thought about their children? They would have just enough to send their son to the primary school and make their daughter a post office clerk. Even for that they would be terribly pinched.

LUCIE. Yes.

MME. BERNIN. You see I'm right. I can't say I'm proud to confess so much, but what are we to do? Life is ordered by things as they are, not like a novel. We live in a shrewd, vain, selfish world.

LUCIE. You despise it and yet sacrifice everything to it.

MME. BERNIN. I know that everybody's happiness practically depends on the consideration he has in it. Only exceptional people can disregard social conventions, and Jacques is not an exception.

LUCIE. If I were you, I don't think I should be proud of it. If he were a little more than commonplace, his love would give him strength to stand up against the jeers of the crowd.

MME. BERNIN. His love! Love passes, poverty stays; you know the proverb. Beauty fades; want grows.

LUCIE. But you yourself — you and your husband are the living proof that one can marry poor and make money! Everyone knows how your husband began as a small clerk, then started in a small business of his own, then won success. If that spells happiness, you and he must be happy.

MME. BERNIN. No; we have not been happy, because we have used ourselves up with hunting for happiness. We meant to " get there "; we have " got there," but at what a price! Oh, I know the road to fortune. At first miserable, sordid economy, passionate greed; then the fierce struggle of trickery and deceit, always flattering your customers, always living in terror of failure. Tears, lies, envy, contempt. Suffering for yourself and for everyone round you. I 've been through it, and a bitter experience it was. We 're determined that our children shan't. Our children! We have had only two, but we meant to have only one. That extra one meant double toil and hardship. Instead of being a husband and wife helping one another, we have been two business partners, watching each other like enemies, perpetually quarrelling, even on our pillow, over our expenditures or our mistakes. Finally we succeeded; and now we can't enjoy our wealth because we don't know how to use it, and because our later years are poisoned by memories of the hateful past of suffering and rancor. No; I shall never expose my children to that struggle. I only stood it to preserve them from it. Good-bye.

LUCIE. Good-bye.

Madame Bernin goes out. After a moment Lucie goes slowly to Annette's door and opens it.

ANNETTE [*coming in*] You 've been crying! It 's because I 'm going away, is n't it? There 's nothing to prevent us, is there? [*With rising emotion*] Lucie, tell me there 's nothing!

LUCIE. You love him so much?

ANNETTE. If we were not to be married, I should die.

LUCIE. No; you would n't. Have all the little girls who said that died?

ANNETTE. But there is nothing to prevent us, is there?

LUCIE. No, no!

ANNETTE. And when is it to be? Did you talk of that?

LUCIE. My dear, my dear, what a state you 're in! You really must be less nervous.

ANNETTE [*restraining herself*] Yes, sweet, yes; I 'm a little crazy.

LUCIE. I think you are.

ANNETTE. Tell me, then, everything! How did she begin?

LUCIE. Are you in such a hurry to leave me? You don't love me any more?

ANNETTE [*gravely*] Oh, if I had n't got you, what would become of me? [*A silence*] But you 're not telling me anything. There must be something. You 're keeping the truth from me. If there was n't something, you 'd say there was n't — you would n't try to put me off — you 'd tell me just what Madame Bernin said.

LUCIE. Well, then, there is something.

ANNETTE [*breaking into tears*] Oh, heavens!

LUCIE. You 're both very young. You must wait. A year, perhaps longer.

ANNETTE [*crying*] Wait! A year!

LUCIE. Come, come, you must not be so uncontrolled, Annette. You 'll make me displeased with you. Why, you are barely nineteen. If you wait to be married till you are twenty, there 'll be no great harm.

ANNETTE. It is n't possible.

LUCIE. Not possible? [*With a long look at her*] Annette, you frighten me! If it were not you — [*With tender gravity*] I can't have been wrong to trust you?

ANNETTE. No, no! What can you be thinking of? I promise you —

LUCIE. What is it, then?

ANNETTE. Well, I've been foolish enough to tell some of my friends that I was engaged.

LUCIE. Before telling me about it?

ANNETTE [*confused*] Don't ask me any more questions. Please, please don't!

LUCIE. Indeed, I must scold you. You deserve it. You have hurt me very much by not letting me know what was going on. I could never have believed that you would keep me so in the dark, whoever had said it of you. I thought you were too fond of me. I was wrong. We see each other every day, all the time, and you could still hide from me what was in your heart. It was very, very wrong of you. Not only because I am your elder sister, but because I am in mother's place towards you. And then, if only that, because I am your friend. A little more, and I should have heard of your engagement from strangers. Well, my dear, you've made a bad choice, and now you'll need all your courage. These people are n't worth your tears. I 'm going to tell you everything. They don't want you, my poor dear; you 're too poor for them.

ANNETTE [*staring*] They don't want me! They don't want me! But he — Jacques — he knows they don't?

LUCIE. Yes; he knows.

ANNETTE. He 'll do what they say, if they tell him to give me up?

LUCIE. Yes.

ANNETTE [*madly*] I must see him! I 'll write to him! I must see him! If they don't want me, I 've nothing but to kill myself!

LUCIE [*forcing Annette to look at her*] Look at me, Annette! [*Silence. Then in the same grave, tender voice*] Have you not a secret to trust me with?

ANNETTE [*disengaging herself*] Don't ask me anything [*very low*], or I shall die of shame at your feet.

Lucie forces her to sit down at her side and takes her in her arms.

Lucie. Come, come here, in my arms. So! Put your head on my shoulder, as you used when you were tiny. Tell me, what is it? [*Quite low*] My sweet, my little darling, are you terribly, terribly unhappy? Speak out, from your heart, as you would to our poor mother!

Annette [*very low, in tears of shame*] Oh, mother, if you knew what your little girl had done!

Lucie [*almost nursing her*] Tell me; whisper, quite low, in my ear. [*She rises and breaks loose, then hides her face in her hands*] Oh, you, Annette, you!

Annette [*on her knees, her arms stretched out*] Forgive me! Forgive me! My dear one, forgive me! Oh, I deserve it all, everything you can say; but, oh, I am so unhappy!

Lucie. You, Annette, you!

Annette. Forgive me! Do you want me to be sorry I did n't kill myself without telling you? Forgive me!

Lucie [*raising her*] My dear, my dear! You 've suffered too much not to be forgiven.

ACT II

The same scene.   Evening.   Electric Light.

LUCIE.   Now you know.   I sent for you as soon as possible.

MADELEINE [*who is in evening dress*]   There is only one thing to do.   Tell your husband everything and make him go to the Bernins.

LUCIE.   My God!

MADELEINE.   The doctor is a long time with him.   I absolutely must go to this party.

LUCIE.   Yes, go.   But you'll come back?

MADELEINE.   As soon as I can.   Don't despair.   Poor little Annette!

LUCIE.   Do you think —

MADELEINE.   Good-bye for the moment.   Don't move.

Madeleine goes out, and the servant is seen giving her her cloak.   Lucie, alone, walks restlessly to and fro.   As she comes to the door of Brignac's study, she stops to listen.

LUCIE [*aloud, to herself*]   How loud the doctor's speaking.   One would think they had quarrelled.

Fresh pause.   The study door opens.   Enter Hourtin and Brignac.

BRIGNAC.   I can assure you, Dr. Hourtin, that I have reached years of discretion.

HOURTIN.   It was my duty, sir, to speak to you as I have done.

289

BRIGNAC [*showing him to the door, drily*] I am obliged to you.

HOURTIN. I have something else to say to Madame Brignac.

BRIGNAC. About me?

HOURTIN. About herself and the children; but if you object —

BRIGNAC. I hardly imagine it is indispensable.

LUCIE. What is it? Dr. Hourtin, I beg you will tell me what you think I ought to know.

BRIGNAC. I have n't time to waste over this subject. I repeat I am exceedingly busy, and I have to make a speech this evening. You must excuse my leaving you. Good-bye.

Hourtin bows. Brignac goes out, slamming the door of his study.

LUCIE. I trust you will forgive my husband if he has annoyed you.

HOURTIN. A doctor cannot be annoyed at the symptoms of a disease. I would no more be indignant at M. Brignac's temper than bear malice against him for having fever in an attack of pneumonia.

LUCIE. You wanted to speak to him. Is there something about the children?

HOURTIN. If you see that the children are treated as your own doctor and I have prescribed in our consultation, I am confident that their condition will improve. But I have something more to say to you yourself. Not long ago I was called in to a married couple, one of whom was a victim to morphia and refused to give up the use of the poison. The children of the marriage were degenerate, and there was every reason to think that should others be born they would be even less healthy than the first. I had to inform the other parent concerned of the facts, in order, if possible, to discover some means of cure. Towards you I have the same duty. With the difference that here the poison is alcohol instead of morphia, the cases are identical. Like my other patient, M. Brignac refused to listen to me; and although his obstinacy is due to his poisoned condition, I confess I was unable, in spite of a physician's philosophy, to see without irritation the way in which he is rushing to ruin, intellectual and physical. Now your nerves are strong. I was unwilling to go away without speaking to you.

Lucie. My children?

Hourtin. Your children are suffering from a nervous complaint which was born with them.

Lucie. As the result, you mean, of their father's intemperance? Our own doctor and another besides have already told me the same thing.

Hourtin. They should have begun by telling M. Brignac.

Lucie. They did.

Hourtin. Well?

Lucie. He listened no more to them than he did to you.

Hourtin. Is he not fond of the children?

Lucie. In his own way he is. But he will never change his way of living.

Hourtin. So much the worse for him.

Lucie. He did try once. He was incapable of work and became sad, weak, restless.

Hourtin. Like a morphinomaniac deprived of his drug.

Lucie. To his mind the experiment was decisive. He simply cannot study a brief or speak in court without the help of his usual stimulant. He thinks it does him no harm.

Hourtin. He has only to look at the children.

Lucie. What he says is that at their age he had nervous convulsions, and that now he is perfectly well.

Hourtin. Precisely. He received from his father a

legacy that he has transmitted to them in a graver degree. His father drank, but his life was the healthy,
active, open life of a peasant, and his power of resistance greater because he probably did not inherit a
morbid tendency. Your husband's life is sedentary and
feverish. Moreover, he does inherit the tendency. You
tell me that he had convulsions in infancy; yesterday
he said he was a backward child. These are symptoms
just as much as his desire for drink and his irritability.
He had a taint at birth that he has increased. His
children suffer from a cumulative degeneracy. The
grandfather drank, the son suffers from alcoholism, the
children are nervous invalids.

Lucie. Horrible!

Hourtin. You must use your influence with your
husband to cure him.

Lucie. He won't listen to me.

Hourtin. You must insist. You must make him see
his duty as a father.

Lucie. It would be so useless that I shall not even
try.

Hourtin [*rising*] Then I have only one further piece
of advice for you both: don't have any more children.

Lucie. No more children?

Hourtin. No.

Lucie. Why not?

Hourtin. Because it is to be feared that any you
might now have would be more diseased than the first.

Lucie. Is that certain?

Hourtin. In medicine there are no certainties; only
probabilities. The chances are, perhaps, five to one that
I am right. Would you venture to give any creature
so doubtful an existence?

Lucie. I! No, indeed! Most likely you have said
as much to my husband. Won't he believe you?

Hourtin. You must make him realize that the responsibility of having a child, great as it always is, becomes terrible when, so far from its being born into normal circumstances, it runs the risk of going into the world worse equipped than usual. To give birth to a child doomed to unhappiness or likely to be an invalid or incapable of growing up is like crippling someone. It is as much a crime as robbery or murder. Children ought to be deliberately and soberly brought into the world by parents healthy enough to give them health and of sufficient means to ensure their complete development. You must forgive me. When I get on this subject I hardly know how to stop. But really there is so much unavoidable misery and distress that we ought not to add to the sum of general suffering for which there is no remedy.

Enter Madeleine. She wears an opera cloak and a mantilla over her evening dress. During the following scene Josephine helps her off with her things.

MADELEINE. How do you do, Dr. Hourtin? I 'm so glad to find you still here. I 've only just been able to get away from the party. I had to go. There 's nothing serious the matter with the children, I hope?

HOURTIN. Nothing serious. With the care of a mother like theirs, I have every confidence. Now I was just going. Good-bye.

MADELEINE. Good-bye. Thank you.

LUCIE. I 'm extremely grateful to you, Dr. Hourtin.

HOURTIN. Don't mention it. Good-bye, good-bye. [*He goes out*].

LUCIE. Oh, Madeleine!

MADELEINE. What is it?

LUCIE. Do you know why the children are ill? Because of Julien's intemperance.

MADELEINE. My poor darling! But you knew that before. Our doctor said so; and when they went to Paris with me, the man there said the same.

LUCIE. I tried to make myself believe it was n't true.

MADELEINE. And Annette?

LUCIE. Has anything fresh happened?

MADELEINE. Yes; the Bernins have announced Jacques' engagement to his cousin. They want to put an end to the business. People were talking of the engagement this evening.

LUCIE. Ah! And they 're still going away this evening?

MADELEINE. At ten o'clock. How does she take it?

LUCIE. She is in her room, waiting as though she expected something. She said just now she knew the Bernins would not go this evening. What can she hope?

MADELEINE. We must tell her about the engagement. She must n't be left to hear of it from strangers.

LUCIE. No, no!

MADELEINE. And your husband?

LUCIE. He 's working in there. There 's to be a political meeting, a smoking concert or something, after the dinner at the Préfecture to-night. He heard at the last moment that he was expected to speak, on the budget of the Department, I think. I don't know, exactly. Anyway, he 's there.

MADELEINE. Fetch Annette, then.

LUCIE. Yes. [*She goes out. A short silence. Then calls outside*] Madeleine! Madeleine!

MADELEINE [*running to the door*] What is it?

LUCIE [*returning*] She is n't there.

MADELEINE. Where is she?

LUCIE. Gone! She 's left a note. She 's gone to look for him. Quick! Your carriage is here. Go and find her! Help her!

MADELEINE. Gone!

LUCIE. Yes. Quick! Go!

Madeleine goes out. Enter Brignac.

BRIGNAC. What is all this noise about?

LUCIE. Julien, I've something very serious to say to you. A disaster has fallen on us.

BRIGNAC. The children!

LUCIE. No; it's about Annette.

BRIGNAC. Is she ill?

LUCIE. Not ill, but in cruel, horrible grief.

BRIGNAC. Grief at her age! A love affair, eh? She's been jilted?

LUCIE. That's it.

BRIGNAC. Whew! I breathe again. You frightened me. Not so very serious.

LUCIE. Yes; it is. My dear, you must listen with all your heart and with all your mind — and be kind.

BRIGNAC. But what's the matter?

LUCIE. Annette has fallen in love with a scoundrel who has deceived her. The poor child committed the mistake of trusting him completely. He promised to marry her and took advantage of her innocence to seduce her. [*Low*] Understand me, Julien, she is going to have a baby in six months.

BRIGNAC. Annette!

LUCIE. Annette.

BRIGNAC. Impossible! It's —

LUCIE. It was she who confessed to me. She is sure of it.

BRIGNAC [*after a silence*] Who's the man?

LUCIE. Jacques Bernin.

BRIGNAC. Jacques Bernin!

LUCIE. Yes.

BRIGNAC [*furious*] Here's a fine piece of business! Ha, at the moment of my election, too! Magnificent! Oh, she's done me to rights, your sister has! All's up with me now! We may as well pack our trunks and be off.

LUCIE. You exaggerate.

BRIGNAC. Do I? I tell you if she had been caught

stealing — stealing, do you hear? — it would n't have been worse. Even that would have compromised me less — thrown me less absolutely out of the running.

LUCIE. Leave that till later. Now the thing is to save her. You 'll go to-morrow morning, won't you, Julien, and find this fellow? Make him see what an abominable crime it would be for him to desert our poor little girl.

BRIGNAC. Much you know him, M. Jacques Bernin! But I do! He 'll laugh in my face. His one idea is to get on in the world. Why, he was talking of his engagement to Mademoiselle Dormance two months ago and chortling over her shekels. Good lord, what a man for your sister to hit upon!

LUCIE. But you won't abandon her?

BRIGNAC. Yes; I 'm in a nice place. Who 'd have thought it? So this is the thanks I get for all I 've done for her!

LUCIE. Don't fly into a rage!

BRIGNAC. Her! Her! A child brought up in the strictest principles, brought up at home here by you and me, not allowed to read novels or go to the theatre! She has n't even the excuse of having been to a boarding school. Why, sometimes we could hardly help laughing at her ignorance of life.

LUCIE. Perhaps if she had been less ignorant, she would have run less risk.

BRIGNAC [*breaking out*] That 's right! Now it 's all my fault!

LUCIE. Don't get into a passion!

BRIGNAC. I shall if I like! And I think there 's some reason, too! Annette!

LUCIE. Annette is only a victim.

BRIGNAC [*shouting*] A victim! I tell you there 's only one victim here! Only one! And do you know who?

LUCIE. You, I suppose.

BRIGNAC. Yes; it is. Look here! Can't you see the jokes that will be made about me, the ironical congratulations — me, the apostle of repopulation? Ha, they'll say that if I don't give an example myself, my family does!

LUCIE. Julien, Julien, please!

BRIGNAC. Just when I thought I had done with vegetating as a provincial lawyer, when my patience and ability had got me accepted as candidate!

LUCIE. You might not have been elected.

BRIGNAC. I should have been! Even if it were not me, our side would win. Once in the Chamber, I should have done with this wretched obscure existence.

LUCIE. And then?

BRIGNAC. Then? A deputy gets any amount of work, and wins his cases, too! Judges listen very differently to a man who any day may become Minister of Justice. It means something to them. And now this catastrophe! I tell you that here, at Chartres, it spells ruin!

LUCIE. How you exaggerate! Who's to know?

BRIGNAC. Who's to know? Next Sunday every person in the town'll be talking of it. And my political opponents, do you think they'll scruple? Not only them, either. M. de Forgeau and his committee won't give the electors the chance to turn me down. Within a week I shall be shown the door. You see! It'll be lucky if no one insinuates that I seduced the girl myself!

LUCIE. Oh!

BRIGNAC. This is a provincial town! This is Chartres!

LUCIE. So when an unhappy woman is seduced by a scoundrel, her shame, if shame there is, falls on her whole family! Is that the system you uphold?

BRIGNAC. Society must defend itself against immorality. Without the guarantee of social punishment, there would soon be hardly any except illegitimate children.

LUCIE. If anyone is guilty, two are. Why do you only punish the mother?

BRIGNAC. How should I know? Because it's easier.

LUCIE. But you can't sit still and do nothing. You must do something! You're the head of the family.

BRIGNAC. Something! Something! What? The only logical thing I know is to take a pistol —

LUCIE. Julien!

BRIGNAC. And go coolly and put a bullet through the man's head. No? A crime, is it? Ah, if we lived in an age with a little more guts! [*As if to himself*] No; I'm not sure it's not my duty to go and do justice myself.

LUCIE. Julien, you're not dreaming of that!

BRIGNAC. And why not?

LUCIE. Think of the scandal, and then —

BRIGNAC. And then I should be tried for murder? Well, do you think I'm afraid of that? What then? I should defend myself, and I can tell you not many people have heard such a speech as I should make! Think of the effect on the jury! I should be acquitted, and the public would cheer till the court had to be cleared. [*A pause*]. He's in luck's way, the brute, that I've too much respect for human life. If I were n't a bit old fashioned — ha, so much for him. [*A pause*]. No, no; the weak point in these folk is their pocket. That's what I'll go for. That's it. We'll bring an action, an action for the seduction of an infant.

LUCIE. Publish her shame like that!

BRIGNAC. He'll have his share of it. I'll make him sing another tune, so I will. We'll ask twenty, fifty, a hundred thousand francs damages! It'll be a dowry for Annette. Yes; we can do that, an ordinary civil action, or else, if we like, prosecute him criminally. I could show you the law about it; it's all in the reports. And besides, the way I'll conduct the case, the papers will boom it sky high.

LUCIE. You can't surely want to have the papers talking about us, printing poor Annette's story, discussing her honor?

BRIGNAC. Reflecting on me, too. If only we were n't related!

LUCIE. We should be just as much dishonored.

BRIGNAC. If you had n't made me take Annette to live with us when your parents died, none of this would have happened.

LUCIE. It was you who suggested it to me!

BRIGNAC. I know I did. All the stupid things I've done in my life — not that there have been many — come from my having too good a heart. All people from the South have; we can't think twice before doing a kindness. So much the more reason why you should have looked after her carefully.

LUCIE. Oh, it's too much! When you yourself wanted her to make friends with the Bernins!

BRIGNAC. Because I hoped that old Bernin would be useful to us!

LUCIE. You always kept urging Annette to go to them.

BRIGNAC. So it's all my fault, is it?

LUCIE. I don't say that, but I must show you that I'm not so culpable as you make out. What are we going to do?

BRIGNAC. In any case Annette can't stay here.

LUCIE. Good heavens, where can she go? Madeleine can't have her. Perhaps our old nurse, Catherine —

BRIGNAC. If she went to Madeleine or Catherine, it would be exactly as if we kept her here. The important thing is that no one should know anything about it. She must go to Paris, to some big town, till the birth of her child.

Lucie. It's not possible.

Brignac. The only thing not possible is to let it be known, to keep her at Chartres. Can't you imagine what it would be like for her if we did? Think of her going to a concert or to Mass when her condition became evident! She would n't be able to go out of the house without being exposed to insult and insolence. And the way our acquaintances would look at her! Why, it would be purgatory!

Lucie. And everyone will welcome M. Jacques Bernin.

Brignac. Of course they will. And when the child is born, what then? I 'm not thinking of the expense: fortunately for her she has us to fall back on, so she would n't starve. Suppose she put the baby out to nurse? Afterwards she 'd have to keep it with her — imagine what people would say! She might pay for it to be brought up elsewhere, but that 's only a way of deserting it. She would never be able to marry. All her life she would be a pariah. No; the only thing is to send her away.

Lucie. Send her away — where to?

Brignac. How should I know? We 'll find some place. There are places for that at Paris. Yes; I remember now, special places. We 'll pay whatever is necessary. Establishments where you 're not required to give your name at all. The difficulty will be to find a plausible reason of Annette's absence. However, we 'll find one.

Lucie. And the child?

Brignac. The child? She can do what she likes with that. You don't suppose I 'll have it back here with her, do you?

Lucie. Then that 's what you 're proposing to do?

BRIGNAC. That's what we must do.

LUCIE. How does one get into these places you were speaking of?

BRIGNAC. I don't know, exactly. I'll find out. Don't worry. If necessary, I'll go to Paris and take the proper steps. Of course without saying that it's to do with anyone I know.

LUCIE. Of course.

BRIGNAC. Of course.

LUCIE [*rising and touching him on the shoulder as she passes*] You are a fine fellow.

BRIGNAC [*modestly*] Oh, come; only a little thought was wanted.

LUCIE. I think you have no conscience at all.

BRIGNAC. What do you mean? You speak as if I were a monster.

LUCIE. Nothing but respect for public opinion.

BRIGNAC. Respect for public opinion is one form of conscience.

LUCIE. The conscience of people who have n't got any!

BRIGNAC. Anyway, one can't do anything else.

LUCIE. Can't you imagine what my poor darling's life would be like if we did what you said? Turned out of here —

BRIGNAC. No, no; not turned out.

LUCIE. Sent away unwillingly, if you like, coming to this place, suddenly thrust into contact with all the sadness and the misery and the vice of Paris! Think of her waiting all those months, in the midst of the women there, while a poor little creature is growing into life that she knows beforehand is condemned to all the risks and cruelty suffered by children whom their mothers abandon! And when she is torn with the torturing pain that I know so well, at that moment of martyrdom when a woman feels death hovering over her bed and watching jealously for mother and child, when the full horror of the sacred mystery she has accomplished is on her, then she'll only have strangers round her! And if her poor eyes look round, like a victim's, perhaps for the last time, for a friendly glance, if she feels for a hand to press, she will only see round her bed unknown men performing a duty and women carrying on their trade. And then? Then she must resist her highest instincts, stifle the cry of love that consoles all women for what they have gone through, and say she does n't want her child — look aside, and say: " Take him away! I don't want to see him." That's the price for which she will be pardoned the crime of someone else! That's your justice! Justice! Social hypocrisy, rather — that's what you stand up for. Nothing but that. And that's why, if Annette stayed to bring up her child here, she would be an object of reproach; whereas, if she is confined secretly in Paris and gets rid of the baby, nobody will say anything. Let's be frank about it. If she had a lover, but no child, she would be let off. It is n't immorality that's condemned, but having children! You cry out for a higher birth rate, and at the same time you say to women: " No children without marriage, and no marriage without a dowry." Well, so long as you don't change that, all your circulars and your speeches will only succeed in arousing laughter of pity and of rage!

BRIGNAC. Well, is it my fault?

LUCIE. No; it's not your fault. It's the fault of all of us, of our prejudice, our silly vanity, our hypocrisy. But you stand up for it all and justify it. You have the typical window dressing, middle class virtues. You publicly preach the repopulation of France, and then find it in your conscience to get rid of a child whose only fault is that its parents had it without first going through a stupid ceremony, and without the whole town being told that Monsieur X and Mademoiselle Y were going to bed together! [*A pause*] Go and make your speech. Go and defend the morals of society. That's about what you're worth.

Enter Madeleine.

MADELEINE. She's not come back?

LUCIE. No. Have n't you seen her?

MADELEINE. No.

BRIGNAC. Since you take it like that, then, you will kindly find another home than my house for your sister from now onwards.

LUCIE. Ah, yes; say it outright! You long to get rid of her!

BRIGNAC [*talking all the time while he goes into his study and comes back with his portfolio, hat, and coat*] I'm off. It's too much! Yes; I'm off! And for my part, I refuse to be the victim of your sister's pranks!

LUCIE [*to herself*] Wretch! Wretch!

BRIGNAC. Do what you like, but I won't have that sort of thing here. [*He goes out*].

MADELEINE. I don't know which way she went nor where she is.

LUCIE. You've been to the Bernins?

MADELEINE. They were dining out.

LUCIE. Did they leave the town by an afternoon train?

MADELEINE. I don't know.

LUCIE. Oh, I'm afraid.

MADELEINE. Annette must have known where they were dining, because I got to their door before she had time to get there herself.

LUCIE. You should have gone to the station.

MADELEINE. I made up my mind to, but then I saw that I should n't have time before the train went. So I thought she must have come back.

LUCIE. Here she is! Thank God!

Enter Catherine and Annette.

CATHERINE. I will! I will tell! So as they may stop you trying again.

Annette, her teeth clenched, her eyes fixed, shrugs her shoulders. Throughout the ensuing scene no tear comes to her eyes.

MADELEINE. In heaven's name what has happened?

LUCIE. You're here, you're here! [*She tries to take Annette in her arms*].

ANNETTE. Let me go! Let me go! [*She picks up her hat and coat, which she has thrown on to a chair, and sits down, hard and reticent*].

LUCIE. What is the matter? What have you done?

ANNETTE [*in a broken voice*] I wanted to put an end to myself. Catherine stopped me.

LUCIE. To kill —

MADELEINE. Annette!

LUCIE. And us, had you forgotten us?

ANNETTE. My death would have brought less trouble on you than my life will.

MADELEINE. Catherine, what has happened?

CATHERINE. I was getting out of the train. I saw her start to throw herself under the wheels.

MADELEINE and LUCIE [*terrified*] Oh!

ANNETTE. You'll be sorry one day you stopped me.

CATHERINE. You hear her! That's the way she's been going on as we came back, all the time she was telling me her story.

LUCIE. Swear you'll never try again, Annette.

ANNETTE. How can I tell?

MADELEINE. Was she alone?

CATHERINE. No. When I saw her, she seemed to be having a dispute with M. Bernin's family. I stopped to watch. Then M. Jacques got into the train and Annette stood there crying; and just as the train went away, she gave a cry and ran to try and throw herself under the wheels. I caught her by the dress and brought her away; and I would n't leave her till I knew she was back here and I had told you what she 'd done.

ANNETTE. All right. Don't let 's speak about it. I tried to kill myself and I failed. If they saw me, no doubt they shrugged their shoulders.

MADELEINE. You went to wait for them at the train?

ANNETTE. No. I knew where Jacques was dining — at a restaurant — a farewell party. His parents were having dinner at the station. I went to the restaurant and asked for him, like a girl off the streets. I could hear his friends laughing and joking from where I was, when the waiter took my message.

LUCIE. Did he come?

ANNETTE. Yes. He told me afterwards he thought it was some woman from a café chantant who sent for him. Oh!

MADELEINE. And when he saw that it was you?

ANNETTE. He took me into the street, so that I should n't be recognized. That 's where we had our talk. The passers-by laughed and made horrible jokes.

MADELEINE. And then you told him?

ANNETTE. Yes.

LUCIE. Well?

ANNETTE. You could n't guess what he answered: that it was n't true.

LUCIE. Oh!

ANNETTE [*still tearlessly*] Then he lost his temper and said he saw through my game; that I wanted to force him to marry me because he was rich. Much he spared me! I tried to put my arms round him: he threatened to call the police. Then I cried, I implored him — I asked him to come with me tomorrow to a doctor to prove I was n't lying. He answered quite coldly that, even if it was true, there was nothing to prove that it was him. Ah, you can't believe it, can you? It's too much! I could n't have, unless I had heard it with my own ears; and how I could without dying, I don't know. You don't know what depths of shame and cowardice I sunk to. Then he looked at his watch, saying he only had time to catch the train. He said good-bye and dashed off to the station. I had to half run to keep up, crying, and begging him not to desert me — for the sake of his child, of my happiness, my love, my very life! Horrible! Horrible! Loathsome! And how ridiculous! I had him by the arm. I could n't believe *that* was the end. At the entrance to the station he said, brutally: "Let me go, will you?" I said: "You shan't go." Then he rushed to the train and got into the carriage, nearly crushing my fingers in the door, and hid behind his mother; and she threatened, too, to have me arrested. Gabrielle sat there, looking white, and pretending not to notice and not to know me. Catherine's told you the rest.

A silence.

LUCIE. You must swear, Annette, never to think again of suicide.

ANNETTE. I could n't swear sincerely.

MADELEINE. You must be brave, now that you know what life is, brutally as it has been revealed to you. Almost all the women you think happy have gone through an inner catastrophe. They make themselves forget it because their very tears give out. Suffering is reticent, and they conceal theirs. But there are few women whose lives have not been broken, few who don't carry within them the corpse of the woman they would have wished to be.

ANNETTE. You say that to console me. I don't believe it.

MADELEINE. It's the truth; and I've learnt it by experience.

ANNETTE. I'm tired of life. I feel as if I were a hundred.

Lucie. Keep up your heart. We won't desert you.

Annette. What can you do? I shall be turned away from here.

Lucie. If you are, I 'll go with you.

Annette. And your children?

Lucie. I 'll take them, too.

Annette. He 'll fetch them back. Besides, what should we live on?

Lucie. Ah!

Annette. You see! You can't do anything either, Madeleine, for all your love. Your husband would n't let you take me in. Nor you either, Catherine. You could n't afford to. Well, then?

Catherine. Eh! eh!

Fresh silence.

Annette. What a terrible thing life is!

Madeleine. For all women.

Annette. Not for anyone as much as for me.

Madeleine. You think so, and that 's why you think of dying. Well, I 'm alive. You see me laughing now and then. If you only knew!

Catherine. And what about me, Annette?

Annette. You have your children to console you.

Catherine. It 's they that make it hard for me.

Annette. For other women it 's a refuge to have children. What will it be for me?

Madeleine. You think that I am happy, Annette?

Annette. You have a husband who loves you, you 're rich, you can afford to dress beautifully, you go everywhere, and everyone wants to have you. That 's some happiness, is n't it?

Madeleine. That 's all you see. If you only knew what you don't see!

Catherine. Do you think being a mother has made me happy?

Annette. I know you 're poor. You have to work,

to work hard, to bring up your children; but you can look the world in the face and love them.

CATHERINE. If you knew!

MADELEINE. Then you must know! Even Lucie does n't know what I 'm going to say. You think I 'm happy because the money my godmother left me enabled me to marry the man of my choice, a man who was well off. Listen, then. My husband married me because I was good looking. He wanted a son. I gave him one, but my child cost me his love. You can't be a wife and a mother at the same time. I lost my elegant figure, I was ill, I suffered the woes that woman's flesh is heir to and — he left me for another woman! Don't be too quick to condemn worldly women who shrink from motherhood, Annette. Man's baseness is such that they must often choose between their husbands and their children. And if some choose their husband, let those who have never loved throw the first stone at them! I felt that if I nursed my baby I should lose my husband for good, and to win him back I put my child out to nurse. He died, Annette; and I have the agony of thinking that if I had kept him with me he would be alive. Do you understand? It 's as if I had killed him. Now I don't mean to have another child. I lead a worldly life, laughing, dining out, going to parties, because that 's what my husband wants, and that 's how he loves me. I shall have a lonely old age. My arms are empty — mine, whose joy would have been to rock my children to sleep in them — and I 'm ashamed of what I 'm doing. I despise myself. You 'd think I 'd paid enough for my husband's love, would n't you? Oh, no. He 's gone to Paris, ostensibly on business, really to another woman. I know it. I pretend not to know because I 'm afraid of forcing him to choose between her and me. That 's my life, Annette. Many women whom you think happy live like that.

Annette. Poor Madeleine!

Lucie. And I. One of my little girls is an invalid, the other is ailing. Perhaps she 'll die.

Catherine. Two of mine died of want.

Madeleine. I don't want to have another child for fear that my husband would leave me altogether. A divorce, if I got one, would leave me a kind of half-widow and make my girl an orphan.

Catherine. If I had any more, it would only mean taking away food from those who have n't enough as it is.

Lucie. I 'm guilty enough already. Two children of suffering owe their existence to me.

Madeleine. Think of my torture! I adore my husband: when he comes back I long to feel myself in his arms and I dread the consequences.

Catherine. Mine will leave me if I have another. And then what would become of me, all alone with all my children?

Lucie. Your children who are grown up will support you, Catherine.

Catherine. Those who are grown up! Grown up! I 've just been hearing about them. Edmond is in hospital, ruined for life by going into what they call " a dangerous trade " because he could n't get work in any other. There are too many workmen. My daughter, she 's on the streets. [Sobbing] Oh, it 's too much! There 's too much misery in the world!

Madeleine. Yes, there 's too much misery!

Annette. And I thought I was the most miserable!

Lucie. There 's too much unhappiness!

Catherine. The children of poor folk are unhappy, all of them, all.

Annette. The child of an unmarried woman, too, is born only to suffering.

Lucie. Children who are born sickly or ill ought not to be born at all.

CATHERINE. You see, Annette, we must bear it. God's
given us eyes; it's to cry with.

ANNETTE. To cry with!

*The four women cry silently. Catherine is in Made-
leine's arms. Lucie has her head on Annette's lap.*

CATHERINE [*making ready to leave*] Please to forgive me.

MADELEINE. We have the same troubles.

ANNETTE. Yes; we have the same troubles.

CATHERINE. Yes; whether one's rich or poor, when
one's a woman —

Annette kisses Catherine. Catherine goes out.

MADELEINE. I must go, too. Your husband will be
coming back.

LUCIE [*to herself, terrified*] My husband coming
back — coming back!

ANNETTE. I won't see him. Madeleine, you're alone;
take me with you!

MADELEINE. Yes. You can come to-morrow, Lucie.
We'll talk then.

LUCIE. Yes. [*Suddenly*] Here he is! Go out that
way.

*She pushes them out through Annette's room. After
a moment Brignac comes in, flushed and happy.*

BRIGNAC. What, still up! Aha, my dear, I'm going
to be elected! Absolutely certain, I tell you. Here,
I've brought you a bunch of roses.

LUCIE [*without listening*] Thank you. So you're
going to turn Annette out?

BRIGNAC. I'm not turning her out. I simply ask her
to go somewhere else.

LUCIE. I shall go with her.

BRIGNAC. You're going to leave me?

LUCIE. Yes.

BRIGNAC. You don't love me any more, then?

LUCIE. No.

BRIGNAC. Ha! Another story beginning. Since when?

LUCIE. I've never loved you.

BRIGNAC. All the same you married me.

LUCIE. I didn't love you.

BRIGNAC. This is nice news. Go on.

LUCIE. You're only another victim of the morals you were championing just now.

BRIGNAC. I don't know what you mean.

LUCIE. When you asked me to marry you I was tired of waiting in poverty for the man I could have loved. I didn't want to become an old maid. I took you, but I knew you came to me because the girls with money wouldn't have you. You were on the shelf, too. I made up my mind to try and love you loyally.

BRIGNAC. Well, then?

LUCIE. The first time I was going to have a child you left me for other women. Since then I have only put up with you. I was too cowardly not to. You may as well know it. I wanted my first child; the others I've had only because you made me. Each time you left me — I was so ugly! Yes; ugly through you! You left me at home, alone, dreary, repulsive, to come back from the arms of some prostitute, full of hypocritical solicitude for my health! After the fatigue of nursing I begged for a rest, to have a breathing space, so that I might have some life of my own; and when I demanded only to have children at my own wish, you laughed like a self-satisfied fool. Oh, your fatuous pride, your base egoism, your utter want of thought for the future of your children and the life of your wife! So you forced on me the labor and the agony and the danger of having another child. What did it matter to you? It flattered your vanity to make merry with your friends and give yourself the airs of a fine fellow. Idiot!

BRIGNAC. I've had enough of this. You're my wife!

LUCIE. I won't be your wife any more. I won't have any more children.

BRIGNAC. Pray why?

LUCIE. Did n't Dr. Hourtin tell you anything?

BRIGNAC. Yes. All right. I 'll do what he said. There, does that content you? Come to bed.

LUCIE. No.

BRIGNAC. You have n't looked at my roses. Come, is n't he a loving husband, your little Julien?

LUCIE. Leave me alone. You 're drunk.

BRIGNAC. You know I 'm not. Come and give me a kiss!

LUCIE. You stink of alcohol. Let me go!

BRIGNAC [*low*] I want you. [*He kisses her*].

LUCIE [*tearing herself away*] Faugh! [*She wipes her mouth furiously*].

BRIGNAC. Enough of that, do you hear? [*He seizes her brutally*]. That 's enough!

LUCIE. You hurt me! Let me go!

BRIGNAC. Be kind now. How well you look when your temper 's up! Pretty pet! Must n't be naughty! Come!

LUCIE. I won't!

BRIGNAC. Then I 'll make you! [*They struggle, with low cries, panting*].

LUCIE [*at the end of her strength*] I can't! I can't!

He puts her on a chair; then goes to open the door of the bedroom and turns on the electric light. The bed is seen, a vision of white sheets. Brignac comes to his wife.

LUCIE [*mad with terror*] The cave man! The cave man!

He seizes her. She gives a cry and faints. He carries her towards the bedroom.

ACT III

The Cour d'Assises. Only two of the four sides of the hall are visible. The footlights nearly correspond with a line drawn diagonally across it. To the left and in front is the seat of the Ministry of State. Further back, to the left, the Court.

Facing the audience, successively, are seated counsel, above them the defendants, and, lastly, the gendarmes. In the middle, in front of a table placed for exhibits in the case, the witness stand.

To the right three or four benches for the accommodation of the audience, but only a small part is visible. The jury, which is unseen, is supposed to occupy the place of the prompter's box.

There are present the Advocate General, the President of the Court and his assessors, counsel for the defence and his learned friends. In the dock are Madame Thomas, Marie Gaubert, Tupin(Catherine's husband), Lucie, guarded by gendarmes. Among the public, Madame d'Amergueux, Brignac, the clerk.

At the rise of the curtain Madame Thomas is standing in the dock.

PRESIDENT [*authoritatively, to counsel for the defence*] Maître Verdier, this is not the moment for you to address the Court. And I take this occasion to warn you: I tell you plainly I will use all the authority in my power to prevent you from attempting to set up a theory of justification, as I see you are about to do, for the crimes with which the defendants are charged.

313

Counsel for the Defence. You are mistaken, President. I have no intention of the sort. On the contrary, I declare publicly that in my eyes abortion is a crime because it destroys the existence of a creature virtually in being. To allow it would infallibly lead to allowing infanticide. But what I shall try to show is that by not permitting affiliation, and by not respecting all motherhood, however it is caused, Society has lost the right to condemn a crime rendered excusable by the hypocrisy of its morals and the indifference of the law.

President. This is not the moment for your speech. The defendant Thomas: we shall now pass to the second part of your examination. [*He hunts in his notes, says a word or two in an undertone to the assessor on his right, then to Madame Thomas*] So you admit the abominable crimes with which you are charged?

Mme. Thomas. I must admit them, as you have the proofs.

President. And you feel no remorse for the lives of human beings you have destroyed from the sole motive of gain? The jury will appreciate your attitude.

Counsel. Except that you have spared them the trouble!

President. Maître Verdier, I cannot hear you now. [*To Madame Thomas*] You have crippled the work of nature, you have offended against the principle of life, and you never said to yourself that among the beings you stifled before their birth might be one destined to benefit humanity by his greatness! Did you? Well?

Mme. Thomas. No.

President. You did not say so! Very well.

Mme. Thomas. If I had thought about that, I should have perhaps said that there was as much chance — more, perhaps — that he might be a thief or a murderer.

President. Indeed! I will not argue with you; I am

not going to give you the chance to expound your criminal ideas here.

MME. THOMAS. My counsel will do it better than me.

PRESIDENT. We 'll see about that.

COUNSEL [*with a smile*] It might, perhaps, be well for you, President, not to contemn in advance the rights of the defence.

PRESIDENT [*irritated*] Maître Verdier, you have no right to address me! And you will be good enough to moderate your expressions. I regret to say that from the opening of this case you have adopted an attitude that you can, perhaps, carry off at Paris, but that I shall certainly not countenance here. Pray take notice of that.

COUNSEL. At the Paris bar —

PRESIDENT. I cannot hear you now.

COUNSEL. At the Paris —

PRESIDENT. I cannot hear you now! Kindly be seated.

MME. D'AMERGUEUX [*among the public, to her neighbor, M. de Forgeau*] What an excellent judge M. Calvon is. He is to dine with us to-morrow: I shall congratulate him.

M. DE FORGEAU. A judge of the old stamp.

MME. D'AMERGUEUX. He recognizes us. Did you see him give a little nod? [*She directs her smiles at the President*].

M. DE FORGEAU. Yes. Hush!

PRESIDENT. Marie Gaubert, stand up. [*A thin little woman rises to her feet*]. Your name is Marie Gaubert? How old are you?

SCHOOLMISTRESS. Twenty-seven.

PRESIDENT. Profession?

SCHOOLMISTRESS. Schoolmistress.

PRESIDENT. Do you admit the facts with which you are charged.

SCHOOLMISTRESS. Yes.

PRESIDENT. What have you to say in your defence?

SCHOOLMISTRESS. I did n't think I was doing wrong.

PRESIDENT. Your levity astounds me. You are a schoolmistress, and you do not understand that the sacred mission entrusted to you of preparing men and women for the glory and responsibility of the future entails on you the duty of giving an example yourself! It is your business to conduct the course of elementary instruction in civic morality, and this is how you practise it! Have you nothing to answer? According to my notes you undertook the nursing of your two children yourself. Do you love them?

SCHOOLMISTRESS. It was just because I loved them.

PRESIDENT. But you decided that two were enough. You made up your mind to limit the work of the Almighty.

SCHOOLMISTRESS. I should have asked nothing better than to have four or five children.

PRESIDENT. Indeed! Then let me tell you that you did not take the best means to arrive at that result. [*He laughs and looks at his assessor on the right, then at Madame d'Amergueux. She signals her congratulations to him*].

SCHOOLMISTRESS. You have to be able to feed your children.

PRESIDENT. Ah, there! No! At a pinch I could understand that excuse — a very bad one — being employed in the case of other women; but not in yours, who enjoy the incomparable advantage of being protected by the State. You are never out of work.

SCHOOLMISTRESS. I earn eighty-three francs a month. My husband, who is a teacher, too, gets as much. That makes a hundred and sixty-six francs a month to live on and bring up two children. When there were four of us, we could almost do it; with five it would have been impossible.

PRESIDENT. You omit to say that during your confinement you have the right to a month's leave with full salary.

SCHOOLMISTRESS. That used to be true, President. It is so no longer. A department circular of 1900 informed us that the funds were insufficient for more than half salaries to be paid, as a rule, at such times. To obtain the whole salary, a detailed report from the inspector is required, and you must petition for it.

PRESIDENT. Then why not petition?

SCHOOLMISTRESS. It's hard to seem like a beggar simply because you have feelings.

PRESIDENT. Proud, are you?

SCHOOLMISTRESS. There's no law against that.

PRESIDENT. So that is why you went to the defendant Thomas?

SCHOOLMISTRESS. Yes, sir. My husband and I arranged our little finances so: the evening our salaries were paid we used to divide the money into different parts and put them by; so much for rent, so much for food, so much for clothing. We just managed to get along by calculating carefully, and more than once having to cut down expenses that seemed inevitable. The prospect of a third child upset everything. It made our existence impossible. We should have all gone hungry. And then the inspectors and the head mistresses don't like you to have many children, especially if you nurse them yourself. The last time I was nursing I was made to hide myself — I only had ten minutes during the break at ten o'clock and again at two; and when my mother brought the baby, I had to take him into a dark closet.

PRESIDENT. That has nothing to do with it.

COUNSEL. Yes, President, it has. It ought to be known how the State, which preaches the increase of the population, treats its servants when they have children,

PRESIDENT [*furiously*] I can't hear you now! [*To the schoolmistress*] You haven't anything more to say?

SCHOOLMISTRESS. No, sir.

PRESIDENT. Sit down.

MME. D'AMERGUEUX. I think M. Calvon lets their counsel talk too much.

M. DE FORGEAU. He's rather afraid of him.

PRESIDENT. Tupin, stand up.

TUPIN [*a man of mean and wretched appearance*] After you, Calvon.

PRESIDENT. What's that?

TUPIN. I said, "After you, Calvon." That's your name, is n't it?

PRESIDENT. I warn you I shall not stand the least insolence from you.

TUPIN. I said, "After you, Calvon," just as you said, "Stand up, Tupin." If that's insolence, I did n't begin it.

PRESIDENT. I will have you removed. Stand up.

TUPIN. All right. It 'll let me stretch my legs a bit.

PRESIDENT. Your profession?

TUPIN. Electrician.

PRESIDENT. You were once. It' a long time since you worked regularly.

TUPIN. There's no work to be had.

PRESIDENT. Because you look for it at the wineshop. The police give the worst account of you.

TUPIN. I 'm not surprised they don't like me: I never liked them. [*Laughter*].

PRESIDENT. Silence there, or I shall have the court cleared. [*To Tupin*] The name of your wife has been found among the papers of the defendant Thomas. Catherine Tupin, maiden name Bidois. Where is Catherine Tupin? Stand up. Very well, sit down again. [*To Tupin*] You tried to conceal your wife from the police.

TUPIN. I did n't think they were good company for her.

PRESIDENT [*pretending not to hear*] You then gave yourself up on your own confession that it was you who took her to this abominable woman's house.

TUPIN. You speak like a book.

PRESIDENT. You persisted in the confession of your guilt. Did you want to go to prison?

TUPIN. Why, that 's an idea! You get fed and sheltered there, anyway.

PRESIDENT. The prison conditions are certainly better than those you are accustomed to.

TUPIN. Now you 're talking.

PRESIDENT. When you were arrested you were completely destitute. The remains of your furniture had been sold, and you were on the eve of finding yourself without a roof over your head. Doubtless you will blame Society, too. Your insubordinate character leads you to frequent Socialist clubs; and when you do not affect, as you do now, a cynical carelessness in your speech, you are used to repeat the empty phrases you have learnt from the propagandist pamphlets that poison the minds of the working classes. But we know you. If you are a victim, it is to your own vices. You are a hardened drinker.

TUPIN. Lately, that 's true.

PRESIDENT. You admit it. Extraordinary!

TUPIN. What 's that prove?

PRESIDENT. Your eldest daughter is known to the police of Paris as a prostitute. One of your sons has been sentenced to a year's imprisonment for theft. Is that true?

TUPIN. Possibly.

PRESIDENT. A little less proud now? That 's right. Well, now, you took your wife to this woman. Why?

TUPIN. Because I thought it was enough to have brought seven wretched creatures into the world.

PRESIDENT. If you had continued to be the honest and industrious workman you were once, you might have had another child without its necessarily growing up wretched.

TUPIN. No, sir. Not with five. It's impossible.

PRESIDENT. I don't understand.

TUPIN. I say that a working man's family, however much they work and economize, can't support itself when there are five children.

PRESIDENT. If that is true, there are — and it is to the credit of the Society that you despise — there are, I say, numerous charitable organizations which are, so to speak, on the watch for the victims of misfortune and make it a point of honor to leave none without succor.

TUPIN [excitedly] Oh, and that seems all right to you, that a working man, who hasn't any vice and does his duty, which is to work and — we're told, too — have plenty of children, it seems all right to you that that should simply lead to beggary.

PRESIDENT. Yes, yes; I recognize the wineshop orator. So you say that a household can't exist with five children. Thank God, there is more than one in that condition which goes neither to ask for charity nor to an abortionist.

MME. TUPIN. You're wrong.

TUPIN. Shall I prove that you're wrong?

PRESIDENT. That doesn't seem to me to have much to do with the case.

MME. TUPIN. Yes, it has.

TUPIN. Pardon me. If I prove it, people will understand how I came to do what I did.

PRESIDENT. Very well. But be short.

TUPIN. I've given my counsel my accounts for a month. Let him read it to you.

PRESIDENT. Very well. [The counsel rises].

COUNSEL. Here it is.

PRESIDENT. You are not Tupin's counsel.

COUNSEL. No, President, but my learned friends have done me the honour — for which I thank them — to confide to me the task of dealing in my speech with the case as a whole, reserving to themselves to deal with particular aspects of it as they relate to their clients.

PRESIDENT. I will hear you now solely for the purpose of reading these accounts. But this is not the time for you to address the court. You understand? I will hear the accounts and nothing more.

COUNSEL. Certainly, President. [*He reads*] The daily nourishment of five children consists of a four-pound loaf, soup of vegetables and dripping, and a stew which costs ninety centimes. Total, 3f. 75c. This is the expenditure of the father: Return ticket for tram, 30c. Tobacco, 15c. Dinner, 1f. 25c. The rent is 300f. Clothing for the whole family, and boots: sixteen pairs of boots for the children at 4f. 50c. each, four for the parents at 8f.: total again, 300f. Total for the year: 2,600f. The expenditure then must be set down at 2,600f. Tupin, who is an exceptional workman, earned 160f. a month, that is to say, 2,100f. a year. There is therefore an annual deficit of 500f. As I have promised, I will not add a word. [*He sits down*].

MME. D'AMERGUEUX [*to her husband*] He might well have saved the three sous a day for tobacco.

COUNSEL. Does the Court wish to have this paper put in?

PRESIDENT. There is no object in that. [*To Tupin*] I will not quarrel with your figures: I accept them. But I repeat, there are charitable institutions.

TUPIN. And I repeat that I don't want to beg.

PRESIDENT. You prefer to commit what is almost infanticide. A man whose daughter is on the streets and whose son is a thief can accept charity without degradation.

TUPIN [*excited*] They were n't then. If they 've
fallen to that, it 's because with so many other children
besides, I could n't look after my son as rich people
look after theirs, and because my daughter was seduced
and abandoned — because she was hungry! No, but
you must have a heart of stone to bring that up against
me!

PRESIDENT. And it 's not your fault either that you 've
become a drunkard?

TUPIN. I 'll tell you. You know the proverb:
" When there 's no hay in the manger — " Well, when
the pinch came at home, I and my wife began to quarrel
over each new baby. Each of us accused the other of
having made things worse for the first ones. Well I 'll
cut it short. If I went to the wineshop, why, it 's
warm there, and you don't hear the brats crying and their
mother complaining. And the drink helps you to forget,
so it does, to forget!

MME. TUPIN. It 's good to forget, so it is!

TUPIN. It 's my fault if you like, but that 's how we
got poorer and poorer.

PRESIDENT. And when you had your last child, did n't
that serve as a lesson to you?

TUPIN. The last one did n't cost anything.

PRESIDENT [*absently*] Ah!

TUPIN. He came into the world deformed and sickly.
He was conceived in misery, in want — his mother was
worn out.

PRESIDENT. And his father a drunkard!

TUPIN. If you like. Well, he came badly into the
world — he could never have been anything but a cripple.
But he did n't want for anything! They took him in at
the hospital and begged me to let him stay there.

MME. TUPIN. He was a curiosity for the doctors.

TUPIN. They looked after him, I tell you. They
did n't leave him for a minute. He was made to live in

spite of himself, so to speak. The other children, who were strong, they let them perish of want. With half the care and the money that was spent on the sickly one they might have made fine fellows of all the rest.

PRESIDENT. Then that is why you made away with the next?

TUPIN. For all the good he'd have had in the world, if he could, he'd say, thank you.

PRESIDENT. You ought not to have had him.

TUPIN. That's true. But we poor folk, we don't know the dodges rich people have so as only to have the children they want, and take their fun all the same: worse luck!

PRESIDENT. If everyone was of your opinion our country would be in a bad way. But your country, doubtless, is nothing to you?

TUPIN. I've heard say: "A man's country is where he is well off." I'm badly off everywhere.

PRESIDENT. And you are equally lost to any interest in humanity.

TUPIN. If humanity can't get on without a set of wretches like me, let it go smash!

PRESIDENT. Well, the jury can estimate your sense of morality. You may sit down.

Night has come. The ushers bring lamps.

MME. D'AMERGUEUX. I shouldn't like to meet that man of an evening in a lonely place.

M. DE FORGEAU. Nor I. Now for Madame Brignac — that was. My dear lady, what a dreadful thing!

MME. D'AMERGUEUX. Dreadful!

PRESIDENT. We have now only to examine the facts concerning Lucie and Annette Jarras. [*To the defendant Thomas*] Stand up! This girl, Annette Jarras, was your victim. What have you to say?

MME. THOMAS. Nothing.

PRESIDENT. You don't trouble yourself about it? Well, we know your heart is not easy to move.

Mme. Thomas. If I told you that I was led to do what I did by pity, you would n't believe me.

President. Probably not. But you can try to make us believe. The defendant has the right to say whatever he thinks fit — always under the control of the court, of course.

Mme. Thomas. It 's not worth while.

President. Yes, yes; go on. The jury is listening to you.

Mme. Thomas [on a sign from her counsel] A girl came to me one day. She was a servant. Her master had had her. I refused to do what she asked me: she went away and threw herself into the water. Another, whom I would n't help, was tried here for infanticide. So, since then, when others have come to me, I have agreed; I have prevented more than one suicide and more than one crime.

President. So it was from pity, out of charity that you acted. The prosecution will reply that you never forgot to exact heavy payment.

Mme. Thomas. And you, are n't you paid for condemning others?

President. Those whom you condemned to death and executed yourself, were innocent.

Mme. Thomas. You prosecute me; but the surgeons who guarantee sterility get decorated!

President. You forget this young girl who died as the result of your action, Annette Jarras. She was eighteen, in the full enjoyment of health; now she is in the grave. [Lucie breaks into sobs] Look at her sister by your side; listen to her crying. Ask her now if she does not curse you.

Mme. Thomas. She would bless me if I had succeeded.

President [to Lucie] Defendant Lucie Jarras, stand up!

M. de Forgeau [to his neighbour] Brignac must think himself lucky to have got his divorce.

MME. D'AMERGUEUX. Speak lower; he's behind us. I am against divorce, but in this case —

PRESIDENT. You have heard the defendant Thomas. What have you to say?

LUCIE [*through her sobs*] Nothing. Nothing. [*She sinks back upon her bench*].

PRESIDENT. Do you admit —

LUCIE. Yes, yes; I admit everything. I 've told you so already.

PRESIDENT. You did not want your child to come into the world?

LUCIE. I did n't want it to.

PRESIDENT. Why?

LUCIE. Out of pity for him. I knew what sort of a life he would have, and I risked my own to save him from it. I acted like a good mother.

PRESIDENT. What you say is simply monstrous. [*Silence*]. You, now, have not the excuse of poverty. Your child would not have suffered from want.

LUCIE. He would have suffered from disease, and that is as bad as want.

PRESIDENT. No theories, please. Only facts.

LUCIE. Yes; facts, nothing but facts. You can see the theory of it yourself. I had two children, two little girls. One is a deaf mute, the other had convulsions. She is dead now. The doctors told me that that was due to the alcoholized condition of my husband, whose father had been in the same state.

PRESIDENT. Most unfortunate.

LUCIE. Be pleased to let me speak!

PRESIDENT. Very good. I will answer you.

LUCIE. One of the doctors is famous — Dr. Hourtin.

PRESIDENT. A specialist who sees alcoholism everywhere!

LUCIE [*more vigorously*] Those doctors told me that if my husband did not change his mode of life, any further children I had by him would, perhaps, be worse than the first, nervous degenerates. The very evening that Professor Hourtin came to see me, my husband came back from some festivity in a state of excitement — [*She stops*].

PRESIDENT. Well? Is that all?

LUCIE. No; I 'll have the courage to say everything. I have nothing to lose now.

PRESIDENT. Please take note that it is not I who make you go on.

LUCIE. No; you would probably prefer if I did n't. [*Controlling her voice*] During the day something had happened — something serious — that revealed to me all the hideousness of his moral character. I determined no longer to be his wife. He came in, gay with drinking. In spite of my prayers and resistance, my cries of hatred and disgust, he chose that evening to exercise his rights — his rights! He took me by force; he outraged me.

PRESIDENT. He was your husband?

LUCIE. Yes.

PRESIDENT. Then —

LUCIE. Of course. The next morning I left his house.

PRESIDENT [*starting*] M. Brignac is not in question.

LUCIE. I bring him in question!

PRESIDENT. I shall not allow you to bring charges against persons unconnected with the case.

LUCIE. He ought to be in my place.

PRESIDENT. His name does not figure in the indictment.

LUCIE. Because your justice does n't want to put responsibility on the right shoulders!

PRESIDENT. I forbid you to speak like that of M. Brignac.

COUNSEL. Pardon me, President.

PRESIDENT. I cannot hear you now.

COUNSEL. That is why I ask to be heard.

PRESIDENT. What do you want?

COUNSEL. M. Brignac is called as a witness.

PRESIDENT. We have already heard him.

COUNSEL. Allow me to remind you of the terms of Article 319 of the Criminal Code, which authorizes me to say against him as well as against his evidence whatever may help the defence.

PRESIDENT. And let me remind you of Article 311 in the same Code, which enjoins you to express yourself with moderation.

COUNSEL. I ask you, President, kindly to recall M. Brignac to the bar. I have a question to put to him through you.

PRESIDENT [after consulting with his assessors] Usher, ask M. Brignac kindly to come here.

BRIGNAC [coming forward to the bar] Here, President.

PRESIDENT. What is your question, Maître Verdier?

COUNSEL. M. Brignac has heard all that has just been said?

BRIGNAC. Yes.

COUNSEL. Then I beg M. Brignac to review all the factors in his memory. I make a supreme appeal to his conscience, and I beg you, President, to put this question to M. Brignac: does M. Brignac not recognize himself as morally responsible for the crime imputed to Madame Lucie Jarras, his divorced wife?

PRESIDENT. I shall not put the question. Is that all?

COUNSEL. For the moment, yes.

PRESIDENT [to Brignac] You may return to your place, Deputy. But since the defence, with an assumption of excessive liberty, appears desirous of incriminating you, the Court may, perhaps, be permitted to express to you here the high esteem in which it personally holds you. [He half rises from his chair, bowing to Brignac].

BRIGNAC. I thank you, President. [*He goes back to his place*].

MME. D' AMERGUEUX [*to her neighbour*] Then it's true what they say, that Brignac is to be Minister of Justice in the next Government?

PRESIDENT [*to Lucie*] Defendant Jarras, have you finished?

LUCIE. No, President.

PRESIDENT [*with a gesture of weariness*] Go on, then; I'm listening.

LUCIE. When I felt a child coming to life within me of a man who was nothing more to me, whose name even I no longer bore, and whom I hated with my whole soul, I prevented it from being born to a destiny of misery. I consider that I had the right to refuse the task of motherhood when it was forced on me against my will.

PRESIDENT. I shall not allow you to justify an act which is a crime by law.

LUCIE. I have nothing on my conscience to reproach myself with.

PRESIDENT. Then you have a singularly indulgent conscience. All this comes from your pride. If you had not entered into a struggle with your husband, you would still bear a respected name and you would not be there.

LUCIE. I knew that any child of his would be a degenerate. Had I not the right to refuse?

PRESIDENT. No.

LUCIE. I loved him no longer. Had I not the right to refuse?

PRESIDENT. No.

LUCIE. Well, then, have the courage to say that woman in the marriage of to-day is a slave whom man can reduce to be the instrument of his pleasure! Just as he likes he can leave her sterile or give her children

— imperil her happiness, her life, or her health, and pledge her whole future without having to render more account to her than a bull who is put to a cow! If that's it, very well! But say so! At least, let innocent girls know the shameful bargain that men offer them, with love for a bait and the law for a trap!

PRESIDENT [*coldly*] You were the cause of your young sister's death. You took her with you.

LUCIE [*calmer*] Yes. [*She stops*].

PRESIDENT. Well?

LUCIE. Our money was soon spent. Annette got some music lessons to give, but they sent her away when they found out her condition. I did sewing.

PRESIDENT. Then you earned some money.

LUCIE. I could not get work every day. When I did, I earned fifteen sous for twelve hours. It's true I was not clever; there are women who earn one franc twenty-five. We were seized by despair at the thought of the child that was coming.

PRESIDENT. That was not a reason to take your sister and her child to their deaths. [*Lucie is seized by a nervous shudder and does not answer*] Answer me.

COUNSEL. Let her take a minute, President.

LUCIE [*pulling herself together*] I wanted to get her into a hospital, but they only take you in at the end of pregnancy. At Paris there are institutions, it seems, but not in the provinces.

PRESIDENT. You might have asked for relief.

LUCIE. We had not been the requisite six months in the town. And afterwards, what could we have done with the child?

PRESIDENT. If she was unable to bring it up, your sister could have taken it to the " Enfants Assistés."

LUCIE. Yes, abandoned it. We did think of that. We made inquiries.

COUNSEL. A certificate is required that the applicant

to the society is without means. An inquiry is made and the application may be accepted or refused. In the meantime the child may die.

LUCIE. They only take in children on condition that the mother shall not know where the child is, that she shall never see it or have news of it. Once a month only she is told if it is alive or dead; nothing more.

PRESIDENT. Go on, madam. But facts, if you please.

LUCIE. Yes. I begged my husband to take Annette and me back. He would not.

PRESIDENT. Kindly come to the defendant Thomas.

LUCIE [*with constantly rising emotion*] Annette reproached herself for having accepted what she called my sacrifice. She said that she was the cause of all my trouble. [*Pause*] One day I was fetched; I found her dead at this woman's. [*A fit of sobbing seizes her: her nerves break down completely. She cries*] My little sister! my poor little sister!

PRESIDENT [*Compassionately, to the usher*] Take her away. Call the doctor. [*Lucie, still crying out, is led away. Her emotion has communicated itself to everyone in court. The President continues to the defendants*] Has no one else among you anything further to say in his defence?

TUPIN [*excited*] Oh, if we said everything we should be here till to-morrow!

MME. TUPIN [*equally excited*] Yes, till to-morrow, so we should!

TUPIN. And then we should n't be done, I can tell you!

PRESIDENT. Then I will hear the Advocate-General.

SCHOOLMISTRESS. But you 're not going to condemn us? It is n't possible. I have n't said everything —

TUPIN. It 's not we who are guilty!

SCHOOLMISTRESS. I was afraid of getting a bad

name. We had n't the means, either, to bring up another.

MME. TUPIN [*greatly worked up*] So that's it! So that's all the children that we bring up get by it! What's the use of talking? The men have n't thought of changing it — well then, we must do it! We women! We must strike! We — the mothers! The great strike — the strike of the mothers!

Cries among the public, " Yes, yes."

PRESIDENT. Silence!

MME. TUPIN. What's the good of using ourselves up to make more wretched men and gay women! For others to use!

TUPIN. It's not that we are guilty!

PRESIDENT. Sit down!

TUPIN [*drowning his voice*] It's the men who 've not given us enough to feed our children that are guilty!

PRESIDENT. Sit down!

TUPIN. The men who tell us to have other children, while those we have are rotting with hunger!

COUNSEL. The criminal is the man who seduced little Annette!

PRESIDENT. Silence!

MME. THOMAS. Yes, where's he? Where's he? You have n't taken him up! Because he's a man and your laws —

PRESIDENT. Guards!

MME. THOMAS. And your laws are made by men!

PRESIDENT. Guards!

MME. THOMAS. And all the men who got with child the girls I delivered, did you prosecute them?

During the following an anger which becomes a fury seizes the accused. They are all on their feet, except the schoolmistress, who continues to sob and utter words that no one hears. The President is also on his feet; he tries vainly to restore silence by knocking on his desk

*with a paper-knife, but he cannot make himself heard.
The tumult increases till the fall of the curtain, the
voices of the counsel for the defence and his clients
drowning those of the President and the Procuror.*

PRESIDENT. I will have you removed to prison!

MME. THOMAS. The fine gentlemen who take mistresses! And the young ones who humbug little work-girls!

PRESIDENT. I 'll have you removed to prison!

PROCUROR. Guards, can't you keep that crowd of fanatics quiet?

COUNSEL. You have no right to insult the defendants!

TUPIN. That's all they 've done from the beginning!

PROCUROR. Make that howling mob be quiet! The defendants have no respect for the Court!

COUNSEL. And you, Advocate-General, have no respect for justice!

PROCUROR. If their crime inspires you with sympathy, it only fills me with indignation.

COUNSEL. They are right. They are not guilty. The respect that you lack —

PROCUROR. I demand —

COUNSEL. The guilt is at the door of the morals that brand the unmarried mother.

THE PUBLIC. Bravo!

PROCUROR. I ask that counsel for the defence —

COUNSEL. Every woman with child ought to be respected in whatever circumstances her child has come into being.

Applause.

PRESIDENT. Maître Verdier, by virtue of Article 43 of the Rules —

COUNSEL. Their crime is not an individual, but a social crime.

PROCUROR. It is a crime against nature!

COUNSEL. It is not a crime; it is a revolt against nature!

PRESIDENT.   Guards, remove the defendants!   [*The guards do not hear or do not understand*].   Maître Verdier, if I have to employ force —

Tumult in court.

COUNSEL [*succeeding by the force of his voice in imposing a short silence*] It is a revolt against nature! A revolt that fills my heart with pity, at the cause of which all the force of my mind is roused to indignation! Yes; I look forward with eagerness to that hour of freedom when the storehouse of science shall give to everyone the means, without a restraint that is only hypocrisy, without the profanation of love, to have none but the children he wants! That will be indeed a victory over nature, that cruel nature which sows with criminal profusion the life that she watches die with indifference. But meanwhile —

The tumult begins again.

PRESIDENT. Guards, clear the court! Guards! Guards, remove the defendants! The sitting is adjourned.

The judges put on their caps and rise.

MME. THOMAS.   It's not me who kills the innocents! I'm no murderess!

SCHOOLMISTRESS.   Mercy!   Mercy!

MME. TUPIN.   She's no murderess!

TUPIN.   She's right.   She's no murderess!

MME. THOMAS.   It's the men that are guilty!   The men!   All the men!

The judges leave by the narrow door leading to their room.   During the last words their red robes are seen gradually disappearing.

THE END